Julie + Tim
xmas
2014

IRONCLAD DOWN

IRONCLAD DOWN

The USS *Merrimack*-CSS *Virginia*
From Construction to Destruction

CARL D. PARK

NAVAL INSTITUTE PRESS
Annapolis, Maryland

Naval Institute Press
291 Wood Road
Annapolis, MD 21402

Library of Congress Cataloging-in-Publication Data

Park, Carl D., 1926–
Ironclad down : the USS Merrimack-CSS Virginia from construction to
destruction/by Carl D. Park.

    p. cm.

Includes bibliographical references and index.
ISBN 978-1-59114-659-9 (alk. paper)
1. Merrimack (Frigate)—History. 2. Virginia (Ironclad)—History. 3. Armored
vessels—Confederate States of America—History. 4. Shipbuilding—
Confederate States of America—History. 5. Naval architecture—Confederate
States of America—History. 6. Confederate States of America—Biography.
7. Confederate States of America. Navy—History. 8. Confederate States of
America—History, Naval. 9. United States—History—Civil War, 1861–1865—
Naval operations, Confederate. I. Title.
E599.M5P37 2007
973.7'52—dc22.

                                                   2007004064

Contents

Illustrations

CHAPTER TWELVE: Two Days of Glory

CHAPTER THIRTEEN: Ironclad Down

Preface

Why did I write another book about the most famous epic in Civil War naval history? To explain that, I have to tell you about myself. I seem to have been born a Civil War buff in the little town of Columbia, Tennessee, where as a boy I played on Civil War battlefields. Nathan Bedford Forrest killed one of his own officers in Columbia. John Bell Hood, the "Mighty Hood of Texas," marched through town twice: first on his way north to fight the battles of Franklin and Nashville, which should have been one of the Confederacy's most decisive victories, and again as he retreated south into Alabama after inexcusable and humiliating defeats. My maternal great-grandmother stood at the door of the family home on South Garden Street and wept as she watched Hood's haggard and starving troops march away, leaving bloody footprints on the icy road. I revel in the heritage of Dixie, and rejoice in the victory of the Union.

I am also a master model builder—some would say an obsessive model builder. I don't build many models—only one or two a year—but I do strive for accuracy in those I construct. And that brings us to this point. A few years ago I decided to build a model of the CSS *Virginia*. Instead of tracking down some plans and documentation and then starting from scratch, I ordered a model kit from a well-known producer of scale ship models. As I got into the project, some things were not completely clear, so I did a little research. Of course, for serious model builders and history buffs, there is really no such thing as "a little research." From the moment you read the first line or scan the first drawing telling you that what you had presumed to be fact is in reality someone's best guess, then the floodgates open! After a careful analysis of the text and engravings in my copy of *Battles and Leaders of the Civil War*, I knew I had a problem, which grew after more research at the Phoenix Public Library. Finding more and more contradictions, I had to accept the fact that, even at this late date, it was entirely possible that no one knew exactly what the *Virginia* really looked like on that fateful March morning in 1862 when she slipped her moorings and steamed away from Gosport Navy Yard. The *Virginia* was a mystery ship, and there was no way that I could build a truly accurate model, exterior and interior, unless I started at the beginning. I would have to track down every reliable description and drawing of both the *Merrimack* and the *Virginia* and then try to separate fact from fiction.

I realized that this was no longer just a model project. I was going to attempt to unravel some historical assumptions that may have been muddled for more than a hundred years and also develop new information that apparently had never been documented. This was going to be a daunting research project—one that was crying out to be a book. I had written historical pamphlets and magazine articles, as well as how-to articles for model magazines, but I had never written a book. In the beginning, I was going to keep it simple, more or less a glorified how-to project. But as I dug deeper into the history, I found some fascinating characters who would have important roles to play in the story: Stephen R. Mallory, secretary of the Confederate Navy; John Mercer Brooke, naval officer and inventor; and John Luke Porter, shipbuilder. These men were the *Virginia*; they were mother, father, and midwife. To tell the *Virginia* story, I would have to tell their stories, a complex mixture of inspiration, genius, and possibly deceit. In Stephen Mallory I found a complex man with dogged determination and intense loyalty. He was either admired or detested by his contemporaries. Mallory's prime place in history is as the catalyst for the Battle of Hampton Roads. He knew that the Confederates had neither the time nor the means to build ships of the line to battle the Union Navy. He had a general idea of what might be done, and he knew how to find the people to do it. He enlisted the talents of John Mercer Brooke, a young naval officer with great energy and imagination. Brooke was an inventor and, in his own estimation, the person responsible for the *Virginia's* most outstanding feature. He claimed that it was his concept to make the *Virginia* a semisubmersible in order to protect its vital parts. John Luke Porter was a naval constructor, or naval architect in modern parlance; his part in this story was building the *Virginia* and other ironclads during the war. As we will see, his statements about the design and construction of the *Virginia* do not match Brooke's remembrances. In reading the statements of some of his contemporaries, we can safely assume that Porter could be opinionated and abrasive. In later years, he considered himself the sole designer of the *Virginia* and Brooke his enemy and a usurper. These three men had all taken oaths to defend the United States of America and its Constitution. Why did they, along with Robert E. Lee, Stonewall Jackson, Jefferson Davis, and others, become what some consider traitors to their country?

The notion of secession was nothing new in 1860. For more than twenty years, the South had threatened to secede over the issue of slavery in the new territories. An argument about state versus federal authority had gone on incessantly since the framing of the Constitution. This passion for states' rights almost had destroyed the efforts to form a country during its beginnings. The dark cloud of slavery hung over a nation where no compromise was possible: the United States of America would be either "slave" or "free"; it could not be both. Many Southerners believed that abolition of slavery would cause the death of their agrarian economy rooted in cotton. The Old South would be politically bankrupt. The abolitionist Yankees would rule the land. For years, the South had threatened to take its ball and go home if the North would not play the game its way.

By the election of 1860 this ploy had been used far too many times. The new Republicans, waning Whigs, and Northern Democrats heard the old song of secession, but none believed it. There were loyal Southerners and Northern copperheads who sincerely believed that the new Republican Party in Washington would treat the states as cavalierly as the British Crown had treated the original thirteen colonies, and they would not stand for it. The Republicans narrowly won the election of 1860, and far too many Southerners decided that to "secure the blessings of liberty for ourselves and our posterity," as the Preamble to the Constitution promised, they would have to separate themselves from the Union. In December 1860 the nation began to dissolve.

For men in the government and the military, the inner conflict was agonizing, but there was no middle ground; they had to choose sides. Every military officer knew that if he chose the South, he had everything to lose and nothing much to gain. But through no fault of their own, these military officers had a decision to make. Mallory, Brooke, and Porter chose the South. They severed their ties to the Union and gathered in Richmond to plan for and build a navy for a new country. There they faced problems unlike any they'd encountered before. There was an acute shortage of seamen, skilled labor, weapons of war, and money. There were complex logistics problems to solve. Where would they find the material to build ships? How would they transport it where it was needed, and what would they do with it after they got it there?

Early on, I realized that it would take me longer to find out how Mallory and company solved their problems than they actually took to do it. I didn't even know how they got the coal on board the *Virginia*. Did they hoist it over the ship with a crane and pour it down a chute, or did slaves struggle up gangways and down ladders deep into the hot, steamy hold with gunnysacks of coal tearing into their shoulders? For every riddle I solved, I exposed two more. I knew from the start that my book could never be totally complete. Much of the end product would have to be based on detective work and supposition, and I hoped my hypotheses would be proven right or wrong by future researchers. My ship model project had taken on a new life. I had fascinating people confronting monumental challenges in a chaotic time and place in history. My quest would take me down new pathways in history. The central characters of my book were on the verge of writing a new chapter in naval history. I journeyed to find my ghost ship and the stories of the men who built her, so join me now in my search for the *Virginia*.

Acknowledgments

After pestering librarians and museum personnel all across the country for many years, it's difficult to know exactly where to start saying "thank you." Probably the best starting place would be to thank the seventy-some authors, living and dead, who wrote the books that became the foundation for my research. Many of those books came to me through the efforts of Bill Kummer at the Maricopa County Northwest Regional Library. Through the interlibrary loan system, Bill tracked down and obtained books for me from all over the country. Sally Stephenson, from the Haverhill Public Library, provided invaluable information about the Merrimack River, the Merrimack Valley, and ship building in the region. John Hightower's great staff at The Mariners' Museum—in particular, Greg Cina, Josh Graml, David Dick, Anita Smith, Laura Huff, Marc Nucup, and Sidney Moore—spent hours tracking down information that made large portions of this book possible.

The Museum of the Confederacy in Richmond was another great source of information. John Coski, Robert Hancock, and Heather Milne devoted much of their time to answering my endless questions. John Ahladas, a former staff member, was also helpful. Crista LaPrade, of the Virginia Historical Society, sent some valuable reference source information about Porter, Brooke, and Jones. Molly Hutton-Marder, at the Chrysler Museum of Art, and Gordon Calhoun, Hampton Roads Naval Museum, tracked down information on one of the *Virginia* bells. Gordon also provided information about *Virginia* armor plates.

The ship plans and records I obtained from the National Archives in Washington, D.C., and College Park, Maryland, were the "mother load" in terms of the information I needed to prepare my drawings and scaled plans. My thanks and gratitude go to Raymond Cotton, Richard Smith, Keith Kerr, Stephanie Richmond, John Petralia, and Rebecca Livingston.

I would like to thank each of the individuals of the research staff at the Library of Congress for the hours they spent answering my numerous questions. Unfortunately, that's almost impossible; as a general rule, when you go online to the "Ask A Librarian" link you receive an answer signed "The Digital Reference Team": so, thank you, Paul Conner and the Digital Reference Team, whoever you are.

Information I requested from the Smithsonian Institution came from Chris Cottrill, Jim Roan, and Kathleen Golden. Alice Hanes sent information from the Portsmouth Naval Museum. Glen Helm, Jean Hort, and Bernard Cavalcante answered the questions

I posed to the Navy Department Library, Washington Navy Yard. I discovered Mabry Tyson at his CSS *Virginia* home page, and we corresponded by e-mail for months.

In addition to the above, I also got information from the following: Jennifer Bryan, Nimitz Library, United States Naval Academy; Geoff Chester, United States Naval Observatory; Paul Clancy, *The Virginian-Pilot;* Stuart Frazer, the Perry Library, Old Domino University; Hanna Goss and Rebecca Owens, National Oceanic and Atmospheric Agency; Ann Hassinger, United States Naval Institute; John Kelley and Steve Milner, Norfolk Navy Shipyard; Steve Pagnano, Naval History Center, Boston, Massachusetts; Gregory Stoner, Virginia Historical Society; and Dana Wegner, Naval Surface Warfare Center.

The one individual who is most responsible for the successful writing of this book is my wife Polly. I can't spell, and I scatter punctuation marks across a page like a farmer sowing grain. Polly spent hours poring over page after page, correcting much of my outlandish spelling, unscrambling my punctuation, and un-splitting numerous infinitives. If I had sent the original draft to a publisher, they would have had a good laugh and that would have been the end of *Ironclad Down*.

My thanks to Michael Shally-Jensen, project manager, and Joy Matkowski, copy editor. Both were the official hand holders who guided me through this unfamiliar maze. Joy chiseled off the rough edges and took a hatchet to many of my picturesque but rambling sentences in order to make the book more readable. Judy Loeven, proofreader-cum-editor, further polished the book's prose.

And a special thanks to Eric Mills, acquisitions editor at the Naval Institute Press, who believed that my in-depth research and discoveries made this book worth publishing.

PART

I

The People

Chapter One

The Secretary:
Stephen Russell Mallory

hen the South Carolina militia opened fire on Fort Sumter, the fledging Confederacy had no army, no navy, no reliable transportation system, an inadequate manufacturing base, and no idea of how to go about waging a war. If, as the saying goes, necessity is the mother of invention, then the Confederate States of America was the mother of necessity. The Confederacy needed to find ways to manufacture huge quantities of powder and shot, mass-produce small arms and engines, and build vessels capable of attacking the Union Navy. They were undaunted by this herculean task because they were confident of two things: "One Southern soldier is worth five Yankees," and "God is on this side of the Confederacy." Logistically, this "lost cause" (a campaign in which defeat is inevitable, often said of the Southern side of the Civil War) was lost before the first shot was fired. But the boiling emotions of February 1861 prevented Confederate leaders from bothering with petty details.

The provisional Confederate Constitution gave the pro tempore Congress, meeting in Montgomery, Alabama, the power to raise armies and (in art. 1, sec. 5, par. 13) "provide and maintain a Navy." On February 12, using executive power prior to the seating of President-elect Jefferson Davis, the Confederate Congress instructed its newly appointed Naval Affairs Committee to immediately commence organizing the Navy. At that point, the committee—four captains, four commanders, and not one capital ship or a single seaman—*was the*

Stephen Russell Mallory.
The Century War Book

Confederate Navy. As coastal states seceded, each seized Union ships when possible. Texas took the revenue cutter *Dodge*. Florida captured a coastal survey schooner, and Alabama took a revenue cutter, a tug, and the Pensacola Navy Yard. There were probably no more than ten small, lightly armed vessels available throughout the Confederacy.[1]

On Monday, February 18, 1862, Jefferson Davis was sworn in as president of the provisional government of the Confederate States of America. A week later, he informed the Confederate Congress by special message that Stephen Mallory had accepted the post of secretary of the Navy. Despite some protests, Congress approved the appointment on March 4. Contemporaries and historians have criticized President Davis for many of his decisions, and this appointment was no exception. Mallory had made enemies in politics and in the U.S. Navy, but Davis felt he was the right man for the job.

President Lincoln chose Gideon Welles as his naval secretary for reasons of political expediency. Welles was a Connecticut lawyer, journalist, and editor. He was an early member of the Republican Party and his state's representative to the party's convention in Chicago. He supported Salmon P. Chase for president but on the third ballot changed his vote to Lincoln. Welles did not meet Lincoln until the morning of the inauguration, when he learned, to his surprise, that he had been nominated as secretary of the Navy. Politicians considered this cabinet post to be the least desirable, and Welles knew very little about the overall operations of the Navy. In 1845, as a reward for his help in getting James Polk elected president, he had been appointed chief of the Naval Bureau of Provisions and Clothing. Welles was an excellent judge of character and a quick learner who knew how to delegate. He had completely reorganized this small purchasing bureau and made it a model of efficiency. Success has few rewards in politics, however, and Zachary Taylor dismissed him in 1849.[2] Recalled to national service by Lincoln, along with his experienced naval aide and adviser, Gustavus Fox, Welles became a competent secretary of the Navy and a trusted friend and confidant of Lincoln.

Stephen Mallory had the same personal assets as Welles, plus the advantage that salt water ran in his veins. He had never served in the Navy, but the sea and ships had played a vital role in his life. Stephen Russell Mallory was born in Trinidad, West Indies, in 1811 or 1812. His father, John, was a construction engineer from Connecticut who in the early 1800s met and married Irish-born Ellen, who as a girl had been sent to Trinidad to live with her two planter uncles. The Mallory family then briefly lived in New York and Mobile, Alabama, before settling down in Key West in 1820 with their two sons, John Jr., age twelve, and Stephen, age nine.

When they arrived on the island, it was an outpost in every sense of the word, and Ellen was the only white woman there. The Keys offered Mallory everything Tom Sawyer had on the Mississippi River and more. He roamed the islands and played in the crystal-clear waters. There were fish and turtles to catch and great sailing ships drifting past on the horizon. Old men enchanted him with stories of the noted pirates Jose Casper and Jean Lafitte, of General Andrew Jackson (soon to be president) and his battles with redcoats and with Seminoles who lurked in the dark mainland swamps. Another advantage for small boys living in the Keys was the absence of a school within a hundred miles, but this was not to last.

Mallory was sent to live with family friends and attend a country school near Blakely, across the bay from Mobile. There he found himself in the midst of a wilderness of great shadowy woods crisscrossed with creeks, inlets, bayous, and still lakes. Birds—both plain and exotic—soared through the treetops. Deer grazed in meadows, and raccoons, opossums, foxes, squirrels, and pumas lived beneath the green canopy. This uninhabited area was Mallory's refuge from a school that was less than idyllic. Mallory was by far the youngest student; the others were young men who engaged in fistfights with the headmaster, an old Scot with dubious academic credentials and a fondness for good whiskey and a stout hickory stick. Frequent holidays were required to allow the headmaster to recover from fisticuffs with the students or bouts with John Barleycorn. Mallory later said that he learned to read but little else at this strange school. Having little in common with his classmates, he spent most of his time alone in the woods, riding, swimming, and hunting, or walking in the surf along the beach, catching crabs and watching the ships pass by in the bay. Then, as suddenly as this strange new life had begun for Mallory, it ended. His father and older brother died at Key West, and Mallory left Blakely to return to the Keys.

To support herself and Stephen, Ellen Mallory turned their home into a boardinghouse for seamen. Her long hours, hard work, and isolation seemed to take a heavy toll on Ellen. In later years, Mallory wrote in his diary that "she was passionate, and punished me severely and unreasonably at Times; and this, from my peculiarly sensitive appreciation of wrong rankled and Festered in my heart, and was never entirely rooted out until after her death." But he also wrote that she spared no sacrifice in his care and upbringing. It was obvious to Ellen that her son lacked education, and at the age of thirteen he was once again sent away to school, this time to one that meant business.

He found himself again in completely alien surroundings at the Moravian settlement in Nazareth, Northampton County, Pennsylvania. A lush, gently rolling agricultural land, with quiet, meandering streams and fields of waving grain, replaced the tropical seas, jungle, and wilderness he was accustomed to, and the Spanish architecture of the Deep South was replaced by high gables, hooded chimneys, and tiled roofs on houses along cobblestone streets. The people around him were industrious, hardworking, and pious. Mallory boarded and studied at Nazareth Hall, a large, medieval-looking limestone building with impressive oak rafters. Here Mallory's formal education began. He studied Latin and Greek, mathematics, history, and music. The Moravians were famous for their organist, trombone choir, and orchestra. Mallory learned to sing and play the violin. Next door to Nazareth Hall was Whitefield House, where he attended religious services and Bible class. Mallory began to love the academic world as much as he did the sea and the wilderness. But once again his life changed, because in the fall of 1829, his mother could no longer afford the expense of his schooling. Stephen Mallory would cherish for the rest of his life these few years of formal education.

Back in Key West, the sixteen-year-old boy worked hard to help his mother run the boardinghouse. He wrote her business letters, ran errands, and did other chores. Whenever possible, he liked to mingle with the rougher elements among the Keys' residents. He learned to fence and box, hunted in the adjacent islands, rowed, and sailed, while he occasionally stole away to the sophisticated society of Cuba. He took up dancing, played the flute, and learned to speak and read French and Spanish. He was particularly taken with the Spanish girls. For a while he and a friend worked to establish a plantation at New River on the Florida coast. He befriended the Indians there, who helped him hone his skills in woodcraft, hunting, and fishing. After these months in the absolute freedom of the swamps and forest, he considered staying in the wilderness as a hunter and trapper.

Early in 1830 Mallory returned to Key West and found employment in a minor position as customs inspector. At that time, nothing was brought through the customs office in the Keys that had much value from a tariff standpoint. For the most part, taxable items were "imported" via rivers and bayous far from the customs officials' view. In his new position, Mallory spent most of his working hours at the docks. Years later, in a letter to his son Buddy, he described an incident that would change his life: "On a pleasant spring morning, sitting upon a wharf at Key West, I first saw your mother. She was dressed, I remember, all in white." That young lady, Angela Moreno, the daughter of wealthy Spaniard Joseph Lopez Moreno, was on her way from her home in Pensacola to a school in Bridgeport, Connecticut. She was spoiled, haughty, and conceited. At the time she spoke no English and would not have deigned to speak to young Mallory even if she had. She was not a beauty, being a plumpish brunette of medium height. In later life, her personality became complex and unpredictable. She could be sweet and childlike at one moment and a harpy the next, brave today and a coward tomorrow, gentle and loving in the morning and in a screaming, jealous rage in the afternoon.[3] She resembled Mary Todd Lincoln in many ways. At this first encounter Mallory saw Angela for only a few moments, but for him it was love at first sight. Naively and egotistically, he determined that he would win her as his wife. In his letter to Buddy he also said, "I made up my mind to study law, become a lawyer, and some day go to congress." Abraham Lincoln set himself on this same path, but for Lincoln the process took much longer. Surprisingly enough, Angela remembered seeing Stephen that morning. She later wrote, "I remember that he was the only well-dressed young gentleman I saw, and he was very hansom [sic]."[4]

As was his nature and since he lacked a tutor or adviser, Mallory set to work to accomplish his career goal by studying on his own. He read book after book on every conceivable subject, some of which would be helpful and others worthless for his long-range plan. At night, locked in his room and fighting sleep, he pored over his books, took notes, read more books, and wrote more notes. Education became his obsession. Later in life, by his own admission, he looked down on others around him who were not improving themselves. He became more retiring and sensitive, and in conversation he could be a bore. He recognized his faults but could never completely keep himself from wearing his learning on his sleeve. He could discuss nearly any subject: training carrier pigeons, the origin of political nicknames, theories on generation, belief in ghosts, lunar rainbows, the Koran, the sayings of Sancho Panza, stones found in the ancient quarries of Palmyra, and history, history, and more history. The keystone of his self-education system was copious note taking. As he read, he wrote on sheets of paper what he felt were the most important points, and after accumulating a stack of pages, he bound them. He continued this process throughout his life.

In 1832 Mallory was elected to the office of town marshal, which was at most a parttime job. His major duties were to ring the curfew bell at 9:30 PM and to enforce the law that "Negroes, whether free or not, were not permitted to play the fiddle, beat a drum, or make any other kind of noise . . . without the written permission of the mayor or an alderman." It was also his duty to see that all stores were closed. In addition to being the customs inspector and town marshal, Mallory was also "reading law" with Judge William Marvin as preparation for starting his own practice.

At this time the population of Key West numbered less than a thousand, and some citizens joked that half of them were lawyers. The local paper, *The Register*, printed the flippant comment in 1828 that a certain ship had arrived "with an assorted cargo of goods and seven lawyers."[5] These were maritime lawyers, coming to the Keys because of the area's most lucrative business: the peculiar indigenous occupation of "shipwrecking." Key West was the nearest port to a hundred-mile stretch of the most treacherous reefs on the Atlantic and Gulf coasts. Rough seas and dangerous reefs equal shipwrecks, and shipwrecks equal big salvage profits. The shipwreckers—or salvagers, as they were more politely called—would go to the scene of a wreck and claim the vessel, the cargo, or both in accordance with the strict code of maritime law. Legend has it that in the early days shipwrecking was carried out by the method described in the popular book *The Moon Rakers*: Lighthouse lights and other beacons were hidden or extinguished, and false lights were placed to lead ships onto the reefs.

In 1828 an admiralty court was established in Key West under the auspices of the Superior Court of the Southern Judicial District of Florida. Mallory's tutor, Judge Marvin, sat on this court and wrote many of the decisions governing the salvage business. The laws on wrecking became very detailed and complex: Wreckers had to be licensed by the court. No salvage operations could begin without the consent of the stricken ship's master. The first wrecker to arrive on the scene became the only one who could request and be granted wrecking rights. At his discretion, he could then invite others from among the salvage crews (or "jackal packs") to move in and assist. The rights and privileges of the wrecking master and the master of the imperiled vessel were carefully prescribed and delineated. But during a raging storm, with sailing ships simultaneously struggling to salvage property and stay off the reef, there was a lot of room for confusion, contradiction, and deceit. After a successful salvage operation, the admiralty court determined how the spoils were to be distributed. What risk did the wreckers take? What might have been saved without them? Were the procedures followed correctly? After the testimony, cross-examination, and arguments by lawyers for the wreckers and for the lost vessels' owners, the court granted an award to the wreckers that, on average, amounted to about a sixth of the salvaged property. Next to shipwrecking, the second largest business on Key West was auctioning the salvaged goods. No school in the nation at the time could have given young Mallory a better foundation in maritime law.

In 1834 Angela Moreno returned to Key West to visit her friend Lydia McIntosh, who was Mallory's cousin. Mallory arranged to be introduced to her, and a few days later he proposed marriage. In his best courtroom manner, he stated his love for her and observed that he had thought of her constantly for four years and had selected her for his wife. She measured up to what he thought his wife should be, he declared, and he saw no reason why she would not reciprocate his feelings. Because his proposal might have been a bit sudden, he explained, she could take a couple of years to think it over. A startled and angry Angela told him in no uncertain terms that she didn't require two seconds to think it over. Convinced she was in the presence of a madman, she fled the room—and Key

West! Crestfallen but undaunted, Mallory returned to his work as customs inspector, marshal, and law student. He would bide his time and try again later.

In 1836 Mallory wrote to Angela to reaffirm his love and proposal of marriage. If she gave him no encouragement, he said, he would join the army and go to the Everglades to fight the Seminoles. Angela quickly replied that she thought an Everglades trip was an excellent idea! With her letter of rejection in his pocket, he set out on an expedition into southern Florida. For the next two years, in command of a fine crew, he sailed the coast and bayous in his own centerboard schooner-rigged whaleboat named the *Angela*, attacked Indian villages, and in general enjoyed his wild and adventurous life.

In April 1838 the campaign ended. Whether by accident or design, his command was to be mustered out at Pensacola, Angela's home. He and a fellow officer took up quarters in a hotel directly across the street from the Moreno residence. The first morning there, Mallory ordered horses for himself and his friend to visit his cousin Lydia, who now also lived in Pensacola. Waiting for the mounts outside the hotel, he saw Angela on her piazza and pretended not to notice. When his horse arrived, he took a great deal of time rearranging the saddle and stirrups. Suddenly, from the window behind Angela came the strains of a guitar; Mallory recognized his favorite song being played by Angela's sister and knew it had been arranged by Angela. Without giving her a glance, Mallory rode away to see his cousin. He explained to Lydia that he had come to Pensacola to see Angela, but first he wanted her opinion on his chances. Lydia simply stated with a smile that he should find out for himself. He considered this a favorable response, leaped on his horse, and dashed back to town. During the entire trip back he repeatedly rehearsed his speech, a "very sensible, frank, feeling and manly address of about two minutes," he later said. At the Moreno residence he was shown into the parlor, where he paced nervously as he waited. Suddenly a voice behind him said, "So, sir, you have come at last, have you? After not even looking at me this morning?" Mallory immediately forgot his speech and desperately tried to think of something to say. He remarked that he felt uncomfortable in confined places and would like to walk outside; Angela smiled, picked up her bonnet, and led the way. Outside she coyly asked, "What in the world has brought you here?" Mallory interpreted this as his cue and began to remember parts of his speech: "You have. I came to see you alone. Refuse me and I go back at once: but not to give you up, for I am determined to marry you in spite of your biting teeth!" Angela showed no surprise and answered in a matter-of-fact tone, "I had determined to accept your offer if you ever renewed it. Why don't you kiss me, Stephen?"[6]

In July 1838 Stephen and Angela married and settled down in Key West, where Mallory soon had his own law practice, primarily in pleading wrecking and salvage cases. He soon gained a reputation as one of the best and fairest attorneys in the state. To amuse himself, he took on the assignment of Key West correspondent for the *New York Tribune*. In 1846 a devastating hurricane hit Florida. Mallory wrote a two-part account of the disaster that was not only good journalism but also an excellent appeal for relief funds for the storm's victims. Slowly, he was building a national reputation for wisdom and integrity. He was still collector of revenue at Key West and well liked and respected by Treasury Department officials. He was nominated as a delegate to the national Democratic convention in Baltimore and was mentioned as a congressional candidate for his district.

Until the mid-1840s the Whig Party held virtual control of the state of Florida, but times were changing. Florida had a Democratic senator, David Yulee, in Washington, and in 1850 the Democrats won a majority in the state House and Senate. The seeds of rebellion were being sown throughout the South, and in Florida, as elsewhere, politicians were proclaiming themselves as unionist or secessionist. Senator Yulee was a firebrand who espoused secession on the floor of the Senate, in the halls, and in the press. The moderate Democrats of Florida were in a dilemma. They feared losing their newfound power, there were no public opinion polls to point the way toward political success, and Yulee was up for reelection in March. John C. Calhoun had called for a convention in Nashville the following June to consider secession. The conservative Democrats appointed Stephen Mallory as an alternate to this convention. In a letter concerning this appointment, Mallory took the middle ground: He was grateful to be chosen, thought that meeting and discussing the subject was a good idea, believed in the state's right to recover fugitive slaves, and felt the North did not take the South's demands seriously. Not once did he use the word "secession." Because of previous commitments, Mallory could not attend the convention.

The conservative Democrats decided to try to calm the waters. They withdrew their support from the radical Yulee and endorsed Mallory, a move that astounded everybody, including Mallory, who had never spoken out against any of Yulee's positions. In fact, he had quietly supported practically everything Yulee espoused, with the exception of secession, and he could not see what attraction he had for the anti-Yulee faction. Mallory's entry into national politics was not going as he had planned. Instead of becoming a popular candidate when the time and place were right, he found himself on the brink of a bitter intraparty power struggle. Mallory declined the nomination. The party pressed him to reconsider; he resisted for a time but finally acceded, and a bitter fight erupted.

In those days, U.S. senators were elected by their states' legislatures, so Mallory's and Yulee's names were introduced on the floor of the state senate, thus precipitating the battle. Ballot after ballot was cast, and finally Yulee was declared the winner, even though many of the delegates had cast blank ballots. Yulee had more votes than Mallory but not a majority. In the past, the legislature had held that a blank vote was a "vote against" in the decision that had given Yulee victory against an opponent when he was first nominated and elected. The body held that if such a decision had applied to Yulee in the past, it must also apply to Mallory. Consequently, the legislature overturned its decision and declared Mallory the winner. The stage was set for more fighting, and Yulee threatened to carry the case to the U.S. Senate. Mallory's supporters used this threat to their advantage, as reported in the Jacksonville *Florida Republic* on December 4, 1851: "A more glaring contravention of State privileges, of which Mr. Yulee is a zealous advocate, could hardly be conceived than that involved in the act which he now invokes the Senate to commit." For the most part, the Florida press took Mallory's side, and the Whigs had a field day poking fun at this family feud among the Democrats. In the end, Mallory was victorious, and on March 25, 1851, at age thirty-nine, he accepted the office of senator from the state of Florida. On December 13, 1851, he took the oath of office on the floor of the U.S. Senate.[7] None of this had happened as he had planned, but the deed was now done.

Mallory's plans had come to fruition: He had married Angela, had become a successful lawyer, and was going to the U.S. Senate. He and Angela had two children, a boy, Stephen Jr., called Buddy, and a girl, Margaret. They had lost another son at age three and a daughter at age two. Stephen and Angela were regarded as a happily married couple, yet she would always be mercurial—at turns willful, mettlesome, and unpredictable, and just as suddenly sweet and good natured. She was never entirely sure of Mallory's judgment or of his love for her. James McPherson mentions that Mallory "was snubbed by high Richmond society because of his penchant for women of questionable virtue."[8] Perhaps Angela knew of Richmond society's opinion, and that contributed to her feelings. She impressed people as "a polished lady of the world, a devoted mother and an attractive and witty matron."[9] Washington society was made for her. Though feelings ran high between North and South during the first half of the Franklin Pierce administration in the mid-1850s, the surface of social life was always peaceful and smiling. The Southern ladies were the clear leaders of this exclusive world, and the Mallorys fit into it perfectly. Stephen, of course, was no longer the swashbuckler of the Florida swamps, now described with the gentlemanly term "portly." One observer remarked that he was "a stumpy, 'roly-poly' little fellow, for all the world like one of the squat 'gentlemen farmers' you find in the south of England."[10] His eyes were large and blue, with an air of deep concentration. He had a firm mouth, slight jowls, a round face, and a cleft chin. His hair was dark and curly, and a beard wreathed his face from sideburn to chin (the rest of his face was clean-shaven). He was the perfect host, possessed a fine sense of humor, and loved the English language.

Mallory was in Washington only a short time before his peers began to critique his ability as an orator. Some thought he was superb; others found him dull and verbose. There was little middle ground in people's feelings for Mallory; they either loved him or hated him. Mary Chestnut wrote in July 1862, "And now, too late by one year, when all the mechanics are in the army, Mallory begins to telegraph Captain Ingram to build ships at any expense. We are locked in and cannot get 'the requisites of naval architects,' says a magniloquent person."[11] In October 1863 Catherine Edmondston of North Carolina wrote, "And that bag of wind, Sec. Mallory, listens to him [Flag Officer Lynch] in preference to men of sense & capacity, but he is so stuffed with conceit, so empty headed himself, that I suppose he cannot distinguish good counsel from bad. I have seen this Secy. Mallory, seen & heard him, & he is just the man to be blinded by a dose of flattery skillfully administered."[12]

Mallory had a certain delicacy of manner that his enemies mistook for weakness, but as had been proven in the past, he was a superb and skillful fighter who would never accept defeat as long as there was the slightest glimmer of hope. His loyalty to his friends was legendary. He stood by Jefferson Davis and the Confederacy long after all others had abandoned hope. Durkin, Mallory's biographer, said that "he was careful and deliberate in considering important matters, but sometimes his conclusions lacked range and depth. He was considered competent but never great." No one would have ever pointed him out on the floor of the Senate and say . . . See that man? Some day he will be the catalyst that changes naval history throughout the world. Many of the older naval officers considered him a joke and an embarrassment. Yet, he became the Senate chairman of the Committee on Naval Affairs, and in this post he introduced all naval legislation to the floor.

The legislation Mallory favored often tended toward radical modernization. He opposed the time-honored system of promotion through seniority and recommended a plan of merit advancement. At the time, the highest rank in the U.S. Navy was captain, and this low ceiling prevented young men from rising in the ranks. In Mallory's mind, the U.S. Navy and many of the men who ran it were obsolete. When his merit plan was defeated, he tried a new tactic. Holding a Navy commission guaranteed lifelong employment, and the only form of retirement was voluntary. In 1855 Mallory set the wheels in motion to establish the Naval Retiring Board, which was to check the records of all officers and, if no suitable postings could be found for them, to "prune the dry branches." The outcome was successful but brought a storm of protest and made Mallory naval enemies for life.[13] For political expediency, Congress amended the law to the point where it had no teeth. Edward A. Pollard, editor of the *Richmond Examiner* and nemesis of Jefferson Davis, said that Mallory had been "the butt of every naval officer in the country."[14]

Mallory was looking to the future and was opposed by many men who were living in the past. Through dogged determination, he was bringing about necessary changes, ignoring his critics and continuing to work for naval improvement and modernization, while at the same time doing anything he could to head off secession. By December 1861 he knew that all attempts to save the Union had failed, and at the eleventh hour he sided with his secession-minded Southern colleagues. As Alabama, Georgia, Florida, and Mississippi left the Union, Mallory's political career came to an end.

Determination, hard work, and luck had made Mallory's dreams come true. He was where he wanted to be and doing what he wanted to do. Because of an archaic code of gentlemanly honor, where emotion was required to outweigh logic, he was going to throw it all away. On Monday, January 21, he and Jefferson Davis made their farewell addresses on the floor of the U.S. Senate. Could he ever have imagined then that he would soon be called upon to wreck the navy he had worked so hard to build?

Chapter Two

The Constructor:
John Luke Porter

John Luke Porter was born on September 19, 1813, and grew up with ships as an important part of his everyday life. While young Stephen Mallory was playing on the beaches and wharves of the Florida Keys, John explored the docks at Norfolk and Portsmouth, saw the merchantmen and men-of-war sail in and out of Hampton Roads, and watched the craftsmen at work in the shipyard owned by William Dyson and Joseph Porter II, his father. John, the youngest of the Porter children, had four brothers and four sisters. The Porter family was respected in Virginia for its involvement in government and church work.[1] Unlike Mallory, who was first introduced to formal religion at the age of fourteen, John was born into a devout Methodist family, and religion

was important to him throughout his life. He was a good student, particularly gifted in mathematics, and seemed to have an instinctive understanding of ship construction. As soon as he was old enough, he started working part-time in the shipyard. In 1820 his father bought out his partner and became the sole owner of the firm. While John was growing up, he was involved in the construction of canal boats, sailing vessels, and steamboats. By his teens, he had decided that shipbuilding would be his life's work. His delighted father foresaw the day when his youngest son would take over the family business. In August 1831, however, a few months before John Luke would be eighteen, his father died, and his life changed drastically, just as Stephen Mallory's life had

John Luke Porter.
The Mariners' Museum photo

changed when his father died. To compound the tragedy, his brother Fletcher, a ship carpenter, developed eye problems that would eventually lead to total blindness. The Porter shipyard and family home had to be sold, and the Porter boys became responsible for supporting the family. John and his brother Joseph were skilled ship carpenters who could use this talent to earn a living. Relatives offered assistance, and John's mother moved into the home of her brother, Isaac Luke, in Portsmouth.[2]

In September 1834 John married seventeen-year-old Susan Buxton. We know nothing about his courtship, and no diarist or published accounts tell us anything about Susan's personality, habits, or appearance, though we can safely conclude that their relationship did not match the operatic overtones that surrounded Stephen and Angela Mallory. The newlywed Porters lived in the Luke home for many years while John and his brother Sidney tried to improve the family's financial condition. They borrowed money from an uncle and a cousin and built a ship for the flourishing trade between Norfolk and the West Indies. The two were skilled shipbuilders, but not being sailors, they employed the services of a master and a crew. Their well-built brig was loaded and put out to sea. Before reaching the West Indies, the ship ran into a severe storm that proved too much for the captain and new crew. The ship and cargo, which were inadequately insured, went to the bottom of the Atlantic, and John Luke went from shipowner to debt-ridden ship carpenter. He found employment in shipyards around Portsmouth and Norfolk, including the Gosport Navy Yard. The yard managers and master carpenters liked him, and his shipbuilding skills continued to improve. Eventually, he decided to leave the carpenter shop and become a ship constructor.[3] He understood the construction of both wind- and steam-powered vessels and was an excellent draftsman. With these skills and his excellent references, he soon found work as an assistant constructor. But John wanted to be more than just any constructor; he wanted to be a U.S. Navy constructor. A Navy constructor had to know about armament, understand the stress and strain to a ship during battle, and be able to design both sailing and steam-powered vessels. A U.S. Navy constructor was a civil service employee who worked exclusively for the Navy but held no military rank. The position required experience working on naval vessels, followed by a rigorous and demanding examination at the naval headquarters in Washington. Although not a member of the Navy, the constructor was still subject to the basic laws and regulations that applied to a naval officer.

In 1842 Porter moved his wife and four children to Pittsburgh to work in its shipyard, where a friend stationed there, U.S. Navy engineer William W. Hunter, had helped him get employment. Hunter's main claim to fame was the conception of the *Allegheny*, launched in 1847, a strange new iron paddle-wheel steamer with submerged wheels under the center of the ship. For all practical purposes, the experiment was a failure, the last paddle-wheel ship the Navy would ever build. John worked with Hunter on the design and construction and for a while took pride in the accomplishment. At one point in 1852 the ship was scheduled to go to Japan with Commodore Perry in the government's effort to open trade. As fate would have it, she failed her performance test and was put in ordinary at the Washington Navy Yard. Eventually she was brought to Norfolk and, after the Civil War, remained to haunt Porter as a rusting hulk on the Elizabeth River.

In preparation for the constructor's exam, John would have read everything he could find about new and improved ship construction. The hot topic of the day, although nothing really new, was ironclad ships. In 1846 while working on the *Allegheny*, according to his son, "Mr. Porter conceived the idea of an iron-clad vessel which would be able to go to sea and still be shot proof." He made drawings of his idea and submitted them to the Navy. The Navy was under siege by inventors and crackpots offering everything from unsinkable ships to Greek fire, and it acknowledged receipt of his plans but took no further notice.[4]

In 1847 John failed his first attempt to pass the constructor's examination. I have been unable to learn a great deal about this exam, but given the complexities of both sail and steamship construction, the test would have been daunting, perhaps the modern equivalent of the bar examination that many law school graduates fail on their first attempt. For ten more years, Porter continued to work as an acting constructor and study for his next examination.

While John was building ships, his brother Joseph was busy with a totally different project at the Gosport shipyard. In a civilian shipyard, the chain of command was simple and forthright. The constructors and craftsmen performed their duties as directed by the owner. In a Navy shipyard, there was no owner per se, just civilian employees and naval officers and their oil-and-water relationship. In 1842 Joseph advocated petitioning Congress to turn the yards over to the civilian employees, who knew what they were doing, and "divest Officers of the Navy of the power of controlling the mechanical operations of the various yards"; Joseph wanted a Navy yard without the Navy. The petition further stated, "Nor do [we] wish to see Negro laborers substituted for white mechanics." Needless to say, the petition never went beyond local newspapers, and it couldn't have done much for Joseph's popularity with the naval personnel around the yard. John doesn't mention his brother's petition in any of his writings, but by 1862 he appears to have been in total agreement with the idea of throwing the naval officers out of the yards.

In 1850 Porter returned to Norfolk with his family. The debt he had incurred in the shipping business disaster had been paid, and the family "no longer had to live plainly and hire out the slaves," said his daughter Brent. In 1852 John became active in politics and, when Portsmouth was incorporated, was elected president of the town council. He continued his lifelong association with Memorial Methodist Church, which caused him considerable soul-searching. He had concluded that Christianity and slavery were not compatible, yet he was a slave owner. If he freed his slaves and went public with his opinions, he would be ostracized in the community and probably in the church. He became a silent abolitionist and, to compensate, treated his slaves, and all blacks, kindly and even broke a long-standing Virginia law by allowing his daughter to teach a slave to read.

John returned to work at the Gosport yard, which was a beehive of activity that had improved considerably since he had last been there. New storehouses were being built, as well as an extensive saw shed and large foundry. The hundred-acre facility was fast becoming the Navy's finest shipyard and was doing large-scale construction work. One of John's first assignments upon his return was on the USS *Constellation*. The old frigate had been slowly rotting away at Gosport for seven years. John Lenthall, the navy's chief constructor, drew up plans for the *Constellation* to be "repaired," which required a change in the ship's classification from a frigate to a sloop of war. The plans were sent to the Gosport yard just after John Porter was named master shipwright for the yard and assigned responsibility for overseeing this project.[5] The old ship was in deplorable condition, and salvaging her would require major surgery. The ship was badly hogged (sagged at the bow and stern) so a new keel was put down in ship house B, and the old hull was then disassembled and rebuilt, piece by piece, on the new keel. All of the armament was removed. Twenty new shell guns were placed on the gun deck, with no guns on the spar deck. The ship was one foot wider and twelve feet longer than before, and the square stern was now rounded. Any old parts that could be reused were reapplied to the new ship, and other good lumber was reconfigured into different parts and installed. The old hulk was brought back to fighting trim. On August 26, 1854, the new sloop USS *Constellation* slid down the ways, and the Navy had a new fighting vessel. Assigned to the African Squadron, she took part in antislavery patrols. During the Civil War, fitted with twenty- and thirty-pound Parrott pivot rifles fore and aft, she patrolled the Mediterranean and the Caribbean to protect U.S. merchantmen. After the war, she was a receiving ship and a training vessel. Finally in 1955 she was stricken from the active list, underwent another restoration project, and became a major attraction as a museum ship at the Baltimore waterfront.[6] If John Lenthall and John Porter had not taken the care they had with the reconstruction of the USS *Constellation*, there would be no ship by that name today, but some historians and naval purists continue to criticize the project. The ship in Baltimore is not the original frigate *Constellation.* It is a Civil War sloop named *Constellation* and a cousin, not a sister, of the *Constitution* and the *United States*. It is ironic that John Luke Porter is best remembered for his controversial work in the reconstruction of two ships, the USS *Constellation* and the USS *Merrimack.*

In 1855 the merchantman *Ben Franklin* arrived at Norfolk with a "cargo" of yellow fever. Breaking every rule of maritime quarantine law and good judgment, she tied up at the Page and Allen shipyard, where the crew opened hatches and pumped her bilge. The pestilence was loosed, and in days the residents of Norfolk and Portsmouth were under siege. The ill were taken to pest houses on the outskirts of town to recover or die. Everyone who could leave did so. John Porter sent his family to Washington, D.C., but stayed behind himself to help in any way he could. All business stopped, and the population left behind was fed by contributions from neighboring towns. Committees were formed to care for the sick and bury the dead. In addition to his volunteer duties, John was taking care of his slaves. One slave, Willis, came down with the fever but was nursed back to health at the family home. Soon after Willis recovered, John fell ill, and Willis made himself John's doctor and nurse. He put John in hot mustard baths and then wrapped him in blankets, the prescribed treatment that was followed until the fever broke or the patient died. After three days and nights, the fever broke, and soon thereafter the Washington newspaper reported that John L. Porter was recovering from yellow fever. While he fought the epidemic in Portsmouth, his last child, James, was born in Washington, but the family did not dare return to Portsmouth until after the first frost.[7]

In 1856 Porter worked at the Gosport yard on the USS *Colorado* and *Roanoke*. This was another fortuitous event. The previous year the *Colorado's* sister ship, the USS *Merrimack*, had been launched in Massachusetts.[8] The reconstruction experience John gained on the *Constellation* and his knowledge of the structure of the *Colorado* and *Roanoke* would soon be applied to reconfiguring the *Merrimack*.

In 1857 John went to Washington to once again take the constructor's examination, this time with success. He was now an official U.S. Navy constructor and as such could no longer come and go as he pleased but be assigned to whichever post the Navy required. His first assignment was the Pensacola Navy Yard, and he traveled ahead to find suitable housing for his family and his slaves, Willis and Matilda Hodges. In the fall he returned to Portsmouth and took the group on an arduous sea trip to Florida on a miserable little schooner named *Rebecca*. Everyone became seasick, and eventually they were becalmed in the Gulf of Mexico and spent several days floundering at sea. Finally they made port and settled down in their quarters in the picturesque Pensacola Navy Yard. The family became active in the Methodist church that stood just outside of the yard's northwest gate, and the older Porter children began to go their own ways. The oldest son, George, returned to Portsmouth and married; son John and daughters Martha Brent and Alice left Florida to attend schools in Virginia and North Carolina; and the second oldest daughter, Mary, married the Methodist minister John S. Moore in Pensacola, while their father settled down to his duties as Pensacola Navy Yard's constructor. This yard was far smaller than the Gosport facility but an ideal place for John to start his official Navy career. He designed and supervised the construction of the screw sloop USS *Seminole*, a 188- by 30-foot, bark-rigged steam sloop that carried an 11-inch pivot-mounted Dahlgren gun and six 32-pounders. The ship was launched in June 1869, and soon after claims were made that she was constructed with inferior timbers. Because John was the constructor in charge of the project, charges were filed against him. It was soon determined that the claims were either false or seriously exaggerated, and the court found Porter innocent on all counts. Still, this was not an auspicious way to start a career as a naval constructor. The *Seminole* went on to offer productive service during and after the war. She had three captures to her credit, saw action at Mobile Bay, and ironically, was one of the ships that stalked the *Virginia* at Hampton Roads.

Porter continued his work at the Pensacola yard as tensions between North and South increased. On November 1, 1860, the Navy Department stopped paying the workers at the yard, an inexplicable situation that dragged on into January, by which time the workers and their families were in dire straits. Doing everything he could to rectify the problem, John convinced the base commandant, James Armstrong, to get permission from Navy Secretary Isaac Toucey to give the workers food from the naval supplies stored on the base. At this point, Porter might have been remembering his brother's crusade to throw the Navy out of the shipyards. He knew the country was coming apart, and for him to maintain the position he had, Florida would have to stay in the Union.

On January 10, 1861, Florida became the third state to secede from the Union; two days later, war came to John and his family. A militia group from Florida and Alabama marched into the Navy yard and took command. Not a shot was fired. In a few days, all Union Navy personnel were told to leave. By this time, Susan was back in Portsmouth with daughters Susan and Mary and son James. John left Florida for a new assignment at the Washington Navy Yard, where he was kept busy supervising the outfitting of the USS *Pawnee* and the installation of machinery in the USS *Pensacola*. On February 8, 1861, a court of inquiry was called to determine if Commo. James Anderson should be court-martialed for not defending the Pensacola Naval Facility, and John was called to testify. His testimony was straightforward, without any support or rebuke of Armstrong's actions.

However, after the Confederates took the Norfolk facility, he said that he thought that Commandant McCauley, who was in charge of the facility, should have been court-martialed as well. Anderson was found guilty and suspended from active service for five years. It is not clear just what the court thought Anderson should have done, other than build fortifications before the militia arrived. He was in Confederate territory surrounded by Rebel sympathizers and facing a force of more than 350 heavily armed men with only 60–90 men of his own. Any resistance on his part could have ended in a bloodbath and started the war long before the first shot was fired at Sumter. Apparently the Navy reconsidered on this basis, Anderson's conviction was overturned, and he served with distinction throughout the war. He later returned as commandant of the Pensacola Navy Yard and, in 1867, was promoted to captain.

One of John Porter's old instructors, Samuel M. Pook, who had been the chief naval constructor at the Gosport yard since 1859, saw the handwriting on the wall. As a staunch Union man who wanted to put distance between himself and the Old South, he requested a transfer north and was sent to St. Louis, where he began to design and build the now-famous "Pook Turtle" ironclad riverboats. On April 1 John learned of Pook's transfer and immediately applied to fill the vacancy. Throughout this time, he stated a desire to be assigned to a facility near his family, but, like Pook, he had to know that the time was fast approaching when he could find himself in enemy territory. On April 12 the first shots of the Civil War were fired in Charleston harbor. Three days later Lincoln called for 75,000 state militia troops to be called up for ninety days of service, and on April 17 Virginia seceded from the Union. That same day, John received his orders from the U.S. Navy to report to Commandant McCauley at the Gosport Navy Yard. When he arrived, "Everything within the Yard was disorder and confusion. The workmen were standing around in groups. No one was working." Undoubtedly, these groups were either pro-Union or Confederate. Porter reported to McCauley, sized up the situation, and went home to discuss his future with family and friends. He showed good judgment by being totally pessimistic: "I did not think from the beginning of the War that the Confederacy could succeed, if the Federal Government chose to prosecute the war."[9] But he was a Southerner, and once again it would be Virginia first, the federal government second.

While Porter was at home trying to decide exactly what he should do, Commandant Charles Stewart McCauley was wrestling with a larger problem: He was in command of one of the finest naval shipyards in the country, a shipyard in imminent danger of being lost to hostile forces. In addition to the yard itself, there were ships to be protected. Secretary Gideon Welles was concerned about security and sent additional ships to increase the firepower, if necessary. On March 14 the storm-damaged screw steamer *Pocahontas* put into the yard, ostensibly for repairs, followed by the frigate *Cumberland* on March 23. Already on hand were the five-year-old *Merrimack*, which was having her engines overhauled, *Germantown, Raritan, Columbia, Plymouth*, and the old ship of the line *Pennsylvania*. Parts and pieces of the *Merrimack*'s engines were in various machine shops all around the yard. Her tops had been stripped down to the lower mast, and her guns taken off.[10]

Prior to the start of hostilities in Charleston, the administration had been trying to find a way to keep Virginia loyal to the Union. By the second week in April, McCauley was trying to find a way not to be blamed for losing Virginia by starting the first major battle of the American Civil War in defense of the Navy yard. At age sixty-eight, McCauley had had a long and distinguished career in the Navy. He had served on the *Constellation* as a midshipman, fought on Lake Erie in the War of 1812, commanded major ships in the Mediterranean, Atlantic, and Pacific, and in 1856 was honored with a public dinner at the White House. He had never been reprimanded, and his file was full of letters of praise. Now, in the final days of his distinguished career, he was being ordered to defend the Navy yard and prevent its stores and ships from falling into the hands of the insurrectionists. At the same time, he had been ordered to do nothing that could be construed as a hostile act or that might cause anxiety among the people of Virginia—a classic Catch-22 situation. Because of his superiors' inept decision making, McCauley would eventually have a new assignment: designated scapegoat. If there was going to be a war, Washington wanted the South, not the North, to be seen as the aggressor. The Gosport yard was a vital naval facility that many thought should be defended at all cost, and yet general Winfield Scott had already declared the entire Norfolk area undefendable. The closest Union troops, relatively few in number, were on the other side of Hampton Roads at Fort Monroe. It would take a full-scale invasion of all of the land between Suffolk and the Chesapeake Bay to secure the Navy yard against any massed Southern opposition, and that was not about to happen.

Lack of experience led Secretary Welles to send McCauley the first of a number of ambiguous orders that would prove to be McCauley's undoing. On March 10 the first order read in part: "the Steamer *Merrimack* should be in condition to proceed to Philadelphia, or to any other yard, should it be deemed necessary; or in case of danger from unlawful attempts to take possession of her, that she may be placed beyond their reach." And then came the catch: "It is desirable that there should be no steps taken to give alarm."[11] The next day Welles gave oral orders to Commander Alden to go to Norfolk to take the *Merrimack* to Philadelphia. On April 14 Engineer-in-Chief B. F. Isherwood arrived at the yard with orders, informing McCauley that he had been sent "without creating a sensation, but in a quiet manner, to put the machinery in working condition."[12] After the Confederates had fired on Fort Sumter on April 12, McCauley should have realized that the situation had drastically changed. South Carolina might be at war with the United States, but for the moment Virginia's status was in limbo, and McCauley wasn't about to do anything to change the status quo. By April 16 engineers Isherwood and Danby had the engines of the *Merrimack* in working order, and the ship was basically reassembled and ready to sail, but McCauley refused to let Alden take the ship out of the yard. He thought the Rebels might take the mere fact that the *Merrimack* was leaving the yard to be a hostile act. Moreover, his junior officers told him that ships had been sunk in the channel of the Elizabeth River to trap the *Merrimack* at the yard. At this point, Secretary Welles was desperate to save the yard and the ships; if the yard was lost, then the ships had to be saved. He sent Commo. Hiram Paulding to Portsmouth to ascertain the situation, supervise the repair of the *Merrimack*, and get her ready to sail. To Welles's amazement, Paulding returned the next day to report that the *Merrimack* had been repaired and was ready to depart and that things at the yard were just fine.

To add to McCauley's problems, he was surrounded by spies and turncoats. All of his junior officers were Southerners who in a few weeks would be in the Confederate Navy. For the moment, their primary objectives were to keep their Southern friends informed of the Union Navy's plans and their commander as confused and off balance as possible. To accomplish that end, they devised a clever plan. Locomotives blew their whistles at the depot while crowds cheered to create the impression that Rebel reinforcements were arriving by the trainload. People pretending to be armed troops milled around outside the yard and made an awful racket in an effort to sound like a gathering army. Although the sympathies of the workers inside the yard are not known, they were nearly all Southerners.

By this time, McCauley was panicking, trapped in a confusing situation with orders from Washington that basically told him to defend the yard and ships by force if necessary but not to anger anyone in Virginia. With no friends to turn to, he found solace in a bottle, which, according to later reports, became a constant companion. When Welles finally made a decision, it was already too late. Commo. Hiram Paulding was ordered to return to Norfolk and relieve McCauley of command. He was to save the facility if possible and, if not, to destroy it. Before Paulding arrived, McCauley had already decided that the situation was hopeless and ordered the destruction of the ships and the yard. At about 8:00 PM on Saturday, April 20, Paulding arrived on the USS *Pawnee*. A quick look around told him that all he could do was finish the destruction that McCauley had already started.

With him were 349 troops from the 3rd Massachusetts. With the help of the loyal personnel still at the yard, the yard's Marine detachment, his soldiers, and 100 sailors from the *Cumberland*, he began systematically destroying everything possible. Prior to the arrival of Paulding, the Navy personnel, on McCauley's orders, had proceeded to scuttle all the ships in the water around the yard. If destruction was the intent, it was a bad decision in the case of the *Merrimack*. She sank a short way to the bottom, where she settled upright in the mud with water up to, or slightly over, the berth deck. Later, when the fires were started, the spar deck, gun deck, mast, spars, and rigging went up in a spectacular blaze, but the engines and boilers were safe beneath the water. The overall demolition project was far from a total success. An attempt was made to blow up the dry dock, but evidence later showed that either the fuse to the powder kegs was faulty or someone had doused it. At 1:45 AM the order was given to abandon the yard. Fifty sailors from the doomed *Pennsylvania* went on board the *Cumberland*. McCauley thought he should "go down with his ship" and had to be forced to go on board as well. The *Pawnee* and the tug *Yankee* managed to tow the *Cumberland* down the Elizabeth channel to safety across the sea roads under the protection of the Union guns. A resurrected *Merrimack* and the *Cumberland* would meet again the following year. Every ship in the yard was lost, with one sentimental exception. The old *United States*, far too decrepit to ever again be a ship of war, was left in peace. The two huge ship houses had burned, and the large hoisting shears, or derrick, was destroyed.[13] The fires were spectacular, but the next morning the Confederates were pleased with the cache of usable supplies still on hand.

So what was Commandant McCauley doing while Gosport burned? The information that Paulding, Isherwood, and Alden took back to Secretary Welles and General Scott was that orders had not been carried out because McCauley had been drunk during the crisis.[14] McCauley and his supporters denied it as totally false. He had followed the course he took because he did not believe the facility could have held out against the 2,000 militiamen he had been led to believe surrounded the facility. No one had told him

"Burning of the Gosport Navy Yard." In addition to the ships, two large ship houses and numerous other buildings were also destroyed. Because she had been scuttled before being set on fire, the burning *Merrimack* should have been shown sitting deeper in the water than is depicted here. *The Century War Book*

that reinforcements were on the way, so the only practical solution was destroying the yard to keep the ships out of Confederate hands.[15] If more aggressive action had been taken earlier, the ships might have been saved, but even General Scott believed that the yard was doomed from the start. This situation was a simple example of what Stephen Mallory had complained about for years. Longevity, not logic, dictated which naval officer would serve where and when. The administration had known for days that Portsmouth was a crisis waiting to happen, and they should have replaced their "ancient mariner" long before he was put in harm's way. The official government response to the situation was simplistic: Washington had sent sound advice and orders, but poor old McCauley, drunk or sober, was just not up to the task. John Luke Porter may have thought that McCauley should have been court-martialed, but the Navy disagreed. He had served his purpose as scapegoat, and no salt was rubbed into the wound. Charles Stewart McCauley was retired from the service in December 1861 and died May 21, 1869. History soon forgot his years of loyal service but continues to remember the debacle at Gosport.

Just what Porter was doing during the three days of chaos at the yard is unclear. There is no indication that he ever offered assistance to McCauley or anyone else. He does say that on April 20 "I then resigned my appointment as Constructor in the U.S. Service and reported for duty to Commandant Forrest. The Commandant had assumed command of the Yard for the state of Virginia."[16]

No matter how hard he tried, John always seemed to be a few steps behind his dreams. His business ventures failed, and some of the naval projects he worked on were declared failures through no fault of his own. His attempt to become a registered constructor was long and trying. The Navy rejected his plan for a ship that he thought could have been of great benefit to it. He was accused of malpractice soon after he became a constructor. On the eve of what he perceived to finally be stability, his country fell apart. The nation he had been loyal to was suddenly supposed to be his enemy. At this point, all he could rely on were his family and his faith.

When Virginia joined the Confederacy, John followed his state and became a part of the Confederate Navy. In the beginning, he found himself repairing the Gosport yard and preparing guns for coastal batteries rather than constructing ships. Among the wreckage at the yard were various ships that had been destroyed or badly damaged. John wrote a damage report but was too busy to give a lot of thought to these hulks resting in the river. Within a few weeks, though, he would take his place in history because of the blackened hull and rusting engines of one of them, the USS *Merrimack*.

Chapter Three

The Inventor:
John Mercer Brooke

He was an Army brat, born and raised on military posts where his father commanded regular Army troops. As far as we know, in his youth John had no interest whatsoever in ships or the sea. His father, George M. Brooke, was born - in King and Queen County, Virginia, on October 16, 1785. In 1803 George went into the regular Army as a first lieutenant and served with distinction throughout the War of 1812. After the war, he went south as a major in the 4th Infantry to cope with the justifiably unfriendly Creek and Seminole Indians and became a friend and staunch supporter of Andrew Jackson. In 1819 George married Lucy Thomas of Duxbury, Massachusetts, and took his new bride back to Florida, where his regiment was stationed. The major was instructed to build a fort near the present city of Tampa. Completed in 1823, it was named Fort Brooke in his honor. On Monday, December 18, 1826, John Mercer Brooke was born at Fort Brooke.

When John Mercer was five years old, his father was transferred to Fort Mackinaw in the Michigan territory and a year later to Fort Howard on the Fox River where it joins Green Bay, where John lived with his family until he was ten. Life on a military post in the Northwest Territory was hard on Lucy Brooke. Of her eight children, only John and William survived to adulthood. As a respite from the monotony and hardship of housebound frigid winters, Lucy and the children made occasional summer visits back to relatives in Massachusetts and Virginia. Young John had learned to sail on the Fox River and the bay, but the boat trips on the Great Lakes

John Mercer Brooke.
The Century War Book

and the East Coast were his first exposure to seafaring life. They went by lake boat to Buffalo and then took the Erie Canal to Troy. From Massachusetts, they traveled by boat to Virginia. John could find very few playmates at the fort, and educational opportunities were slim. When he was eight, in the fall of 1835, he was sent to a boarding school to begin a real education. His mother took him east to Milnor Hall in Gambier, Ohio, and John immediately decided that this was not the life for him. He ran away and found his mother, who had traveled only a few miles on her way back to Green Bay. She took him back to the school. He waited a few days until his mother would be well out of range and made another escape, this time back to Green Bay. His father took command of the situation at this point and took John to Detroit to stay with a family friend, who was to put the boy on the next steamer to Cleveland. By this time, John was an expert escape artist; he got out of the house, went to the riverfront, and stowed away on a northbound steamer. He arrived home just as all lake transportation ended for the winter. His dogged determination ended his family's attempts to educate him for another two years.

By 1837 Lucy had health problems, and she and the children went to Philadelphia where she could get proper medical attention. John was sent on to Aaron's School in Burlington, New Jersey, to start an educational program. He was older now and knew that, with his mother's problems, there could be no more nonsense on his part. Here he began the classical education that was typical for boys of that time. In addition to the usual curriculum of Latin, mathematics, and history, he was exposed to science and physics for the first time. He was fascinated with this wonderful new world he had discovered. Whenever possible, John visited his sick mother in Philadelphia; because of their isolation in the northwestern outpost, he had grown very close to her. He also enjoyed being with his brothers, especially his youngest, Charlie. In 1839, tragedy visited John Brooke; on the last day of April Lucy Brooke died at the age of thirty-four, followed by Charlie less than a year later. His father, now a colonel, had been transferred to St. Louis. John wanted to join him there, but family friends convinced him that his education should be paramount, so he remained at school in Burlington. His father and a family friend, John Nicolson (who carried the rank of commodore, which stood between captain and vice admiral), put the wheels in motion to obtain an appointment for him as an acting midshipman in the Navy. On April 30, 1841, John received orders from the Navy Department to "proceed to Norfolk without delay and report to Commodore Shubrick for duty on board the USS *Delaware*." John went immediately to Norfolk and stayed with his father's relatives until the day he was to report on board the *Delaware*. While there, he became reacquainted with his teenage cousin Lizzie, his father's sister's daughter. The two had not seen each other for many years. They were immediately attracted to one another and decided to correspond while John was at sea.

On May 14, John reported on board the *Delaware*. He was fourteen years and six months old, almost two years younger than the average acting midshipman. He was "small . . . had a fair skin, with a ruddy complexion, and dark hair . . . intense blue eyes . . . [and was] a skilled swimmer and fencer."[1] The midshipmen wore natty blue uniforms and carried a dirk as a symbol of authority. In the Navy caste system, these boys ranked above common sailors and had certain responsibilities and privileges. When they first went on board a ship in civilian clothes, they were accepted by the seamen, told about the ways of the Navy, and shown how to tie knots and other nautical skills, but when the uniforms arrived, all of that ended. Overnight, their new friends began to treat them as if they had the plague, and with good reason. They were now recognizable midshipmen; they had risen to a new plane where a seaman could not go.[2] This initial camaraderie had a purpose; the seamen were getting to know the young men's temperaments and who would later treat them fairly and who would be abusive. The midshipmen were taught to think of themselves as superior, but at the same time the officers above them could make their lives a living hell if they were thought to be slacking in their duties. Many midshipmen resigned or were dismissed, and only the fittest survived.

The U.S. Navy in the 1840s was in the transition period from sail to steam and from cannonballs to exploding shells. Because of his inquiring mind and interest in science and technology, John was in the right place at the right time. William Garnett, John's uncle and Lizzie's father, wrote to encourage him to take advantage of the opportunities he had in the Navy to improve on his meager education and learn seamanship, navigation, and mathematics. His uncle also advised him to seek the counsel and advice of his officers whenever he had questions. Young John followed this advice; he applied himself to his studies and made a point of getting to know his superior officers. The captain of the *Delaware* was Charles McCauley, who would play a major role in his future. Another officer who supervised John's training was First Officer David Farragut. Proficiency in gunnery and ordnance was stressed on board the *Delaware,* and the many hours of study and drill would serve John well in the future.

From 1841 until 1846 John's naval career was typical for the period. He served on the *Delaware, Princeton, United States,* and *Cyane.* During this five-year period, he kept up a correspondence with his uncle William and his cousin Lizzie. On November 10, 1846, John's career took a drastic and beneficial turn. As ordered, he reported to Commodore Buchanan at the Naval School at Annapolis, where he was about to get a crash course in college academics. The school, to become the United States Naval Academy, was in only its second year and structured much differently than today. The majority of the acting midshipmen in attendance, like John, had had sea experience. They were called seniors and were to undergo an intensive eight months of instruction in mathematics, physics, modern language, history, composition, ordnance, gunnery, chemistry, steam engineering, navigation, algebra, geometry, sextant use, infantry drill, and fencing. If time allowed, they might be permitted to eat and sleep. The younger men and boys, called juniors, who had just joined the Navy and never served on a ship, studied a two-year course before being assigned to sea duty. The students wore civilian clothes and walked from class to class. There was no military regimentation, but they were "expected to act like gentlemen." From November until July of the following year, John's life was consumed with hard work and study. His father wrote to ask if he was angry at him because he seldom received a letter. His uncle and Lizzie felt the same neglect. Early in July, his months of toil culminated in the midshipman's examination before a board of examiners. For him and his classmates, the following days were a combination of relief and anxiety. On July 21, 1847, the board spoke. Fifty of the men who took the examination had failed; of the 136 students who passed, John stood thirty-fifth. At age twenty-one and after six years of sea duty and study, John Mercer Brooke was now a passed midshipman and soon, after a short stay in Norfolk with his relatives, orders came for him to return to sea.

Again John resumed his correspondence with his cousin, and while stationed in the Mediterranean on board the *United States,* he came to the conclusion that he was in love with Lizzie and wanted to marry her. The Mediterranean cruise ended, and the *United States* returned to Norfolk early in 1849. John immediately told his cousin John Ludlow of his intentions, and Ludlow passed the "secret" along to Lizzie. Lizzie was the same age as John, had deep blue eyes and exceedingly fair skin and, according to her sister Charlotte, "was not without good looks." She was a typical Southern girl of her class. She had attended Mrs. Hickly's school for girls in Norfolk, where she had obtained a typically sketchy education. She liked poetry and novels and knew little about history or geography and absolutely nothing about science. The youngest of five brothers and sisters, she was lighthearted, with a sense of humor, and loved a bit of gossip.[3] Being forewarned, Lizzie coquettishly led John on a merry chase. For several days, she made it impossible for him to ever be alone with her, and frustration was his constant companion. But her actions may not have been all for the sake of fun. She was deeply religious and knew that, at best, John was agnostic. She also dreaded the idea of leaving her family and friends to become a sailor's wife and live in far-distant places. At last her feelings for John overcame her misgivings, and on the day John was officially detached from the *United States,* she allowed the two of them to be alone together. According to Lizzie, we can assume that Stephen Mallory and John Brooke had something in common: They were totally inept at the art of proposing! John sat twisting a silk handkerchief around his knees and hands and running it through his fingers. He "had everything so jumbled up together and spoke so fast that I could hardly collect my thoughts." She finally took pity on the poor wretch and told him that she had "never liked anyone else"; her answer was a somewhat reluctant yes.

Lizzie's father was taken by surprise and opposed the marriage. In that time, marriage between cousins was not unusual but not an everyday occurrence. William was also devoutly religious, and knowledge of John's attitude toward religion may have been a factor in his objection. Lizzie's mother, on the other hand, was completely in favor of the union, and she and Lizzie convinced William to consent. No date for the wedding was set, and a few days after his proposal, John was ordered to the Washington Navy Yard to join the crew of the USS *Washington* to prepare the ship for coast survey duty, a perfect assignment. John would be at sea for a few months in the summer and stationed at the Navy yard all winter. His assignment was making observations and calculations at sea for new charts of the eastern Atlantic. In the past, the U.S. Navy had bought its charts from the British Admiralty, but that practice was coming to an end, and John was to play a part. The correspondence between John and Lizzie was primarily about setting a wedding date. John wanted to get married as soon as possible, but many of Lizzie's relatives were lobbying for a long engagement. As the days passed, it became more obvious that the objective of the family's interference was to prolong the engagement indefinitely. The question was still unresolved when the *Washington* put to sea. However, after much correspondence a date was finally set, and John and Lizzie were married at the Garnett home on November 6, 1849.

Brooke's work kept him at sea for most of the summer. During the winter he was back in Washington at the Naval Observatory, where the observations and calculations made on the survey were converted to navigational charts. The man in charge of the observatory was Matthew Fontaine Maury, later known as the "Pathfinder of the Sea." Maury was born in Spotsylvania County, Virginia, on January 14, 1806, but grew up in

Tennessee, where he attended Harpeth Academy near Franklin. He entered the Navy in 1825 where his outstanding abilities were quickly recognized; he made lieutenant in 1836. Three years later, he was in a carriage accident that crippled him, but Maury's loss was the world's gain. The Navy assigned him to the Department of Charts and Instruments, which maintained chronometers, sextants, and other navigation instruments and was the depository for all Navy charts. When a ship was about to leave on a cruise, the necessary instruments and charts would be "checked out," and at the end of the voyage, these items, along with the ship's log, would be returned. Instruments were repaired, if necessary; the charts were filed; and the logs were stored in any convenient place. Legend has it that when Maury came to the department, he discovered that old ships' logs were being burned for fuel to make room for the new ones coming in and that priceless information was literally going up in smoke. The burning stopped immediately, and the staff were assigned to catalog the information in the logs into a specific plan Maury devised. The first item was the vessel's exact location, date of entry, wind direction, current direction, and so forth. The information eventually became a kind of ocean road map that was used throughout the world. Maury devised a new kind of logbook that was not just blank pages in a binder but a printed form with an entry place for all the pertinent facts. This important project became the responsibility of the Department of Charts and Instruments, a department within the Naval Observatory. The observatory had been established in 1844, with Maury in charge.[4]

When John began working at the observatory, Maury already had an international reputation as the world's greatest oceanographer: he had invented a new science. Brooke performed his duties well, and his interest in science grew. In 1850 John was suddenly reassigned to the brig *Porpoise*, to be stationed in the African Squadron to hunt down slave ships. He disliked the assignment intensely. He opposed the slave trade and said that the U.S. efforts to stop it were "a perfect farce."[5] At one point, he decided to resign his commission. His father and Lizzie tried to persuade him to stay, but he was tired of what he considered a useless assignment. He wrote a letter of resignation but before submitting it, he received word that his father had died on March 9, 1851. He was ordered home and landed in Boston on June 25. While settling his father's estate, he wrote to the secretary of the Navy to request assignment to the Naval Observatory. His request was granted, and on October 15 he reported to Matthew Maury. His life was about to take another dramatic turn because of a relatively simple solution he found to a problem that had plagued chart makers and scientists for years.

"Mark Twain" is not only the pen name of the famous author but also a river man's call in sounding the depth of the water under a riverboat. Knots tied at regular intervals along a lead-weighted line were given names so a linesman could stand on the bow, cast his line, and call out to the pilot the name of the knot that showed the depth of the water at that point. "Mark twain" was the knot on the line that indicated deep, safe water. A similar method at sea used a line marked with a combination of knots, colored bunting, and leather at fathom lengths, all the way to twenty fathoms.[6] At even greater depths, the line was simply pulled up and measured on deck. For soundings at ocean depths or areas with strong currents or tides, a cannonball replaced the lead weight so the movement of the water would not cause false depth readings. A sticky substance like wax put on the bottom of the weight or cannonball retained some sand, mud, or gravel stuck to it, and both the depth of the water and the nature of the bottom were determined in one operation. At greater depths, problems began to develop. A line that was too light broke from the weight of the ball. A line that was too heavy put so much rope in the water that the heavy, waterlogged line continued to sink after the ball had touched bottom. To overcome this problem, a special light line, with the proper amount of threads and twist and with a specified tensile strength, was tied to an eye in a cannon ball. Where the line passed through the eye, it was intentionally slightly weakened. When the linesman was satisfied that the ball had hit bottom, he jerked the line, which would break it at the eye, and then brought up the line and measured it. One problem was solved, but the cannon-ball was lost, and with the weight gone and no bottom residue, there was no proof that the weight had hit bottom and no information on the composition of the bottom.

While doing coastal survey work, John had taken hundreds of depth readings and was all too familiar with the problem. He recalled Maury having "expressed the wish that some means of detaching the sinker might be devised and positive evidence of having reached the bottom obtained."[7] John had an idea, made some sketches, refined the idea

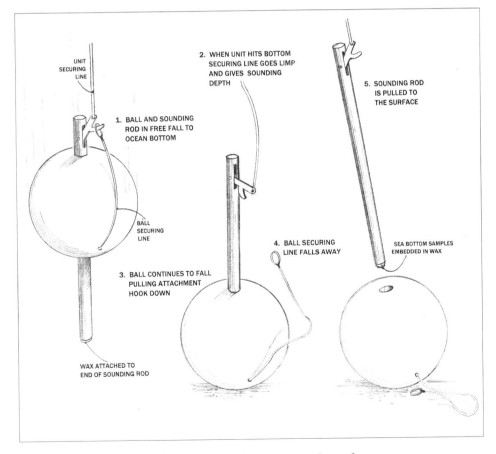

UNIT SECURING LINE

2. WHEN UNIT HITS BOTTOM SECURING LINE GOES LIMP AND GIVES SOUNDING DEPTH

5. SOUNDING ROD IS PULLED TO THE SURFACE

1. BALL AND SOUNDING ROD IN FREE FALL TO OCEAN BOTTOM

BALL SECURING LINE

4. BALL SECURING LINE FALLS AWAY

SEA BOTTOM SAMPLES EMBEDDED IN WAX

3. BALL CONTINUES TO FALL PULLING ATTACHMENT HOOK DOWN

WAX ATTACHED TO END OF SOUNDING ROD

Brooke's sounding device. *Drawn by author*

further, and eventually made a simple model with an old clock's brass ball weight representing the cannonball. Like most great ideas, the concept was relatively simple. A three-quarter-inch hole would be drilled in a cannonball. A rod, with the sounding line attached to a pivoting hook at the top, was passed through the ball. The rod had tallow or grease on the bottom and protruded several inches below the ball. A single linesling supporting the ball was attached to the pivoting hook. When the device struck bottom, the rod stopped, but the ball continued to drop. The pivoting hook that secured the ball was pulled down, and the ring and sling fell loose. The ball now rested on the bottom, but the rod, with the material trapped in the wax, was free and could be pulled to the surface.

With his fellow officers looking on, Brooke demonstrated his invention to Maury. The commander was delighted and had William R. Gable, the instrument maker at the observatory, make a full-scale prototype. The prototype worked perfectly, and the device, with minor changes, was soon being manufactured and used by the Navy.

Scientists like Maury had long been interested in the consistency of the deepest ocean bottoms, but there was no practical reason for this knowledge until the early 1850s. If telegraph lines could connect Boston with Richmond, people reasoned, why not a telegraph line to connect Boston to London? Scientists and engineers began researching how to lay a transatlantic cable to join the continents and quickly hit the same snag that had plagued the Navy. How deep was the ocean, and what type of surface was down there? Would the cable lie on slime and ooze, on rock, or on some material that had never been seen? In 1853 the Navy used Brooke's deep-sea lead to take soundings in the North Atlantic, and this research proved that a huge plateau, as Maury had predicted, stretched from Newfoundland to Ireland. It had a smooth, uniform floor of perfectly formed microscopic seashells. In 1854 Maury announced that conditions were favorable for the Atlantic cable project. An English firm, the Atlantic Cable Company, was formed to design a cable and develop the technique to lay it. Brooke's invention was acknowledged as the key that made the project feasible. He wanted to be involved in designing and laying the cable, but the Navy had other ideas.

His reputation as a man of science grew, and in 1854 he was appointed astronomer and hydrographer on board the USS *Vincennes* for a north Pacific survey expedition, responsible for synchronizing chronometers, making astronomical observations, and taking depth soundings. This was the first of two expeditions he would make to the Pacific. On this voyage, he went around Cape Horn, through the Indian Ocean, around Australia, through the Coral Sea, north to the Carolines and the Marianas, and on to Hong Kong. At stops along the way, he set up his astronomical instruments and took readings to establish exact longitude and latitude points for the charts that would be made back in Washington. After leaving China, they went through the Sea of Japan and then down Japan's east coast, stopping at Edo (present-day Tokyo). He did the first survey ever taken of as much of Japan's east coast as their time in the area allowed. After leaving Japan, the *Vincennes* went north and in July 1855 passed through the Bering Straits into the Arctic Ocean. John was taking deep-sea soundings all along the way. At one cast, he reached a depth of 2,500 fathoms, more than three miles, and brought up a bottom sample of greenish mud to prove it. Before going south, he made observations on the coasts of both Siberia and Alaska. On October 13, 1855, the *Vincennes* anchored in San Francisco Bay. The expedition was hailed as a tremendous success, but not without cost. One of the five ships that had started on the journey, the *Porpoise*, was lost in the Pacific. The wreck was never found, and there were no survivors.

On March 1, 1856, John Brooke reported to the secretary of the Navy in Washington. He had spent three years circumnavigating the globe, risking his life to make observations that would benefit both the Navy and humankind, and for all this, he was granted two weeks of leave. John hurried to Lexington, Virginia, to join Lizzie, where she had been living with her sister and brother-in-law. When his leave ended, he returned to the Naval Observatory in Washington, where he began work on the new charts of parts of the Japanese islands, the Sea of Okhotsk, and the Bering Straits. By April 1858 all of Brooke's charts had been engraved and published. In the meantime, John brought Lizzie to Washington, and there, on December 12, 1856, their daughter, Anna Marie Brooke, was born.

John had found that the conventional hook-and-eye mechanism for attaching and detaching a ship's boats to and from davit lines was difficult and dangerous. He devised a ball-and-socket mechanism with a swivel that eliminated any twist in the lines; it was simple to handle in a pitching boat and would not detach or reattach, by accident. He patented the device in August 1860 and later made some improvements, which he also patented. The *U.S. Nautical Magazine and Naval Journal* said that Brooke's new device was "a labor and life saving improvement, commending itself to the nautical fraternity." John had not given any thought to patenting his sounding device until someone else tried to claim the credit for it. When Matthew Maury had instructed Brooke to have the instrument maker, William Greble, make a prototype, Greble made some minor suggestions that he thought might be improvements. These "improvements" proved not to be efficient and were dispensed with on later models. When the national and international press began praising Brooke's achievement, Greble stepped forward to claim the invention as his. Because Maury and John's fellow officers had witnessed the first demonstration, proving that Greble was a liar was easy enough. But John's reputation had been besmirched, and he went to considerable trouble to make sure that the public and the scientific community knew the truth of the matter. He would never have guessed then that he would be confronted with a similar problem in the future. After the Greble fiasco, John submitted a patent application for the sounding device to the Patent Office but was told that because drawings of the device had been published, and the Navy and private companies had made and used the device for more than two years, it had automatically passed into the public domain. He was encouraged to ask the Navy for compensation for the invention, and his cause was championed by influential men in the Navy and in Congress, including Matthew Maury and Stephen Mallory. On February 21, 1861, he was awarded $5,000. In 1857 John authorized Charles Mortimer of Charlotte, North Carolina, as his agent in selling his boat hook patent. He was paid $150 at the time and was to receive $1,350 when the patent was sold to a manufacturer, but Mortimer never found a buyer.

In 1858 John Brooke began his last assignment for the U.S. Navy, taking charge of an expedition to plot the best and safest shipping route between San Francisco and Hong Kong. He was to take the schooner USS *Fenimore Cooper* and its crew of twenty-one across the Pacific and back, taking depth soundings and astronomical readings and studying the flora and fauna on any islands encountered. On September 16 he sailed through the Golden Gate and began a voyage that would be stranger than fiction. Because John

was determined to take as many deep-sea soundings as possible, the expedition fell behind schedule. Diamond Head was sighted after six weeks at sea. Between the mainland
and Hawaii, he had obtained readings ranging from 2,000 to 2,900 fathoms. He went
ashore in Hawaii for several weeks to set up his astronomical instruments and check the
chronometers, and in the midst of this operation, he became quite ill. As soon as he could
walk, he set out to chart and explore the islands north and west of Hawaii, all the way to
Midway. This survey lasted thirty-eight days and allowed Brooke to correct errors and
misinformation on the old charts. He also discovered a guano-rich island to claim in the
name of the United States. On March 9, 1859, the *Fenimore Cooper* left Honolulu and
headed west to Johnston Island and then on to Guam. Again, the astronomical instruments were set up on shore. While at Guam, they had a harbinger of things to come when
a severe storm swept the island and "at 9:15 the wind blew so hard that a man could not
stand on deck."[8] One schooner in the harbor was thrown onto the reef, while the *Cooper's*
crew experienced some anxious moments but came through unscathed. They left Guam
on May 3 and headed for the South China Sea, en route to Hong Kong. On the way John
took soundings and bottom samples ranging from 900 to 3,300 fathoms. On May 19, 1859,
the schooner dropped anchor at Hong Kong. The expedition was hailed as a tremendous
success. The *Hong Kong Mail* reported that only about a fifth of the 496 navigational hazards that were believed to lie between California and Hong Kong actually existed. The
paper gave the Brooke sounding device proper credit and pointed out that the Royal Navy
was also using it. John Mercer Brooke had become a world-renowned inventor, scientist,
and explorer who could look forward to a brilliant future.

On June 23 the *Cooper* set sail for Japan, where Brooke wanted to do more coastal
survey work. In ten days they reached Okinawa, and after the observation of proper protocol, the local governor gave permission for the survey. Brooke began working his way up
the coast while taking readings and frequently going onshore to make astronomical observations. Brooke and one of his crew had been inland for several days when they encountered heavy rains. On their way back to the *Cooper,* they received an emergency message:
"We are on shore. I have saved what I could. You had better come quickly."[9] In a violent
squall, the *Cooper* had blown ashore at Yokohama. The crew was safe, but the ship was
damaged. A Russian commodore, commanding a Russian squadron in the area, offered
assistance. The ship was careened, and the Russian, who was also a naval constructor,
made a thorough examination. His findings were frightening: forty-one of the floor and
futtock timbers were rotten, the keelson was rotten at the step of the foremast, and timbers were gone on both sides. In short, the USS *Fenimore Cooper* was a floating coffin,
and they were lucky that it wasn't resting on the bottom of the Pacific. Everything possible was salvaged, and Brooke and the crew found themselves stranded in Japan.

At Yokohama, he met a Captain King of the *Wanderer,* who related a most unusual
story. King was the nephew of Josiah Johnson, who had contracted with a builder, Aaron
Westervelt, to build the *Cooper.* To save money, Johnson had Westervelt construct the
schooner from refuse, the cut-down timbers from the clippers *Golden Gate* and *Sweep-*
stakes. Johnson was not satisfied with the speed of his new ship and sold it to a U.S. Navy
purchasing agent named Ringgold. Apparently, Brooke had some knowledge of Ringgold's reputation; he described the matter in his diary "as one of Ringgold's purchases,
cheap and bad."[10]

Lodgings were found for Brooke and the crew until arrangements could be made to send them home. Unfortunately, the housing was not in the best part of town, and there were sake shops only a few steps away. Idle time and sake began to cause trouble among the bored crew. Because of numerous fights and other problems, Brooke finally arranged for a few of the worst offenders to be housed for safekeeping at Kanagawa prison until they could leave for home. One day a crew member burst into Brooke's quarters to warn him about a fight going on next door in the crew's quarters. Not knowing the severity of the problem, he thrust two pistols into his belt and rushed to the scene of the disturbance, where he found two men fighting. While he was separating the two, and keeping them apart with threatening motions with one of the pistols, the gun discharged. Seaman Robert Weir was hit in the chest. Brooke had cleaned the gun a few days before but later believed that some damage caused in the wreck of the *Cooper* or the soaking in seawater may have caused the gun to misfire. The doctor examined Weir and found that the wound was serious but not fatal. Weir was apparently recovering when suddenly he began having breathing problems and died on September 19. Brooke immediately called for a court of inquiry, and on November 1, with the doctor and crew members as witnesses, he was quickly absolved of any wrongdoing. The incident was classified as an accident caused by unavoidable circumstances. Brooke had all the *Cooper*'s troublesome crew members transferred to the USS *Powhatan* and kept eight reliable men with him to help with the survey.

Brooke was making progress with the survey using the instruments he had set up on land when a new problem developed. The foreign quarter of Yokohama was not only infested with sake shops but also packed with small-frame houses and large warehouses. It was a fire waiting to happen, and in January a huge one ravaged the foreign quarter. For twenty-four hours, everything was in flames. A large warehouse next to Brooke's quarters blazed while he and his men worked frantically to save the instruments. The governor of Yokohama sent men to help Brooke move the instruments and supplies out of the city. Everything was saved, and in a few days the survey work continued. Japanese officials were fascinated and constantly asked questions, particularly about navigation, because they were starting a deep-sea navy and had decided to take a recently purchased ship of their own across the Pacific. Because he knew that the Japanese seamen were primarily accustomed to working between the Japanese home islands, China, and Korea, John was concerned about this project. Global navigation would be a new experience for them. Not only would they be learning navigation, but doing it on a recently purchased Dutch vessel with which they were unfamiliar. This looked like another tragedy waiting to happen.

The Japanese were obviously of the same opinion because when the *Powhatan* was ready to take Brooke and his crew back to California, the Japanese governor asked Brooke come on board their new ship, a bark-rigged screw steamer of 292 tons, now named the *Kanrin Maru*, as navigator. Permission was granted, and he was allowed to make any arrangements he felt necessary to ensure the safety of the voyage. He took on board his navigational instruments, food and supplies, and nine men picked from the *Cooper*'s old crew. On February 10, 1860, the *Kanrin Maru* weighed anchor and made her way into the open sea. One hundred Japanese were on board under the command of Secretary of Naval Affairs Kimura Settsuno-kami, a captain, and an executive officer. The crew wore no uniforms, just a hodgepodge of traditional Japanese clothing mixed with some Western attire. The executive officer wore a breastplate that was probably a badge of authority. It soon became apparent that the crew was woefully unprepared for the voyage. The engineers could handle the hundred-horsepower engine but had only a six-day supply of coal. This was a sailing vessel with a crew that didn't know how to sail.

Three days out, the *Kanrin Maru* ran into the weather that she would face for most of the voyage. Gale-force winds and heavy seas began rocking a ship that now had only a three-day coal supply left on board. The crew was going to have to learn fast, with Brooke as their teacher. The interpreter on board, Manjiro, spoke excellent English, was quick to learn, and would be the key to making this awkward situation work. On the first day out, Brooke had divided his small crew into two twelve-hour watches so that he would be informed, day or night, of any problems that might develop. There were no multiple problems, just one long, unending crisis. The helmsman didn't know how to steer by the wind, and the sailors didn't know one line from another. All nautical instructions, given by the officers, were in Dutch, which most of the crew didn't understand—not that that made much difference because they didn't know what to do when Brooke had Manjiro give them instructions in Japanese. When Manjiro ordered them to go aloft, they threatened to kill him.

By February 15 the storm had become a full-fledged typhoon, and the *Kanrin Maru* was on the brink of disaster. The 2,415-ton *Powhatan* and its crew of four hundred were being pounded by the same storm. Its captain said that "never in all of his twenty-eight years' experience at sea, had he encountered such a tempest."[11] If they were to survive, the ten Americans on board the *Kanrin Maru* would have to sail the ship with little or no assistance. Settsuno-kami and the captain were too seasick to come topside. To maintain some sort of discipline, Brooke had Manjiro tell the crew that he would get the captain's permission to hang any man guilty of disobeying orders. Because of his demeanor and the severity of the situation, they believed what he said. The possibility of falling overboard was preferable to being hanged, so they began to cooperate as best they could. Still, it took them twenty minutes to get on deck when called, and they spent most of their time cooking or eating. When the weather was not too severe, the American crew would take a few of the more promising Japanese crewmen aloft and instruct them as much as possible under the existing conditions. The worst of the storm subsided, but without sun or stars for days, navigation was by compass and dead reckoning.

By the end of three weeks Brooke and his crew were exhausted, and the Japanese officers and crew still showed little discipline. On land, they had been polite and cooperative, but at sea they seemed to be from a different planet. The time had come for some drastic action. On March 1 Brooke informed the captain and officers that, on his orders, the American crew was "on strike." They would do nothing to take care of the vessel unless the Japanese officers and men cooperated. It was a simple case of sink or swim; they could either work together or die together. They must take orders and follow the instructions of the men who were trying to teach them to be sailors; the ship was not about to sail itself. The captain gave his crew a stern lecture and then put them all under Brooke's command. One minute he had been a U.S. Navy lieutenant, and in the next he become an acting Japanese naval captain. He could never have imagined this situation in his wildest dreams. With this new arrangement, the situation improved, and he and his crew were able to teach the Japanese officers and men some practical seamanship and naviga-tion. The weather improved along with shipboard conditions; the ship's exact location was fixed, and spirits rose as they approached California. Brooke predicted that the green and unruly crew would someday make good sailors. On March 17 they passed under the Golden Gate Bridge and celebrated the fact that, despite all of their difficul-ties, they had arrived ahead of the *Powhatan*.

San Francisco was abuzz with the news of the Japanese ship's arrival, and Brooke was thrust into the limelight once again. As he took the Japanese dignitaries on a tour of the city, he was trailed by the press, and peppered with questions about the voyage, the great storm, and his survey work. The Japanese heaped on accolades for his determina-tion and courage in bringing them across the Pacific. They had given him lovely gifts be-fore the voyage began and now gave more. They had wanted to give him a large sum of money, but he explained that, as a naval officer, he was doing his duty, so while he could accept their gifts of appreciation he could not accept pay. The *Cooper*'s crew was dis-charged in San Francisco, and Brooke took passage on a ship to Panama. The *Powhatan* left for Panama nine days later with the Japanese. Brooke arrived back in New York on April 27 and soon received news that Lizzie was seriously ill. He immediately requested and was granted three months' leave and was back in Lexington in early May. He had been scheduled to be on the commission to receive the Japanese in Washington, but be-cause of Lizzie's condition, he could not participate. By June, Lizzie had improved enough for him to take her to Washington.

Although officially still on leave, he spent time with Maury and made plans for the new charts. Brooke was kept informed about the progress of the proposed Atlantic cable project and hoped to participate in some way in either the planning or actual laying of the cable. In 1857 and 1858, he published papers on the subject in science journals. Since his invention and Maury's research had made the project feasible in the first place, he expected an opportunity to be involved, but the work was being done by an English company that had little interest in the aspirations of an American naval officer. The com-pany's first attempt in the summer of 1857 failed when the cable broke as it was being laid. John immediately wrote a letter to explain what he believed had caused the problem and described in detail precisely how to correct the situation. Several weeks later, he re-ceived a polite letter from the Atlantic Cable Company thanking him for his interest and telling him that they had independently solved the problem before they had received his letter. Brooke still hadn't figured out the importance of protecting an idea before he an-nounced it. Just before sailing on the *Fenimore Cooper*, he learned that the second at-tempt to lay the cable had succeeded. It went into operation on August 5, 1858, but soon failed. The project would not succeed until 1866, and when the history was written, Brooke and Matthew Maury's contributions were relegated to minor footnotes.

Back in Washington, Brooke and Maury were distracted from their work by the end-less speculation about secession. Both of their lives were rooted in the U.S. Navy, and their Southern ties were a matter of chance, not choice. But like many around them, they were about to make a very unscientific decision based on raw emotion and not logic. After the November election, hope faded. Brooke waited for the Virginia state legisla-ture to decide his future. One bright spot did appear in February. His request for com-pensation for his sounding device had languished in Congress for years. It had been a rider on various bills but had always been cut before any action was taken. It was attached to the naval appropriations bill of 1861, watched over by Mallory, and President Buchanan signed the bill into law on February 21. As soon as possible, John went to the Treasury Department and picked up his $5,000. He was now faced with a new but not unpleasant problem: How would he invest his newfound fortune? Northern railroads or Southern cotton? Circumstances were moving too fast for him to decide this problem. On April 17, 1861, Virginia seceded from the Union, and the die was cast. On the 20th Brooke submitted his resignation to the Navy. Robert E. Lee and Maury resigned that same day. The Navy ignored his resignation, instead marking him as dismissed with his name stricken from the roles. In essence, he was dishonorably discharged. In later years, Adm. David Dixon Porter said that he had regretted the loss of only two men from the U.S. Navy, Catesby Jones and John Mercer Brooke.[12]

John had written to Lizzie during those long days and nights in Asia and the South Pacific. He had searched his soul and from far away told Lizzie his innermost thoughts: He had a temper, one that could turn to rage. He had killed a man. He was conceited, felt that he was superior to those around him, and he could not bring himself to be truly religious. For Lizzie's sake, he had tried. He had read the Bible and thought long and hard on the words he had read, but they were not clear or concise like the movement of the stars or the unfolding of a mathematical formula. He finally gave up trying to understand and turned away.

John took Lizzie, ill and pregnant, and their daughter, Anna, to Lexington, Virginia, to be with Lizzie's relatives, and then he went on to Richmond to join the Virginia State Navy. He invested his $5,000 in Confederate bonds.

PART
II

The Ship

Chapter Four

A Changing Technology

Many of the dominant officers in the old Navy either could not or would not accept the fact that wooden ships firing broadsides were a thing of the past. Naval ordnance was undergoing a revolution. Henri-Joseph Paixhans, the French artillerist, had perfected a naval artillery shell that could be used in horizontal fire. In land combat or for coastal bombardment, mortar shells had been used from the earliest days of artillery history, but on moving sailing ships they were impractical and dangerous. Mortars were therefore only used for coastal defense and on "floating batteries" in rivers. Exploding shells bursting in the rigging or on the sides of wooden ships were a terrifying concept. In a pamphlet published in 1825, Paixhans declared that nothing less than iron armor could resist shellfire.[1] In 1823 Captain Delisle, a French engineer, proposed that a ship of the line be converted into a screw steamer, using the screw he had invented, and be covered with iron sides and deck armor and armed with a ram and 10- and 12-inch shell guns. In 1831 a French inventor named Esquirol proposed that a ship be built with horizontal beam hoops to be covered with iron armor and carry a ram. The French government took no action on either of these proposals or on numerous others that were pouring in. Dreamers and inventors all over the world were trying to design the indestructible man-of-war. Practically all of these Jules Verne proposals had three things in common: The ship would be made of iron with either curved or sloping sides, be powered solely by steam, and carry the most powerful ordnance possible. The British Admiralty and U.S. Navy were also besieged with such proposals. With all of the talk, newspaper articles, and published pamphlets, the time had to come for someone to pay attention. Throughout Europe in the 1820s and 1830s, experiments were conducted with various types of ordnance fired against every conceivable sort of armor.

The U.S. Navy's reluctance in the 1850s to take too seriously proposals for revolutionary new ideas is understandable; they had been burned too many times in the past. During the War of 1812 Robert Fulton designed and built the world's first steam-powered warship for the Navy, the steam battery *Demologos*. It was intended for coastal defense but was not finished until after the war. In 1829 it was accidentally blown up in New York harbor. Fulton also proposed construction of a submarine, the *Mute*, but the plan was never carried out. In 1814 Uriah Brown claimed to have rediscovered Greek fire, which he would incorporate into a shot-proof steam vessel called the *Navis Conflagrator*. He pestered the Navy for twenty-four years until they agreed to watch a demonstration of his seagoing dragon. It was everything he had said and more! A long tongue of flame shot out across the water as if projected from a fire hose. The observers were terrified when they realized that with a slight shift in the wind, they, and the ship they were standing on, would be the one "conflagrated." In 1847 Brown persuaded Congress to give him $10,000 to perfect the shot-proof vessel that was part of his original proposal, but without the flamethrower. The ship would be 200 feet long and have sloping sides and rounded ends rising up from the waterline; it would be covered with sheet iron backed with heavy oak timbers. There would be a flat upper deck for hatches and other openings, and the engines would turn a "submerged waterwheel." Brown's so-called waterwheel was a screw propeller. Unfortunately, Brown spent the entire sum in experimentation and in the end had nothing concrete to show Congress. Secretary of the Navy John Mason refused to put any more money into the project, thus ending Brown's hopes. Brown's basic design preceded the *Virginia* by more than forty years.

Sporadically throughout the early 1830s the Navy considered various plans for paddle-wheel warships, but for varying reasons nothing substantive ever happened. Finally in 1835 Andrew Jackson, a longtime admirer of steam power, directed Secretary of the Navy Mahlon Dickerson to build a steam battery "of a form and size best calculated for the defense of our ports and harbors."[2] The Navy Commission, predecessor to the Navy Board system, began to explore ways and means. Having no experience in such matters, the commission had to depend on the advice of civilian "experts" who didn't know much more than the committee. The project became an ongoing process of trial and error. On one occasion, a 32-pound cannon was fired across a mock-up section of deck, built on a platform, to see if there might be any unexpected problems. There were: the platform and deck were demolished. There were also flaws in the hull design. One type of engine was started and then scrapped in favor of another. Murphy's Law—anything that can go wrong will go wrong—ruled supreme. Finally, in 1838, the finished product, christened *Fulton II*, was tested on the water and proclaimed a tremendous success. Although unorthodox in appearance, she was extremely fast and easy to manage. The press loved her; she was the pride of the Navy and a joy to the American public. But then problems began to appear. She performed well only on comparatively calm waters. In rough water, the paddle housing was submerged, causing her to "chore" (struggle), with the housing acting as a brake. In high seas, steering her required eight men. The hull design was such that she ran low at the bow in a heavy sea and her deck was constantly awash. She had a voracious appetite for coal and not enough bunker space to keep her stoked for more than seventy hours, and because she had been designed along the lines of a paddle-wheel riverboat, she handled poorly under sail. Efforts were made to correct her faults but failed. In 1842 she was laid up, and the Navy had yet another reason to distrust anything new and different.[3]

Another long-lasting naval embarrassment was the *Stephens Battery*. This design disaster started in 1841 and continued off and on until 1885. Robert L. Stephens and his brother Edwin were commissioned to build a ship of monumental proportions for the defense of New York harbor. The design of the ship took on a life of its own; every time Robert thought of a possible improvement, it was back to the drawing board. The

The *Fulton II*. The *Fulton II* was one of the last three paddle-wheel riverboat-type ships built for the Navy. Because of poor performance, she was laid up after only four years of service. *Naval Historical Center illustration*

envisioned finished size ranged from "not less than 250 feet to 400 feet." It was to be propelled by a "Stephens skull" (a six-bladed screw propeller, one of which was installed on the *Princeton* in 1845) and be built of iron plating three and a half inches to six inches thick. Many descriptions of the ship appeared in newspapers and journals, but no plans survive. All work was done in great secrecy for fear of foreign spies. Because the ship was always promised but never delivered, supplemental contracts were required. New delivery dates were set and never met.

When Robert Stephens died in 1856, the unfinished work was left to Edwin.[4] The project continued to languish, and on December 24, 1861, a naval board of experts voted four to one to scrap the project. The government had invested $1,283,294, to which Stephens had added $228,435 of his own money.[5] Edwin wouldn't give up and continued to raise more funds for construction. When he died in 1868, he bequeathed the unfinished ship and a million dollars for continued construction to the state of New Jersey. The additional money was spent, but the ship was still unfinished. At that point, all who were then involved had had enough, and the *Stephens Battery* was scrapped and broken up where she stood on the ways in Hoboken.[6]

By 1839 the United States was far behind the other navies of the world in developing new technology. The British had fifteen paddle sloops and a steam frigate, and France had at least sixteen steamers. Despite the apparent lack of interest from the Navy, in March Congress directed the construction of two seagoing steam frigates. Actually the Navy had good cause for not being enthusiastic about steamers, given the capability of the ordnance a ship faced; a paddle-wheel steamer was a floating catastrophe in the making. One well-placed shot into a paddle wheel or boiler would end the battle. Poor performance under sail was a hallmark of these vessels, as were their commonplace engine failures. Either one would be a death knell during a battle. The new types of ordnance were turning naval strategy upside down. The number of broadside guns a ship carried became less important against an enemy with one or two long-range shell guns that were powerful and accurate. Naval combat would no longer be a slow chess game but a quick-draw shoot-out lasting minutes instead of hours. The old admirals had little confidence in the new ships or their tactics. Something better was needed, but no one knew what. Whether they were wanted or not, Congress gave the Navy two new steamers in 1841, the *Mississippi* and *Missouri*. Lessons learned from the mistakes made on the *Fulton II* did contribute to better design decisions for the two new ships. Once again the press and general public were delighted with these new symbols of national prestige. The ships were huge, 220 feet between perpendiculars, with a 39-foot beam and a 20-foot draft. They were bark-rigged with 19,000 square feet of canvas. Ten Paixhan-type shell guns made up each ship's battery. The engines and boilers were masterpieces of Victorian engineering, with excellent speed, and they were more economical on fuel than the *Fulton II* had been, with the *Missouri* saving more fuel than the *Mississippi*. As paddle-wheel warships went, these two were among the best ever built. The *Mississippi* was with Perry in Japan, circumnavigated the earth twice, and served with distinction in the Civil War. At New Orleans she was instrumental in the destruction of the ironclad *Manassas*. She ran aground while under Confederate shore battery fire at Port Hudson in 1863. To prevent capture, her crew burned her. The *Missouri's* career was quite different. In 1843 she gained fame for the first transatlantic crossing by a steam warship, but near Gibraltar on August 23, she was accidentally destroyed by fire.

The *Allegheny*, launched in 1847, was the last gasp for the paddle-wheel approach. She was a radical design conceived by Lt. W. W. Hunter (assisted by J. L. Porter): an iron ship with two horizontal paddle wheels that protruded from the hull below the waterline. The project was an expensive fiasco. Her only claim to fame was as the first U.S. iron vessel to cross the Atlantic.

The Navy by then was even less interested in experimentation. Between 1841 and 1844 the Board of Navy Commissioners requested fourteen sailing vessels to be built. The navy was in full technological retreat. With the navies of Europe going in an entirely different direction, the United States was about to be totally outclassed without some drastic changes in the upper echelon of naval command and planning. The Navy's Board of Commissioners was made up of veteran officers of the War of 1812. There were no retirement provisions, and unlike old soldiers who just fade away, the old sailors seemed to last forever.[7]

The drastic changes came on August 31, 1842. Public opinion and the press forced Congress to abolish the Board of Commissioners, and an entirely new naval command and management system was installed. Instead of three appointed officers and the Navy secretary having the final say on everything the Navy did, five separate bureaus were formed: Construction and Repair, Yards and Docks, Ordnance and Hydrographics, Provisions and Clothing, and Medical and Surgery. For all practical purposes, the old American sailing Navy had sailed into history, along with the paddle-wheel steamers, of which the *Mississippi* and *Missouri* were the last.

The Navy was not disenchanted with the idea of steam propulsion; it was paddle-wheel steamers they didn't like. Being able to go in and out of ports regardless of the winds and tides was a true bonanza. Turning on a dime and dashing in all directions during combat was the answer to a captain's prayer. But reliance on a hissing, wheezing, smoke-belching, unpredictable pile of iron and brass sitting on deck and slowly turning

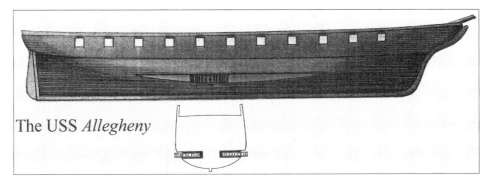

The *Allegheny*. Lt. W. W. Hunter attempted to solve the paddle-wheel problem by designing an iron ship with two horizontal paddle wheels below the waterline. The horizontal wheel concept was a complete failure and spelled the end of the Navy's paddle-wheel experiments. *Drawn by author*

two huge targets on port and starboard was not the answer. There had to be a better way, and the better way was already at hand, or almost. For years, progressively thinking naval officers had known about and lobbied the old board to examine the screw propeller. After years of frustration and endless arguments, they finally prevailed. On September 9, 1843, the screw sloop of war *Princeton*, designed by John Ericsson, was launched, and a new era began.[8] Full-rigged screw steamers would become the mainstay of the Navy for the next forty years. At the time of the Spanish American War in 1898, five of these old ships were still in service.[9]

The screw steamer was no new invention. John Ericsson had successfully demonstrated a screw propeller on the Thames on April 19, 1837. Whether Ericsson, Uriah Brown, Delisle, Robert L. Stephens, or Sir Francis Petit Smith first came up with the idea of a screw propeller can't be proved, but there is no doubt that Ericsson was the first to demonstrate it publicly. A screw-propelled ship had tremendous advantages over a paddle-wheel ship. First and foremost, there were no cumbersome appendages hanging on the side; the propeller and the engine were beneath the waterline, well out of harm's way. In essence, a screw steamer was a sailing ship with an engine. A captain could go to sea in something he trusted, not a glorified Mississippi riverboat. The Navy and Congress began to get the message. Between 1854 and 1859 thirty steam-powered vessels were built for, or acquired by, the Navy. Stephen Mallory was one of the moving forces behind the changes. In 1854, when he was chairman of the Senate's Committee of Naval Affairs, Congress authorized the construction of six large auxiliary screw steamers, one of which would play a pivotal role in Mallory's life. But time was running out for him and his fellow Southerners in Congress and in the military. Soon dire necessity would bring technological changes to the U.S. Navy, and the first technological decision Mallory would make as the secretary of the Confederate Navy would be a mixture of the new and the old. The "old" would be the hulk of the USS *Merrimack*.

Chapter Five

The USS *Merrimack*

About 10,000 years ago the Wisconsin glacier crept across what we now call New England. Glaciers are prone to rearrange things, and this one was no exception. Before the glacier, a river flowed south through present-day New Hampshire, into the northeastern corner of Massachusetts, and emptied into Boston Harbor. The glacier forced the southern part of the river to take a sharp left turn at Lowell and go into the Atlantic at Newburyport. When the glacier receded, it left in the north a rugged, steep-walled valley surrounded by four- and five-thousand-foot mountain peaks. As the river flows south, the terrain becomes less severe and eventually presents a gently rolling landscape with meandering streams and numerous lakes. Some nine to eight thousand years ago, during the Early and Middle Archaic Period, people established permanent residences in this lush river valley.[1] By the Late Woodland Period, when Europeans began to arrive, there were well-established villages with loose-knit alliances. The principal tribes in the southern alliance were the Pawtucket, Pintucket, and Agawam, primarily hunter-gatherers who practiced a little agriculture.

The tribes spoke the same language, but as sometimes is the case, they gave different names to the same places or things in their vicinity. Because they had no written language, we can't now know exactly what the correct word for anything was. English newcomers, hearing residents say the name of a place, then gave it an English spelling that sounded as close as possible to what they heard. A French or Spanish visitor would have spelled the same word differently. Consequently, we do not know the original pronunciation of most Native American words. On the south side of the river, people called the waters something that sounded like "monomack," meaning "the place of islands." On the north bank, it was called "merrimack," meaning "the place of strong currents" or "the place of broken waters."[2] *Indian Place Names of New England* also cites "merrimac" in Penacook as meaning "deep place" and "merrimack" in Abenaki as meaning "at the deep place." Of these five different translations of the same-sounding word, the colonials picked Merrimack. Why with the "k" rather than without it? No one ever said. To add to the confusion, early settlers established a village where the Souhegan River flows into the Merrimack and named it Merrimac. And then just south of Merrimac, there is South Merrimack! Throughout the seventeenth and eighteenth centuries, there was apparently no absolutely correct way to spell the name. Both spellings were used in newspapers, books, and private correspondence. Sometime prior to the Civil War, the South settled on "Merrimac" and spelled it that way in practically all Southern publications and correspondence. Despite that predilection, because the ship we are concerned with here was named for the river, USS *Merrimack* is the only correct identification. Then again, Union Navy secretary Welles and most other Northerners never got it straight either. When Welles refers to the ship in his letters and diary, he uses the "Merrimac" spelling. Salvage contracts prepared by the Navy in 1869 and 1870 also have the incorrect spelling. In a little book titled *The Mystery of the Merrimack*, Edward Barthell goes into great detail about the confusion over the correct spelling of the ship's name.

By the early sixteenth century, the native population had been driven far from the banks of the lower Merrimack, and Yankee engineering and commerce took their place. One of the early industries was boat building. In 1791 the 49-ton sloop *Merrimack* was built at Haverhill. In 1812 two sloops of 59 and 86 tons, both named *Merrimac Packet*, were also built at Haverhill. In 1886 an 88-by-20-foot barge joined the *Merrimac* ranks.[3] In 1799 Cross & Clark of Newberryport built the 467-ton frigate *Merrimack* for the U.S. Navy.[4] The next Navy *Merrimack*, the one that was destined to become the CSS *Virginia*, was launched from the Charlestown Navy Yard on June 15, 1855. Causing more confusion, on March 10, 1864, the U.S. Navy put into service the USS *Merrimac*, a ship the Union Navy had captured on July 10, 1863; it had been an English ship named

"**Launching the *Merrimack*.**" The USS *Merrimack* being launched at the Charlestown Navy Yard on June 15, 1855. *Ballard's Pictorial, 1855*

Nangis that the Confederates bought for a man named Roberts to use as a blockade runner. And then on June 3, 1898, in the Spanish-American War, a Navy collier that the Navy had attempted to scuttle to block Santiago Harbor in Cuba was destroyed by Spanish gunfire before reaching its desired position. Its name was the USS *Merrimac*.[5] Amazingly, the Navy has had two more *Merrimack* ships, a 21,000-ton oil tanker built in 1942 and a 37,000-ton *Cimarron*-class tanker built in 1980.[6]

On April 6, 1854, Congress authorized construction of "Six First-Class Steam Frigates" that would become the USS *Merrimack,* commissioned February 20, 1856; the *Wabash,* commissioned August 18, 1856; the *Roanoke,* commissioned May 4, 1857; the *Minnesota,* commissioned May 21, 1857; and the *Colorado,* commissioned March 13, 1858. The sixth ship in the group, the *Niagara,* commissioned April 6, 1857, is considered a sister to the others but was actually an anomaly. She was 50 feet longer and had a 700-ton advantage in displacement. This big sister was sometimes considered a sloop of war because of her unusual armament, twelve 11-inch, swivel-mounted, smooth-bore Dahlgren guns.[7] In addition, a stepdaughter would head this family of ships. In 1853 Congress funded repair work on the old *Franklin,* built in 1815. This was not meant to be a nostalgic renovation, like the one carried out on the *Constellation.* The Navy planned a real hatchet job, and the statistics tell the story: she increased from 187 feet between perpendiculars to 265 feet at the waterline and from 2,257 tons to 5,298 tons. Two 2,065-horsepower engines and a screw propeller were installed. Constructor John Lenthall's plans for the renovation were completed in February 1854. The hull plans for the *Colorado* and *Roanoke* were finished soon after and are a remarkably close match to the *Franklin's* rebuilt plan. The *Franklin's* resemblance to the other three ships is also quite obvious. It appears that the rebuilt *Franklin* was the prototype for five of the ships and that the *Niagara,* designed by George Steers, was the oddball in the group.[8] It is also obvious that the Navy's constructors hadn't changed their thinking much; these were still traditional sailing ships that happened to have engines.

The *Colorado* and *Roanoke* were both built at Norfolk while John Porter was working there. Porter's daughter Brent mentions in her memoirs, "That winter [1856] my father was building a warship the *Colorado* for the Government over in the Navy Yard, and Mr. Hartt was building another alongside of it, the *Columbia*."[9] The ship she referred to as the *Columbia* was actually the *Roanoke;* the only *Columbia* built in this period was a Confederate ironclad built in Charleston in 1864. On March 3, 1819, Congress standardized the naming of all Navy ships, a process that previously had been somewhat haphazard. Some of the early ships were named for naval heroes or statesmen—the *Franklin,* for example. The alliance with France in 1778 led to such names as *Queen of France* and *Duc de Lauzun.* The act of 1819 put an end to this confusion; the ships were to be named by "the Secretary of the Navy, under the direction of the President according to the following rule: those of the first class shall be called after the States of the Union; those of the second class after the rivers; and those of the third class after the principal cities and towns; taking care that no two vessels in the navy shall bear the same name." This was clear enough, but an additional law in 1858 probably confused things. Steamships with forty or more guns would be considered first class and named for states. Because it applied only to steamships, if the *Merrimack* and her sisters had been built after 1858, the rule would have applied to them. Ships with thirty-nine to twenty guns were second class and fell in the river classification. Any ships with fewer than twenty guns were third class, to be named for a city or town. For some reason, historians and other people writing about U.S. naval ship names have intertwined these two rulings and come up with some bizarre and misleading statements. For example, the *Directory of American Fighting Ships* states that the *Minnesota* was named for the Minnesota territory, organized in 1849, which in turn was derived from a Sioux word meaning "sky-tinted-water." *Roanoke* was named for the town of Roanoke, Virginia; *Niagara* was named for Fort Niagara, which was probably named for the river; and *Wabash* and *Merrimack* were named for rivers. And then comes *Colorado,* and the book made a mess of its explanation: "*Colorado* was named for the state, which was admitted to the Union in 1876." In 1854 even the Colorado *territory* didn't exist; it was established in 1861. Given that in 1854 the Colorado River was the only geographic entity west of the Mississippi with that name, the USS *Colorado* had to be named for the river.

Today you would think there would be no confusion about the correct spelling of *Merrimack*. The construction plans for both the ship and her engines were drafted in 1854, and these plans are on file in the Cartographic and Architectural Branch of the National Archives. In Records Group 19, Bureau of Ships, fifteen construction drawings are on file, and Records Group 19 of the Bureau of Steam Engineering has eighteen drawings of the engines. The majority of these drawings have one thing in common, the spelling of the name. For example Ship Drawing # 40-11-7J (Sheer and Half Breadth) is titled "Steam Frigate – 'Merrimack.' Built at Boston. June 1854." Engine Drawing # 2 (Front Elevation) employs "US Steamer Merrimack." However, the draftsman who did the berth and orlop deck drawing (plan # 40-117M) wrote his plan description and the ship's name as "Plan of Berth and Orlop Decks of the U.S. Steam Frigate Merrimac." Apparently he didn't get the memo. On September 23, 1854, this letter was sent to the Boston yard:

Navy Department,
Bureau of Construction
Sept. 23rd, 1854

Sir:
  The Steam Frigate now in the process of construction at the yard under your command will be called the "Merrimack."

Respectfully,
Comt. F. H. Gregory
Your obt. svt.
Comt. Navy Yard Boston
JOHN LENTHALL,
Chief of the Bureau[10]

What was the ship called before September 23? The construction drawings were sent to Boston on June 27, 1854, and she was laid down on July 11. Apparently for almost three months the ship had no name. How is it possible that drawings made three months prior to the ship being named carry the name *Merrimack*? The only date shown on the sheer and half-breadth drawings, as mentioned previously, is the completion date, June 1854, and most of the ship drawings have no dates at all. Some of the drawings for the engines are dated October 26, 1854, which would obviously be their completion date. As we will see later, John Porter's *Virginia* drawings show two year dates. It becomes obvious that the titles and dates shown on these old drawings were put there after the drawings were made, probably by someone other than the original draftsman. This also brings up another interesting point. Porter's daughter mentioned that a ship named *Columbia* was being built at Norfolk. Is it possible that prior to being given its official name, the *Roanoke* was called the *Columbia*? If this is the case, when were the official names of all of the other ships put on their plans, and what might they have been originally called?

The correct classification of the six sister ships is also in question. The *Register of U.S. Navy Ships* refers to them as the "*Roanoke* Class." *The Old Steam Navy* calls them the "*Merrimack*-Class," and the half-hull model at the Navy's David Taylor Model Basin is labeled "*Wabash* Class." The *Roanoke* plans were probably the first drawings completed, which bodes well for that classification. The *Merrimack* was the first to be built and commissioned, if that has any bearing on the question, but the *Wabash* classification is a total mystery. Because five of the ships were copies of the revised *Franklin* plans, they probably should have been called the *Franklin* class.

On June 27, 1854, John Lenthall's plans for the *Merrimack* were sent to the Charlestown Navy Yard, and on July 11, the construction began there. The commandant of the yard, Commo. Francis H. Gregory, was responsible for the overall supervision, Edward H. Delano was the constructor, and Melvin Simmons was the master carpenter. Secretary of the Navy Dobbin sent instructions for the ship to be built using the live oak frames that had been previously cut, but never used, for the old *Congress*-class frigates of 1839 with a 179-foot length and 45-foot beam.[11] Any additional required timbers were to be "made from promiscuous timber"—in other words, built out of scraps lying around the yard. Dobbin's instructions also called for "no less than 15 ports" each side on both the gun and spar decks. The ports were to be $14\tfrac{2}{12}$ feet on centers, some 3 feet greater than the normal spacing.[12] It is curious that Dobbin would send dimensional instructions several months after the plans had been drawn. When I scaled the dimensions on the sheer and half-breadth plan, I found that they were drawn to within a few inches of the requested spacing. So once again the question is raised as to whether all of the archival drawings are the ones prepared by Lenthall or whether some were made in Boston to reflect plan changes. All of the old ship plans are a nightmare when it comes to in-depth research. On modern plans of both architectural and engineering drawings, a title block always shows the name of the thing depicted, the number of sheets in the overall set, the name of the parts on that sheet, the scale of the drawing, the date it was drawn, the name of the draftsman, the date it was approved, and the name of the person who approved it. If any changes are made, the place or item changed is highlighted and numbered, and the person who approved the change is noted and dated. If this procedure had been followed on the *Merrimack* drawings, the title block would have looked like this:

Steam Frigate USS MERRIMACK
Sheer & Half Breadth—sheet 9 of 15
Scale—¼ inch = 12 inches
Drawn Jan. 25, 1854—"John Doe"

Approved Feb. 3, 1854—John Lenthall

Change #1 Gun port spacing—July 8 by "J.D."
Approved July 10—E. H. Delano

Instead of a clear-cut path like this, we have to find our way through a maze. The title block, if you can call it that, shows the following:

Steam Frigate—"Merrimack"-
Building at Boston. June 1854
Scale 4 feet = one inch

Length bet.per 256—10 ½
Beam moulded—50-2
Depth of Hold—26-2 ½
Frame spaces—2-10 ¼

Another annoying aspect of these old drawings is the weird scales called out. First of all, the scale shown here is written backward. For four feet to equal one inch, the finished drawing would have been forty-eight times larger than the actual ship. The ¼ inch = 1 foot scale is a modern architectural standard, but unfortunately many of the old drawings are scaled at 1 inch = 10 inches, which, for conversion purposes, requires the use of a standard engineering scale that is calibrated only in feet and shows no inches. Then, to really make things look strange, sometimes the dimensions were given in twelfths, as in the 14²⁄₁₂ quoted from Dobbin's memo. Why he couldn't have said, "fourteen feet, two inches" we will never know.

Modern drawings are laterally covered with point-to-point dimensions and notations. The *Merrimack*'s profile drawings are practically devoid of dimensions and notes. The ones that are there, such as "Shell room—Hatch—scuttle and 17-1½," were put on

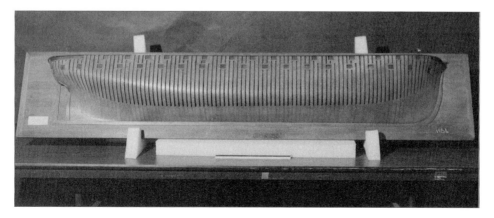

Half-hull model of the USS *Wabash*. This large model, more than five feet long, shows the detail of the framing system for a ship of the *Roanoke* or *Merrimack* class. The detail at the stern shows the opening for the propeller but not the propeller or the rudder. *Naval Sea Systems Command photo*

the drawings in pencil with no lines to show from what points. Dozens of lines and notes have been erased to the extent that they are no longer intelligible on the copies that can be obtained from the archives. The deck plans do have the various compartments noted but, once again, no dimensions. The information on the old plans and specifications were not carved in stone, and the specifications in the nineteenth century were a far cry from the exacting stipulations in the specifications that come out of Washington today. In times past, there was a clear understanding up front that specifications were to be considered as guidelines, unless otherwise stipulated. Even the basic requirements were flexible. A ship could be a little longer or shorter than planned. No one was surprised or annoyed as long as she had the stipulated number of guns and came close to the specified speed and performance (with the early steam ships, the specified speed was wishful thinking). The constructors and carpenters did their work to conform to the general practices in their region; a ship built in Connecticut would not be constructed in the same manner as a Virginia ship. In those days, shipbuilding was a mixture of art and science, but when steam engines came into the picture, the art began to be crowded out.

The Charlestown Navy Yard of 1854 was a first-class facility that sprawled over some sixty acres north of the Charles River across from Boston. It had a large dry dock and was in the vicinity of the Francis Alger and Son gun foundry (later, Cyrus Alger & Co.), where the *Merrimack*'s Dahlgren guns would be cast. The *Merrimack* was primarily a sailing vessel that could unfurl more than 48,757 feet of canvas when all of the sails were set. Her engines were built at the West Point Foundry at Cold Springs, New York, under the supervision of Robert P. Parrott, of Parrott Rifle fame. Her log entries of February 25 and 26, 1855, show that "with strong breeze, sails and engine combined," she did 10.656 knots. A few days later, with only her engines she could manage just a little over 6 knots.[13] Even though these vessels were classified as steam frigates, for the most part their engines were intended only to provide auxiliary power for the sails and to simplify maneuvering in and out of ports. The *Merrimack*'s power plant was two engines and four Martin-type tubular boilers. As the descriptions show, this machinery was massive. The two double-piston engines were huge things, with cylinders seventy-two inches in diameter and a thirty-six-inch horizontal stroke. The piston rods were seven inches in diameter.[14] The distance from the engine base to the uppermost part was more than ten feet, and when both were in line with the drive shaft, they had a spread of more than twenty-eight feet. Each of the boilers, designed by Daniel B. Martin, was fourteen feet wide, twelve feet deep, and fifteen feet high. The four weighed in at fifty-six tons and had an aggregate heating surface of 12,537 square feet.[15] When the ship was traveling at eight knots, the coal consumption was 2,880 pounds per hour. This large-scale production may sound impressive, but actually it was not enough power to drive the ship efficiently. The *Merrimack* had a dead rise (the angle from the keel to the point where the vertical side begins) of only about 15 degrees, but even that small angle restricted the space from side to side in the lower part of the ship to allow for any larger horizontal-stroke, low-pressure, jet-condensing engines. As it was, the floor space required for the engines was fifteen feet in length and twenty-eight feet, six inches in width, with a clear height of twelve feet, six inches.[16] To accommodate larger engines, the ship would have required a bottom that was practically flat. Even with the size restrictions, the engines that were installed provided 869 gross effective horsepower at the propeller shaft. The engines required 103 horsepower just to turn over,

"The USS *Merrimack*." This illustration by Davidson shows the *Merrimack* under sail. The large telescoping smokestack is shown in the retracted position. *The Century War Book*

and another 65 horsepower was lost from the friction of the propeller shaft turning in bearings housed in unstable wooden supports. The segmented propeller shaft was a monster unto itself: several sections fourteen inches in diameter, with a weight of about ten tons each. (One of these sections can be seen on the grounds of the Museum of the Confederacy in Richmond, Virginia.)[17] This huge shaft turned a two-bladed, seventeen-foot, four-inch, fifteen-ton, variable-pitch propeller at about forty rpm. As mentioned earlier, the screw propeller was nothing new, but this variable-pitch monster, patented in England by Robert Griffiths in 1849, was on the cutting edge of nineteenth-century technology.[18] When under steam, the propeller was set at a pitch of about 32 degrees. For sail power only, the blades were set at zero and locked vertically behind the sternpost to reduce drag. A propeller well at the stern allowed the propeller to be detached from the shaft and raised onto the deck for repair or maintenance. Newspapers and periodicals had stories full of praise and admiration for the new ship during its construction and early days of service.

But the truth was that the steam power system was an ongoing disaster. There was little or no insulation on the engines or boilers. Because there was no ventilation system, the vapor-saturated air hung at a sweltering 120-plus degrees. The enormous cylinder capacity caused low pressure on the piston strokes, and the vacuum was poor because of air leaks. The arrangement and proportions of the air pumps were faulty, the hemp air pump packing frequently wearing out only a few hours after repacking.[19] To run fast enough to turn the propeller properly, the engines practically vibrated the ship apart. The cause of all of these difficulties was not so much a construction flaw as an engineering problem. Marine steam engines had originally been designed to turn paddle wheels. When the propeller came along, the engineers simply turned the engine to rotate a long shaft that stuck out of the ship's stern instead of the side, but the physics involved in turning a paddle wheel and a propeller are quite different. The *Merrimack*'s engine problems were caused by using the wrong tools for the job, and years of design and trial and error would pass before the puzzle would be solved.

While there may have some uncertainty about the design and construction of the *Merrimack*'s engines, there was none whatsoever about the design and structure of the hull. It was a sailing ship that happened to have an engine. Everything that had been done a thousand times before was done again. She had a straight keel, curved forefoot, and straight stem. The only sailing ship deviation was the overhung stern with the propeller well that created a gap of more than six feet between the sternpost and the rudderpost.[20]

After being commissioned in December 1855, the *Merrimack* spent a five-year naval career plagued with problems and criticism. She broke down four days out of Norfolk on her maiden voyage and limped into Havana twenty days later under sail only. She struggled over to Key West with a broken rudder and was finally towed back to Boston, where her bearings and bushings were replaced before she crossed the Atlantic to London. The English press had a far better opinion of her than their American counterparts. At home, she was criticized for her slowness and unreliability. Her draft was too great to allow her to enter "nine-tenths of the harbors of the nation's entire east-coast."[21] She was a poor gun platform because of her 15-degree dead rise and high center of gravity that caused her to roll, and she consumed too much coal. The USS *Merrimack* was fast on the way to becoming just another ship whose name would soon be forgotten. But in 1860, when she was on station in the Pacific, it was decided to send her to Norfolk for extensive machinery repairs. We don't know who made it, but that seemingly insignificant decision ended up changing the history of the world.

Chapter Six

Whose Idea Was This Anyway?

O n April 12, 1861, South Carolina opened fire on Fort Sumter. On July 21, the first great battle of the American Civil War was fought at Bull Run (Manassas). And sometime during March or April 1862, John Luke Porter declared war on John Mercer Brooke. The reason for this verbal hostility is not as complex as the underlying causes of the Civil War; it seems to boil down to a simple point of honor: Who should get the credit for the idea of a different kind of ship? There was no money involved, no royalties to be paid, and no long-term contracts. The prize seemed to be the honor of saying, "The CSS *Virginia* was my idea." As is sometimes the case, the catalyst that brought about all of this hostility was the press. Some articles that didn't have the facts quite straight by people who were not directly involved raised hackles, and the rest is history. This conflict of personalities might have been irrelevant except that practically all of the official technical information about the conception and construction of the *Virginia* has been lost. The residue of the Porter-Brooke feud gives us valuable information about the *Virginia* that would not be available had there been no dispute. To put all of this in perspective, we must go back to the time when the people with the idea of building an ironclad ship came together in Richmond, Virginia.

John Mercer Brooke arrived in Richmond and became a lieutenant in the virtually nonexistent Virginia Navy on April 21, 1861. Because there was nothing naval to be done, he was soon ordered to report to General Lee's headquarters and carry out "such duties as he may assign you." Brooke's cousin, Col. Robert Garret, was Lee's adjutant general and probably had something to do with the assignment. Brooke was greatly impressed with Lee, whom he called a "Confederate Washington." On May 2 he received word from Secretary Mallory, who was in Montgomery, that he had been appointed a lieutenant in the Confederate Navy, as he had requested. A few days later, he wrote to Mallory to suggest that "an iron plated ship might be purchased in France loaded with arms and brought into port in spite of the wooden blockade."[1]

John Luke Porter had arrived in Norfolk on May 20, 1861. He had resigned his appointment as a U.S. Navy constructor and began work at the Navy yard as a Virginia naval constructor. Soon after Virginia officially joined the Confederacy, he became a Confederate naval constructor, beginning with the repair of the damaged facilities

and examination and salvage appraisal of the partially destroyed ships. He also supervised the preparation of large guns at the Navy yard, which were to be sent to various
coastal fortifications. The actual design and construction of Confederate naval vessels
would have to wait until the coastal defenses were well under way.

In June his old friend and coworker, William P. Williamson, arrived back at the Navy
yard. Williamson was born in Norfolk on July 26, 1810, and studied mechanical engineering in New York, where his outstanding ability in that field was quickly recognized.
He became an apprentice in the steam engineering division at the Gosport yard and soon
rose to be superintendent of the yard's machine shop. He joined the Navy as a steam engineer and, in time, became the U.S. Navy's chief engineer and worked closely with Porter
on the construction of the *Colorado*. When the war clouds gathered, the yard commander, Charles McCauley, asked Williamson to take the oath of allegiance. As a Virginia
loyalist, he refused, and on March 25 was removed from the Navy and held in prison
from April 21 until his release on May 22. By June 11 he was back at the yard as a senior
engineer in the Confederate Navy. By April 1862 he was the Confederacy's chief engineer.[2] Williamson was about to become a vital part of the *Virginia* story. Meanwhile,
John Porter settled into his duties at the yard and thought about the things that needed
to be done to build a new Navy—no doubt with visions of ironclads dancing in his head.

On March 14, 1861, Mallory's name (along with Davis, Clay, Toombs, and other dis-
loyal Southern notables) was officially stricken from the roll of the U.S. Senate. Mallory
had opposed secession and then, after losing that fight and retreating to the South, he
opposed attacking Fort Pickens, which further infuriated the hawks. His stock was not
high with Southern politicians, so he made it a point to stay clear of Montgomery. He was
willing to serve the Confederacy but didn't seek any high office. However, political expediency required Davis to pick a cabinet member from each of the Confederate states.
When it came to Florida, Davis's old fellow senator, Mallory, was his first choice. Because
the secessionists had all but accused Mallory of treason, there was considerable
opposition to his appointment. As in the North, however, the office of naval secretary was
considered a political booby prize, some of the opposition subsided, and Mallory's appointment was confirmed by a vote of thirteen to six on March 18, 1862. From then until
June, Mallory stayed in Montgomery while the new Confederate Navy took form.

One of the first orders of business was to set up a naval organization departmental-
ized by function. First came the Office of Orders and Detail or, in modern parlance, personnel or human resources. It kept personnel, promotion, and assignment records, and it
assigned civilian pilots for river and harbor duty. For reasons never explained, it also purchased coal and ships' furniture. Next came the Office of Ordnance and Hydrograph. In
March 1863 John Brooke became the head of this department. Third was the purchasing
department, called Office of Provisions and Clothing. A forty-four-year veteran, "old tot-
tering John DeBree," headed this department, but the real administrators were the pay-
masters assigned to the ships and naval stations. There was also the Office of Medicine
and Surgery headed by Dr. W. A. W. Spotswood. In addition to the bureaus, there were
semiautonomous Navy departments to serve specific purposes: the Department of
Steam Engineering, eventually headed by William P. Williamson, and the Department of
Construction that would go to John Luke Porter. The Confederate Marine Corps was a
field unit designated for specialized combat service in cooperation with the Navy. For

expediency, the Marines were placed under Mallory. Because of the Navy's limited activity, the Marines were never assigned their full allotted complement.[3]

The Confederate Congress, where Mallory was short of friends, seemed to take delight in causing him discomfort whenever an opportunity presented itself. They allocated money for naval purposes, but instead of giving the money to the Navy, it was deposited with the Treasury Department.[4] When Mallory needed to pay bills, he had to go to Treasury Secretary Christopher Memminger, with hat in hand, and ask for the Navy's money. In March 1861 the only entity to receive less money in appropriations than the Navy was the executive mansion.[5]

The Confederate railway system was not officially classified as an instrument of torture, but anyone who rode the cars any distance quickly came to that conclusion. On Monday, June 3, 1862, a soot-speckled, rumpled, exhausted Stephen Mallory stepped onto the Richmond Station platform of the Richmond & Danville Railroad and then headed to the Spotswood Hotel, which would be his temporary residence. That evening, he met and talked with John Brooke about the task before them. The next day he went to the Navy's temporary offices, across from Capitol Square, in what had been the U.S. Custom House. He would soon move a block west to 35 Ninth Street, the four-story Mechanics' Institute building that would become the permanent home of the Confederate Navy Department. For the duration of the war, Mallory climbed the two flights of stairs to his offices.[6] His two chief aides were Edward Tidball, described as "a handsome, dapper little robot, seldom guilty of an original thought, but a tireless and utterly reliable weaver of red tape," and Commo. French Forrest, stationed at the Navy yard, who was described as a "fine, white-haired old blusterer of the real old-tar school."[7] There were also four clerks and a runner to deliver messages. In addition to the offices of the various divisions of the Navy Department, the Confederate Navy stored its records here, including the plans and specifications of ships. This treasure trove of American history would go up in flames, along with a good part of Richmond, on April 2, 1865.

On June 4, 1861, John Brooke wrote to Lizzie Brooke that the secretary had arrived in Richmond from Montgomery on June 3 and that he had had "some conversation with him" that night, though the hour was late and Mallory "was very tired."[8] On May 4, before leaving Montgomery, Mallory had sent a telegram to Capt. Lawrence Rousseau in New Orleans to tell him to find iron plates, from 2 ½ inches to 5 inches thick, to be used in building an ironclad ship. Captain Rousseau reported that nothing that thick could be produced. The same response came from inquiries sent to Tennessee and Kentucky.[9] A few days later on May 8, he mentioned an iron-armored ship in a letter to the naval committee: "I regard the possession of an iron-armored ship as a matter of the first necessity. Such a vessel at this time could traverse the entire coast of the United States, prevent all blockades, and encounter, with a fair prospect of success, the entire navy. . . . Should the committee deem it expedient to begin at once—an agent will be sent to England to purchase vessels."[10] At that time, the idea was to buy an iron-plated ship, not build one. In May James Bullock and James North left for Europe on an English ship to try to buy ironclads.[11]

The saga of the *Virginia* actually begins at this point, as Lieutenant Brooke and constructor Porter were about to square off in a never-ending dispute. The story of who, what, when, and why gets quite confusing. For clarity and consistency of the chronological record, some statements made in 1862 are here combined with those written in 1861. Many statements are presented out of context to avoid engulfing a relevant sentence in an immense bulk of quotations; the full texts of the various letters, testimonies, and articles can be found in the periodicals and books cited. I have made every effort not to make a case in favor of either Brooke or Porter, and I will be equally critical of each. I will also point out omissions and contradictions and then leave it up to you, the reader, to decide where credit should go. Below are statements made prior to a meeting in Richmond on June 23, 1861.

> **June 7, Brooke to Lizzie:** Mallory wants me to make some calculations in regard to floating batteries which I shall do today.[12]
> **June 10, Mallory:** directed [Brooke] to aid the department in designing an iron-clad war-vessel, and framing the necessary specifications. [*Confederate Congressional Records, hereafter CCR*]
> **June 19, Brooke to Lizzie:** have been working all day on plans.
> **Mallory:** a few days thereafter [Brooke] submitted rough drawings of a casement vessel, with submerged ends and inclined iron-plated sides. [*CCR*]

Mallory's reference to "rough drawings" makes it obvious that he realized that Brooke was not an experienced naval draftsman and had taken the project as far as he could go without help. The sketches in Brooke's diary are neat but not of professional quality. They show a ship with pointed bow, rounded stern, oval casement with sloping sides, and a hull that is completely submerged with only the casement showing above the knuckle, in other words, a ship with a shallow draft but no details or dimensions.[13] Constructing a ship from this information would not be possible, but anyone looking at the drawing would immediately know what was intended. This having been established, the next step was obvious.

> **Brooke:** He [Mallory] approved the plan and I asked for a constructor to be sent for. [*Official Records of the American Civil War, CCR*]
> **Brooke:** He approved the plan, and I asked him to send to Norfolk for some practical ship-builder to draw out a plan in detail. [*CCR*]
> **Brooke:** In reply to my suggestion that Naval-Constructor John L. Porter and Chief-Engineer William P. Williamson should be called to Richmond, that we might put the plan in action, he [Mallory] replied that a practical mechanic would be sent from the Norfolk yard. [*Battles and Leaders of the American Civil War, October 1887*]
> **Mallory:** His plan was approved by the department and a practical mechanic was brought from Norfolk to aid in preparing the drawings and specifications. [*CCR*]

For a practical mechanic, shipbuilder, or constructor to be sent from Norfolk, Mallory would have gone through channels in the appropriate manner. He would have sent a request to the commandant at the shipyard, Commandant French Forrest, to send a mechanic or constructor to Richmond. Why this person was needed would have been explained, and Commandant Forrest would have acknowledged receipt of the request and informed Mallory that it was being forwarded to constructor Porter to assign a qualified individual from his department. At this point, Porter would have become aware of a ship design project in Richmond. He was *the* contractor and would naturally wonder why someone was infringing on his territory. What was going on in Richmond? Mallory's request to Forrest is lost, so we will never know its exact wording, though to eliminate any confusion, the request should have been for a "constructor." Regardless of the exact wording, there would have been enough information to put Porter on his guard. Did Porter send someone to assist with or to spy on the project? You will have to make that determination based on the following three statements made a year later:

J. W. H. Porter [John Luke's son]: Lieutenant John M. Brooke, of the navy, was considering the question of an iron-clad. He was in a position where he could command the ear of Secretary Mallory, of the Confederate Navy, and as requested Mr. Joseph Pierce [Pearce] then master ship-carpenter at the navy-yard here, and a skilled mechanic, was sent to the capitol to assist him, but nothing came of the conference, and he [Pearce] reported that Lieutenant Brooke had no plan; that he had no practical ideas, and did not know what he wanted. Seeing the failure of Lieutenant Brooke's scheme, Constructor Porter then had another model made like the one he had made at Pittsburgh in 1847.[14]

Brooke: He [Mallory] sent for one [mechanic or constructor], and one of the employees of the yard [Pearce], whose opinion then I did not favor, except that I heard he was a regular constructor there, was sent up. He said he knew nothing of drafting, and although he approved of the general plan, he could not make the drawing. This is what I wanted done chiefly. He was here a few days, and complained of being made sick by the water, and therefore permitted to return to Norfolk. I then determined to go on with the drawing myself.[15]

Mallory: This mechanic aided in the details of timber, etc., but was unable to make the drawings.[16]

If Porter's statement about what Pearce reported to him is true, then Pearce had lied to Porter. We already know from Brooke's letters to Lizzie and from Mallory's statements that Brooke had made a drawing or drawings. Brooke knew the general form of the ship he proposed, and he knew he wanted the hull to be submerged. He also made it quite clear that he wanted someone with the proper training to make *detailed drawings* of the ship. That is about as clear as it can get, and if Pearce didn't understand after "he was here a few days," then Pearce was either a dimwit or, if he wasn't stupid, understood what Brooke wanted and "aided in the statement of detail of timber," then he would have been working with a plan and known full well what was going on. The next question is why would he lie to Porter? Could Pearce have been sworn to secrecy before leaving Richmond and instructed to keep the truth from his boss? Porter had to know what was wanted when he sent a man to Richmond. If they were *designing* a ship in Mallory's offices, they needed a *constructor*; if they were *building* a ship in Mallory's offices, they needed a master ship's carpenter and skilled mechanic. Porter knew that no ship was being built at the Navy Department in Richmond. Did he instruct Pearce to go to Richmond, play dumb, and come back and tell him what was going on? Porter had enough information to know that the subject at hand was an ironclad ship, but that might have been all he knew. It was after Pearce's return that Porter had the model built that he took to Richmond. At this point, he may have been between a rock and a hard place. If he showed up in Richmond with a model that looked like Brooke's drawing, everyone would know that Pearce had disobeyed a direct order from the secretary of the Navy to keep quiet. If Pearce had described Brooke's drawing and explained the logic behind the design, Porter may have thought that the new approach was superior to his Pittsburgh ironclad design. He could have shown the original casement on a barge type of hull that was extended fore and aft and explained that it was to be submerged. Because Porter walked into the meeting with a design that did not have an extended submerged hull, and did not suggest such a thing, the evidence may be strong in Pearce's favor that he obeyed orders and kept his mouth shut. We will never know.

At this point we are presented with a new and bewildering mystery. In all accounts of the first meeting between Mallory, Brooke, Porter, and Williamson, everyone agrees that Porter arrived at the meeting carrying a scale model of an ironclad ship. The only drawing at the meeting ever mentioned is the one that Mallory and Brooke said Brooke had made, the one that Porter claimed didn't exist. There may have been no mention of a Porter drawing, but such a drawing did exist. Porter's drawing of June 1, 1861, has the following identification in his handwriting:

> Floating Steam Battery Bomb proof
> for harbor defense
> scale 4 feet = one inch
> Armament Six XI inch guns
> GNY June 1st 1861
> JL Porter
> V- N.C

This drawing, now in possession of the Mariners' Museum, is remarkable in several details. At the top of the sheet, it shows a ship in profile with a casement that is almost identical to that finally built for the *Virginia*. There is a knuckle that runs around the ship one or more feet below the waterline. The first time Brooke ever mentions a ship design

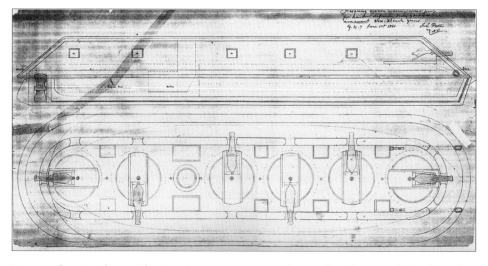

Porter's drawing for a "Floating Steam Battery Bomb Proof." This gun deck plan of an early Porter design with six swivel guns is superior to the plan he used on the *Virginia's* gun deck. *The Mariners' Museum illustration*

is in his June 7 letter to Lizzie: "Mallory wants me to make some calculations in regard to a floating battery which I shall do today." On June 1 Porter had produced a design almost identical to the one Brooke was still working on in the middle of the month. Porter's drawing of June 1 must have been the one followed to build the model. The only thing different about Brooke's concept was that it incorporated a submerged ship's hull that extended fore and aft of the casement, which was the only thing he actually based his patent application on. When the meeting took place in Richmond, Mallory and Brooke had probably moved past the armored battery concept and were dreaming about an oceangoing vessel, which is why the ship would require the protruding bow and stern sections that Brooke planned to submerge. The lower portion of Porter's drawing shows the plan for a gun deck that, in my opinion, is far superior to the plan finally executed. It incorporates six pivot-mounted Dahlgren guns, and there are quarter gun ports in the bow. Brooke later complained that Porter had omitted quarter ports in the bow and stern from his original construction drawings of the *Virginia* and added them only when he, Brooke, pointed out the error and insisted that they be incorporated. Where was this drawing during the early design discussions? Why didn't Porter show it to Mallory or to anyone else? And why didn't he use it later to defend himself against Brooke's charges? Porter failed to produce the strongest piece of evidence he had to support his claim.

THE WAR OF WORDS IN THE PRESS AND IN PRIVATE

Now we must jump ahead in time to a few days after the Battle at Hampton Roads. The *Virginia*'s two days of glory came on March 8 and 9, 1862. The smoke had hardly cleared when newspapers across the country carried stories about how the *Virginia* was designed, built, and fought. Unfortunately, the majority of the information we have about the design and construction of the *Virginia* must be gleaned from letters and articles written well after the fact.

The Charlestown *Mercury* on March 19, 1862, printed an extract from a private letter written by John Porter: "I received but little encouragement from anyone while the Virginia was progressing. Hundreds, I may say thousands, asserted she would never float.—You have no idea what I have suffered in mind since I commenced her, but I knew what I was about, and I persevered. Many of her inboard arrangements are of the most intricate character, and have caused me many sleepless nights, and thanks are due to a kind Providence whose blessings in my efforts I have many times invoked."

This paragraph mainly concerns itself with others' skepticism about the construction of the *Virginia* and how he was ridiculed for what he was doing. He does not refer to Brooke, and he never says "my design" or "my concept." Nothing there offends or calls for a response. Whether because of this innocuous epistle or for some other reason, a party or parties unknown decided to brew a tempest. On March 18, just nine days after the battle, someone calling himself "Justice" wrote a letter and sent it to the Richmond *Whig*: "The Virginia—As the brilliant success of the *Virginia* has attracted the attention of the country, and is destined to cast much glory on our infant navy, it may be of general interest to publish some account of the origin of this magnificent ship." "Justice" then goes on to bestow accolades and glory on John Mercer Brooke: "A plan proposed by Lieutenant John L. Brooke was adopted, —the plan of Lieutenant Brooke could easily be applied to the Merrimac—Experiments to determine the mode of applying the armor and to fix the dimensions of its parts were conducted by Lieutenant Brooke.—The rifled cannon—designed by Lieutenant Brooke. I am a private citizen, wholly unconnected to the Confederate or State government, but think the public ought to know all the particulars, which reflect so much credit on the Secretary of the Navy and his officers."

Who was "Justice" and why did he think Brooke was in need of "justice"? John Luke Porter later stated that "Justice" was "a Dutchman in Lieutenant Brooke's office." Did Brooke play a part in the preparation of this article, or was it all a big surprise? The Richmond *Dispatch* added more fuel to the fire when it published on March 24 an article titled "The Merrimac's Men." It reads in part: "Upon the hulk, according to plans furnished by Lieutenant Brooke, of the Confederate States Navy (though the merit of the design is also claimed for the Naval Constructor John L. Porter), was built a house or shield, etc." Once again, too much Brooke and too little Porter.

John Luke Porter and his son prepared a letter to the *Dispatch* and fired back on March 29: "In your issue of Sunday last, in the communication of Mr. Virginius Newton, headed 'The Merrimac's Men' there appears the following: 'Upon this hulk, according to plans—etc.' This does a grave injustice to a gallant old Confederate and Virginian, who sacrificed his all upon the altar of his country; and had Mr. Newton known the facts it is believed that he would have published his article with the names above reversed."

On March 29 John Luke Porter then sent to the *Examiner* a letter that he alone composed: "Having seen an article in the Richmond Enquirer, and one also in the Whig, claiming the plan of the iron-clad ship Virginia for Lieutenant John M. Brooke, of the navy, thereby doing myself and Engineer Williamson the greatest injury, I feel called upon to make a statement of fact in the case, for the future information of the reading public, in the history of the ship." He then described how he had designed and built the *Virginia* and that Brooke hadn't designed anything and didn't know how to design a ship.

By this time, everybody south of the Mason-Dixon Line knew about the squabble. The Confederate Congress got into the act on March 29 by ordering Mallory to make a full report on precisely what had taken place: "SIR; In compliance with the resolution adopted by the House of Representatives on the 18th instance, 'That the Secretary of the Navy be required to make a report to the House of the plan and construction of the Virginia, so far as the same can be communicated, of the reason for applying the plan to the Merrimac, and also what persons have rendered especial aid in the design and building of the ship.'" Mallory then told the story from Brooke's perspective: Brooke made the first drawings. Porter made tracings of Brooke's drawings. It was Brooke's idea to submerge the hull, and so forth. After that, Porter made detailed drawings and supervised construction.

After the problems Brooke had trying to get a patent for his sounding device and the charges made by William Gable, he wasn't about to go through that again. There was no money involved this time, so it must have been for the principle of the thing. "As neither the Secretary or myself had noticed Constructor Porter's published claims, I thought it advisable to bring the subject before the examiners at the patent office while it was before the public. I therefore applied for a patent, and in order so that there should be no grounds for dispute as to the correspondence of my specific claim with the original plan, I presented tracings of the identical drawings which Constructor Porter made of my plan, as stated by the Secretary in his report to the House of Representatives of the Confederate States. They were filed on May 2, 1862, in the Patent Office."

"As neither the Secretary or *myself* had noticed Constructor Porter's published claim"—why would Brooke lie about not knowing what every newspaper in the state was publishing? He had even written a letter to Porter in April to challenge some of Porter's March 29 statements: "On the 3rd of April, I wrote a private letter to Mr. Porter which, so far as I know, has never been published: 'DEAR SIR: I have observed, with surprise, certain articles in the *newspapers* relating to the Virginia and the origin of the plan upon which she was constructed.' " We will look at this letter in more detail later, but for now it suffices to say that neither Brooke nor Porter was above telling a lie.

Meanwhile at the Confederate Patent Office, Brooke had filed his application for a patent on May 2, 1862. In part, it reads: "Be it known that I, John Mercer Brooke, a lieutenant in the Navy of the Confederate States, have *invented a new and improved form of vessel*, to be iron-clad, and if desired {armed} with cannon; and I do hereby declare that the following is a full and exact description thereof." He then described the *Virginia*. By describing the *Virginia*, Brooke established the uniqueness of his claim. The final paragraph of the patent makes the claim quite clear: "What I claim as my invention, and desire to secure by letter of patent, consists in so constructing the hull of a vessel that her bow and stern shall each extend under water beyond the forward and aft ends of the shield C, which protects the crew and guns sufficiently to give the sharpness necessary to the attainment of high speed and the buoyancy to support the weight of iron applied without an inconvenient increase in draft."

Brooke's claim was recognized, and on June 29, 1862, he was issued Patent No. 100.

The patent inspector let the phrase "invented a new and improved form of vessel" slip past. Brooke had not invented any kind of vessel. In his application, he was claiming only the idea of partially submerging a vessel.[17] Brooke's patent was pending for almost two months. If Porter knew about it, he never challenged it, and after it was issued, he never complained that the patent was invalid; he continued only to say that the *Virginia* was his idea, not Brooke's.

From here on, this squabble gets more confusing. Here are the arguments of the various participants by time, place, and subject. Described are events leading up to, and including, the Richmond meeting of June 23, 1861.

On Thursday, June 20, Porter was given the following message:

Navy Yard Gosport, June 20, 1861

Sir:
    You will proceed to Richmond and report yourself for duty to the Hon. Secretary of the Navy

                              Respectfully,
                              F. Forrest
                              Commandant

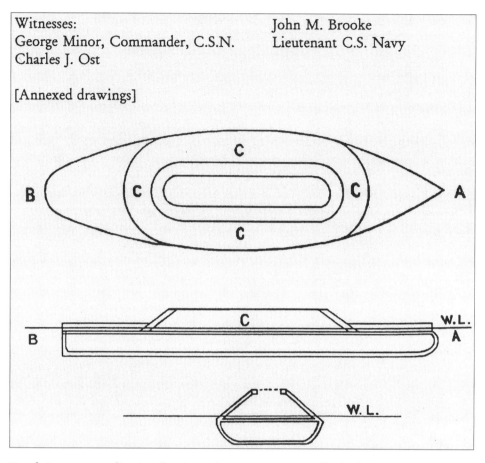

Witnesses: John M. Brooke
George Minor, Commander, C.S.N.   Lieutenant C.S. Navy
Charles J. Ost

[Annexed drawings]

Brooke's patent application drawing. There is no way to tell whether Brooke made this drawing or someone made it for him. *Confederate Patent Office report, 1861*

Both Mallory and Porter give the meeting date as "about the 23rd of June," which was a Sunday. After the meeting, Brooke and Williamson went to the Tredegar offices, which were open for business, so the meeting was probably held on Saturday the 22nd or Monday the 24th.

> *Brooke:* [I] asked the Secretary to send for the naval constructor at Norfolk, and the naval engineer, so they might be consulted in relation to the vessel. They came up and this constructor brought with him a model. I should have said that the name of this constructor was J. L. Potter. This model is now one of the models in the Secretary's room. It consisted of a shield and hull, the extremities of the *hull terminating with a shield,* forming a sort of box or scow upon which the shield was supported.[18]

> *Mallory, February 29, 1863:* Mr. Porter and Liu. Brooke have adopted a thickness of wood and iron, and an angle of inclination nearly identical.[19]

> *Brooke:* When we had examined the model, the Secretary said he wished to show Messer. Porter and Williamson a plan proposed by Lieutenant Brooke. The plan was then placed before them, and the reason for extending the ends of the hull

beyond the shield and under water were stated, and they approved the plan. It had been, as stated above, previously approved by the department.[20]

> *Porter, April 8, 1862:* The report [Mallory's report to Congress] commences by stating that on the 10th of June Lieutenant Brooke was directed to aid the department designing an iron-clad war vessel and framing the necessary specifications, and in a few days submitted to the department rough drawings of a casement vessel with submerged ends and inclined iron-plated sides, the ends of the vessel and the eaves of the casement to be submerged two feet. I do not doubt the statement of the Secretary, but *no such plans were submitted to the board* [by the board he meant the committee consisting of himself, Brooke, and Williamson]; and from the fact that the master-carpenter had returned to the yard without completing any plan of the vessel shows, and myself being sent for immediately, and from the further fact that the Secretary presented us no plans from this source, I stated in my last communication that Lieutenant Brooke failed to produce anything after a week's trial; and I am still of the opinion, so far as anything tangible is concerned.[21]

At this point it seems ludicrous for Porter to continue to insist that Brooke's drawing never existed. If the drawing was on file at the Naval Department office, Tidball and one or more of the clerks had certainly seen it. There is also a similar drawing on a page in Brooke's diary from June 1861. In the article Brooke wrote for the Century Publishing Company to be included in *Battles and Leaders of the Civil War,* he gives a more detailed description of the drawing: "I submitted to the secretary outline drawings—sheer, body and deck, plans, with explanations,—and he approved the adoption of the idea." Porter took an ostrich stance about Brooke's drawing and, when confronted with overwhelming evidence, stubbornly refused to pull his head out of the sand.

> *Brooke:* Mr. Mallory then directed Messers. Williamson and Porter to ascertain if suitable engines and boilers could be had. To me he said: 'Make a clean drawing in ink of your plan, to be filed in the department.' As I placed the paper on the table and was about to begin, Mr. Porter said to me: 'You had better let me do that. I am more familiar than you are with this sort of work.' Accepting his offer I went with Williamson to the Tredger Works.[22]

> *Porter:* The report next states that Mr. Porter approved of the plan of submerged ends, and made a clean drawing of Lieutenant Brooke's plan—the only drawing I ever made of the Virginia was made in my office at the navy-yard, and which I presented to the Department on the 11th day of July.[23]

There is no way to reconcile the discrepancies in these statements. The best witness to these proceedings would have been the engineer William Williamson, but unfortunately he left no record of the meeting that might shed light on the subject.

To further add to the confusion, E. C. Murray, who later built the ironclad *Louisiana,* claimed that he had submitted plans of the *Merrimack* to Mallory in April 1861: "I furnished the plans for the *Merrimack,* though, by some Jeremy diddling, it is attributed to Lieutenant Brooke."[24] He may have submitted a design of some sort of iron-clad, but there are no surviving records to prove it, and it could not have had anything to do with the *Merrimack,* which was in the possession of the U.S. Navy until April 20, 1861. There is also confusion about when it was decided to use the *Merrimack* as the base platform for the *Virginia* and who made the suggestion to do it.

> *Porter:* According to the statement of Messrs. *Williamson* and Porter, there was *nothing before the board* [committee] *or considered by it except that model.* The board decided to recommend the building of a vessel after that plan, and, preparatory to making their report, began discussing the length of time it would take to complete her. Mr. Williamson remarked, "It will take twelve months to build her engines unless we can utilize some of the machinery in the Merrimac." Mr. Porter said, "Why can't you use it all? I can adapt this model to the Merrimac and utilize the machinery in her." Mr. Williamson replied. "I can." It was therefore decided at once to recommend that the Merrimac be converted into an iron-clad.[25]

There are no records showing that Williamson ever made a statement about what was, or was not, considered by the committee. As stated by Brooke previously, while Porter made a tracing of his drawing, he and Williamson went to the Tredegar Iron Works to look for any engines or other equipment that could be used on the project. Finding that Tredegar could offer no help, they then tried the Portsmouth Navy Yard. If it had already been decided that the *Merrimack*'s engines were to be used, there would have been no reason for Brooke and Williamson to go to Tredegar or to Portsmouth.

> *Brooke, while at the Navy yard with Williamson*: Having found no suitable machinery, and determining that new engines would take too long to design and build, Williamson suggested a practical alternative. He proposed that they salvage the engines and boilers of the Merrimac and use her hull to build the armored battery. (From a letter by Brooke to Catesby Jones dated July 10, 1874.)
> *Brooke, in his* "Virginia: Her Real Projector" article, printed in 1891: Upon returning to Richmond, Brook and Williamson discussed the proposal with Porter, who, having worked on the Merrimac's sister ship, the USS Colorado, agreed that it was feasible. . . . I went with Williamson to the Tredegar Works, where we learned that no suitable engines could be had. Williamson then said that the engines of the Merrimac could, he thought, be put in working condition.[26]

Again, we find different statements by Brooke as to what happened. In his account for Battles & Leaders, he also omits any mention of a trip to Portsmouth. The question raised here is did they go, or not go, to Portsmouth?

> *Mallory:* The steam frigate Merrimac had been burned and sunk, and her engine greatly damaged by the enemy, and the department directed Mr. Williamson, Lieut. Brooke and Mr. Porter to consider and report upon the best mode of making her useful. The result of their investigation was their recommendation of the submerged ends, and the inclined casement of this vessel, which was adopted by the department.[27]

Once again, there are widely different accounts of the same event. Porter's account sounds far too simplistic. This was going to be a monumental undertaking, and for them to have immediately concluded to use the wreckage of the *Merrimack* to build a new ironclad seems bizarre. Brooke's account, mentioning his and Williamson's examination of the ship and then later conferring with Porter, reflects logic and good judgment. Mallory's statement also makes it clear that they were instructed to "*consider* and *report* upon the best mode of making her useful." Porter's account gives some of the credit to Williamson for considering the *Merrimack* as a source for parts to be used, but his wording is slanted to give himself the dominant position. Brooke gives all of the credit to

Williamson and then states that only after returning to Richmond, where they conferred with Porter, did the three of them agree that the idea was feasible.

REPORT ON THE FEASIBILITY STUDY

After it was decided that the *Merrimack* could be used as the base for the new ironclad, the next step was to submit a report to Mallory: "In obedience to your orders we have carefully examined and considered the *various plans* and propositions for constructing a shot proof steam battery and respectfully report that, *in our opinion*, the steam frigate Merrimac, which is in such condition from the effect of fire as to be useless for any other purpose without incurring a very heavy expense in rebuilding, etc., can be made an efficient vessel of that character, mounting _____ heavy guns."

Porter always claimed that his plan was the only one ever presented. If there was only his plan to be considered, how had they "carefully examined and considered the various plans and propositions"? The phrase "in our opinion" is important because Porter later wrote that he was the only one who had any knowledge of the condition of the *Merrimack*. In that case, the text should have read "in constructor Porter's opinion." If Brooke and Williamson did not have some detailed information about the condition of the *Merrimack*, would they have signed a document stating they had an opinion on the subject?

The report continues:

> And from the further consideration that we cannot procure a suitable engine and boiler for any other vessel without building them, which would occupy too much time, it would appear that this is our only chance to get a suitable vessel in a short time. The bottom of the hull, boilers and heavy and costly parts of the engine being but little injured, reduce the cost of construction to about one-third of the amount which would be required to construct such a vessel anew. *We cannot, without further examination*, make an accurate estimate of the cost of the proposed work.

Is this an editorial "we," or does it mean that the three men who will sign this document must go to Gosport and carefully examine the wreckage of the *Merrimack*? Porter and Williamson will obviously have to spend a lot of time poring over the battered ship and engine, but did Brooke actually participate?

The report concludes:

> But think it will be about $_____, the most of which will be the labor, the material being nearly all in the navy-yard, except the iron plating to cover the shield. The plan to be adopted in the arrangement of the shield for glancing shot, mounting guns, arranging the hull, etc., and plating, *to be in accordance with the plan submitted for the approval of the Department.*

We are, with much respect, your obedient servants,

WILLIAM P. WILLIAMSON
Chief Engineer Confederate States Navy,
JOHN M. BROOKE,
Lieutenant, Confederate States Navy,
JOHN L. PORTER
Naval Constructor

All three men signed the document, but Porter was the author.

What does "to be in accordance with the plan submitted for the approval of the Department" mean? If we go back to the third week in June, we find this statement by Mallory: "His [Brooke's] *plan was approved* by the department." This is the plan that Porter later said did not exist. If this is what was meant, then Porter signed away all rights to claim the design as his. But once again, it may be necessary to read between the lines: "The plan to be adopted in the arrangement of the shield for glancing shot . . . arranging the hull, etc." These things are depicted in Brooke's design drawing, but what about "mounting guns . . . and plating"? Brooke doesn't show any guns and said only that there would be plating, but none of this is on his drawings. The first guns we see are on the over-all plan Porter makes and on a second drawing labeled "Iron for the Merrimac by John Porter CSNC." The second drawing shows only vertical members and depicts a casement with flat ends. Were they referring to drawings that were to be made and approved in the future? If so, why didn't they say so? Because of secrecy, they didn't want to publicize the number of guns or the estimated cost of construction, which is understandable, but the other omissions are hard to understand.

After this document was submitted to Mallory, Porter returned to the yard and, with the help of his assistant, took measurements of the *Merrimack*'s hulk. He then made a "complete Constructor's scroll, 27 feet long." He later says: "And the only drawing [singular] I ever made of the Virginia was made in my office at this navy-yard, and which I presented to the department on the 11th day of July, just sixteen days after the board adjourned, having been in Richmond on other business."[28] Two interesting points can be learned from this statement. If July 11 was sixteen days after the committee adjourned, then the first meeting was conducted over a period of not less than two days. This time frame supports the case that Brooke and Williamson went to the Navy yard to inspect the *Merrimack* and then returned to Richmond to confer with Porter. The second interesting point is that getting the *Virginia* plans approved was not a high priority for Porter. He had to go to Richmond, so he took the plans along. Had the plans been lying around his office for a few days before he went to "Richmond on other business"?

Later Porter writes:

> So soon as I presented the plan, the Secretary wrote the following order; when everything was fresh in his mind concerning the whole matter:
>
> > NAVY DEPARTMENT,
> > *Richmond July 11th, 1862*
> > *Flag-officer F. Forrest:*
>
> Sir:
> > *You will proceeded with all practical dispatch to make the changes in the form of the Merrimac, and to build, equip, and fit her in all respects according to the design and plans of the constructor and engineers, Messrs. Porter and Williams.*
> > > R. S. MALLORY
> > > *Secretary of the C. S. Navy*

Porter considered this order proof of his claim of having come up with the idea of the *Virginia*. He goes on to say, "What, I would ask, could be more explicit than this letter, or what words could have established my claim any stronger if I had dictated them. The concluding part of this report [Mallory's report to Congress] says; 'The novel plan of *submerging the ends of the ship* and the eaves of the casement, however, is the peculiar and distinctive feature of the Virginia.' This may all be true; but it *is just what my model called for;* and if Lieut. Brooke presented rough drawings to the department carrying out the same views it may be called a singular coincidence." But Porter's model and drawing did not have any protruding ends that could have been submerged; it was a plan for a floating battery, which, for all practical purposes, is a barge with a shielded top. In part, Porter continues, "my model was not calculated to have much speed but was intended for harbor defense only, and was of light draft." This same statement applies to Brooke's design. It had a shallow draft and was not suited to be an oceangoing ship. Porter continues: "I never thought for a moment that, after the many difficulties I had to encounter in making these new and intricate arrangements for the work of this novel kind of ship, that anyone would try and rob me of my just merits." In his arguments, he seems to imply that Brooke was trying to claim that he had come up with the architectural and engineering design for the ship, which was not true. From the very beginning, Brooke went on record saying that he didn't know how to do these things: "I ask him to send to Norfolk for some practice ship builder to draw out a plan."

Then Porter made a statement that he probably wished he had left unsaid: "After the Merrimac was in progress for some time, Lieut. Brooke was constantly proposing alterations to her to the Secretary of the Navy, and as constantly and firmly opposed by myself, which the Secretary knows." Until this point, Brooke had never published a word disparaging Porter's ability and judgment as a constructor. But he was not about to let this go without comment and wrote to Porter:

Richmond, April 3, 1862

Dear Sir:

I have observed, with surprise and regret, certain articles in the newspapers relating to the Virginia and the origin of the plan upon which she is constructed. I will leave it to those qualified to judge the question of whose plan was adopted; for the facts are accessible. But meanwhile I beg to call your attention to one remark of your published letter, which is rather obscure. You say:

"After the Merrimac was in progress some time, Lieutenant Brooke was Constantly proposing alterations in her to the Secretary of the Navy, and as constantly and firmly opposed by myself, which the Secretary knows."

This paragraph conveys the impression that I proposed alterations that were opposed and rejected. As the alterations alluded to affect very materially the efficiency of the ship, I propose to mention them now.

The first alteration proposed by me was the substitution of one plate of two-inch iron for two of one inch; the removal of the ceiling or inner planking of the shield, and the application of four inches of oak outside under the iron, leaving the wood of the shield of the same aggregate thickness; and this alteration was made. I subsequently recommended the substitution of two-inch plates.

The third alteration made by me was to pierce the shield for bow and quarter ports, for you had omitted them, leaving four points of approach without fire. An accident to the engine, propellers or rudder would have placed the ship at the mercy of an antagonist; and this alteration was made.

The fourth alteration was the removal of wheel ropes—chains—from beneath the plates outside, where they were liable to be jammed by a shot. Mr. Robert Archer was present when

I called your attention to this liability. The alteration was not made, however, until Lieutenant Jones called your attention to it a second time.

The fifth alteration was the making of two additional hatches—your plan of detail provided for only one.

The sixth suggestion was that arrangements should be made to permit the use of small arms. You were left to your discretion; but a plan was given if you could not think of a better one. You replied at length: the arrangement was not considered good, and the alteration would have been made but for the delay which would have attended it. The ship is now deficient in that respect.

The seventh proposition was to put six inches of iron on bow and stern. Approved by the Secretary but omitted, from your statement that the ship would not carry it.

John M. Brooke, Lieutenant, C.S. Navy

This letter suggests some very serious flaws in the detailed design of the ship. If Porter had not made the majority of the suggested changes, the *Virginia* would have looked very different. The third point about the lack of bow and quarter gun ports is of tremendous importance and will be examined in detail when we analyze the drawings and plans of the *Virginia*. Just as Porter never challenged Brooke's patent, we can find no challenge or response to this letter.

This verbal volcano did not go extinct after the major eruption in March and April 1862. It smoldered throughout the war and flared up from time to time in letters, articles, and books written by Porter, Brooke, and others. In 1892 John W. H. Porter wrote a book cataloging the military companies and personnel from Norfolk County.[29] The book's last two chapters are devoted to the *Virginia* and the part his father played in her design and construction. As might be expected, nearly every statement ever made by John Brooke on the subject is refuted. Of great interest are the following statements:

> There seems to be a difference of recollection as to what became of Lieutenant Brooke's rough drawings. He says Secretary Mallory laid them before the board. Williams and Porter say they were never before the board, or considered by it, and Mr. Mallory is silent on the subject. . . . Chief Engineer Williamson gave to Mr. Porter a letter certifying to the fact that the Merrimac was converted into an iron-clad after his plans and not after plans of Mr. Brooke. That letter was burned up in Mr. Porter's office in Richmond, but there are witnesses living at this writing who have read it. There are witnesses too, living who were on intimate terms with Chief Engineer Williamson, and to whom he expressed himself freely on the subject of the Merrimac, and to those he always said Mr. Porter was her projector. Mr. Williamson's death prevented Mr. Porter from getting a duplicate of his letter, but its contents and his views upon the subject can be substantiated by living witnesses.

At this point, J. W. H. Porter quotes letters and statements from five men who knew Williamson. The letters basically state that, at one time or another, Williamson had told them that Porter was the one who conceived and designed the *Virginia* in detail and that Brooke had nothing to do with it. Five years passed between the end of the war and Williamson's death. Porter does not explain why, during this time, his father never asked Williamson for a duplicate of the letter. The first time any of this information became public knowledge was twenty-two years after Williamson's death. The Porter family's lack of timing in presenting evidence supporting John Luke Porter's claim and the fact that he never challenged Brooke's patent remain a mystery. The explanation given for not challenging the patent was that "after it [the patent] was granted it was not worth contesting. No naval architect would construct a vessel in that manner from choice."[30] The concept of submerging a ship's ends was all that Brooke ever claimed as his idea. If it was a worthless concept, then what was all the ruckus about? The Porters continued to present evidence to prove that Brooke did not design and plan the *Virginia,* and Brooke never said that he did. In the end, the entire dispute became a rather silly dance around semantics.

After the deaths of John Porter and John Brooke, their descendants and friends picked up the challenge. I could present many more pages of arguments but they would serve no real purpose. The mysteries and myths intertwined in the history of the Civil War that will never be solved or dismissed are just as much a part of history as are the cold, hard facts. By now, we can see that there will never be an undisputed announcement as to who won the Brooke-Porter war of words, and this lack of closure may ironically be appropriate since, in a strange way, this personal conflict was echoed in the actual battle between the *Monitor* and the *Virginia*. From an hour after that battle ended to this very day, people argue about which ship won the battle.

Chapter Seven

Words, Plans, Pictures, and Pieces

I went on a quest to find the facts about the *Virginia*. I inquired at every archive I could think of, borrowed books from libraries across the nation, and made myself a pest to every curator, archivist, and librarian in every institution in the country where I thought some scrap of evidence might be stored. I will never find all of the material I hoped for, but I had enough to make a beginning. To create an internal structural drawing, and not simply copy what had been done before, I would have to base everything on only five sources: verbatim statements made by people who were actually on the ship as craftsmen, crew, or qualified observers; the actual plans for the *Merrimack* prepared in 1854; Porter's *Virginia* plans from 1861 and 1862; pictures drawn by people who actually saw the ship; and artifacts that were recovered and are owned by various museums. I started with the words.

THE WORDS

For years, artists and historians have analyzed and reanalyzed the contemporary texts describing the *Virginia* and tried to visualize an accurate image of the ship. For the most part, there is no reason to dispute the basic conclusions, but examining the written descriptions in close detail creates uncertainty. Many of these descriptions were not written for academic or historical reasons but as part of the Brooke-Porter feud. One person's statements are contradicted by another's, and in these descriptions written months or years after the fact, individuals frequently contradict themselves. These contradictions about the appearance of the ship are usually minor but still prevent a model shipbuilder from determining the size of pieces and how the parts were assembled. As we begin to visualize the internal structure of the casement, we will need to dissect each and every statement and then decide what to keep and what to discard. We have read many of the statements by Brooke and Porter and will examine them further as we consider the various parts of the ship, but other people's statements also deserve attention. One of these was written because of circumstance. In November 1861 the Confederate blockade runner

Fingal, with a large number of English crewmen aboard, slipped into Savannah harbor but became bottled up there by the Union blockade. Trapped behind the Confederate lines, the English crew spent months looking for a way back to England. On April 11, the *Fingal's* British engineer, J. Anderson, was in Norfolk and was invited on board the *Virginia.* As far as I can determine, his is the only detailed description written well after the battle when the ship was in a finished state and shortly before her destruction. James Baxter's *Introduction of the Ironclad Warship* (p. 231) contains Anderson's notes to the British Admiralty.

> You ascend the roof by means of a rope ladder, and at once see the difficulty there would be in boarding her, the roof lying over in such an angle. On the top of the roof there is a kind of platform or grating, on which you can travel to either end, and which is formed in such a manner as to give ventilation below, and at the same time be shot proof. On the gun deck, which had to be lighted by means of lanterns, the guns were not placed opposite one another as the space becomes constricted by the sloping of the roof, and when run in, they are amidship; if they were opposite, loading would be a matter of great difficulty. There are 4 very heavy smooth bore guns on each side, and one very heavy rifled gun in the bow, and another in the stern of the same description, for these two pivot guns there are 6 ports, 3 at each end, the whole of the pivot and broadside ports can be closed in action, by means of shields, made of 3 inch iron, they are on the outside and are worked from within by means of small chains.

This is the only text I have found that describes the actual workings of the shutters. Johnston gives their thickness as three inches, but J. W. Porter says four inches.

> The funnel casing took up a good deal of valuable room. Over the heavy woodwork of the casement were lengths of iron 2 inches thick, and about 7 inches broad—placed fore and aft, and over this is a layer of the same size, but laid cross to the other,—making a resisting surface 4 inches of iron,—which is held together by counter-sunk bolts—showing a very smooth surface. Below the roof and against the ship's side, (under the water line), there is but one layer of iron running fore and aft 4 feet deep,—except where the boilers and engines are—which place is protected by iron knees 2 inches thick, being bitted above, and greatly strengthening that part.

Porter mentioned iron knees that attach the gun deck beams to the rafters but not iron knees on the exterior of the ship as additional armor. It's unfortunate that Anderson didn't go into more detail and describe their overall size and exact placement.

"Her stem was strapped with 2 inch iron, 'building together the stem-head,' over which was fixed the ram, of malleable iron, standing out from the stem about 20 inches, and about the same depth, 6 inches square at the point." This conforms to the description of the original ram but not the description and drawing of a ram said to have been made at Tredegar Iron Works and installed after the battle. We will examine this conflicting description later.

> Her roof, or casement, had resisted well, received very small damage from ricochet shot. Direct hits however, had a much better effect, starting the bolts, and bursting the segments, piercing through the outside layer of iron—then making an indention on the inside layer which arrested its course, there were 7 or 8 such like shots.

The pilot house is placed forward, on the top part of the roof, covered over with a conical shield, which was struck—but made little impression.
—it was thought that she would sink too low in the water &c, but it proved otherwise as an immense quantity of ballast had to be taken on board.

As we examine the structure and parts and pieces of the ship, we will return to these quotations and try to determine what was fact and what was fiction.

THE PLANS

On or about June 25, 1861, John Luke Porter began making drawings of an ironclad ship, but just what ship was it? According to Porter, he made a twenty-seven-foot constructor's scroll that would have shown in detail the changes and additions that he proposed to convert the *Merrimack* into an ironclad. Presumably this is the drawing he took to Richmond on July 11 for Mallory's approval. Mallory approved the drawing and ordered Commodore Forrest to commence construction. Obviously John Brooke did not see this drawing when Porter showed it to Mallory or he would have raised questions about the points he objected to later. In Porter's statement about Brooke's interference, he said: "*After* the Merrimac was *in progress* for some time, Lieut. Brooke was constantly proposing alterations to her." If this was the case, the plan that Porter showed to Mallory would have called for ceiling planks on the interior of the casement. It would not have included the second layer of four inches of oak under the iron. The drawing would have shown the wheel ropes, or chains, running under the iron plates on the stern between the rudder and the casement. There would have been only one exterior hatch, and most important, there would have been no bow or stern quarter ports. Without the quarter gun ports, there would have been no reason to have pivot guns fore and aft and no reason to have the casement rounded on the ends. If these things were not shown on Porter's construction scroll, it had little in common with the drawings that are in existence today or with the descriptions of the finished ship. This drawing probably would have detailed how the casement timbers were cut and assembled, very important information for my purposes, but I assume that the original drawing Porter showed to Mallory is gone forever.

The drawings or specifications that were used to communicate complex fabrication instructions between Portsmouth and the Tredegar Iron Works in Richmond also appear to be lost forever. They could have been discarded at Tredegar, destroyed when the Confederates evacuated the Navy yard, or lost when the Navy Department's offices burned in Richmond.

My first step was to get copies of the *Merrimack* plans. As mentioned earlier, there are fifteen drawings (or drafts, as they were called at the time) of the *Merrimack* and its component parts and several drawings of the engines. These drawings are wonderful illustrations but offer little text to tell the complete story.

A copy of the specifications would round out that picture, but the closest I have come are specifications for the sister ships *Roanoke* and *Colorado*. In the Bureau of Ships, Record Group 19, Dash file 142-4-14, there are eight 8- by 14-inch sheets of blue laid paper, dated July 1854, described as "specifications." The copy is written in both ink

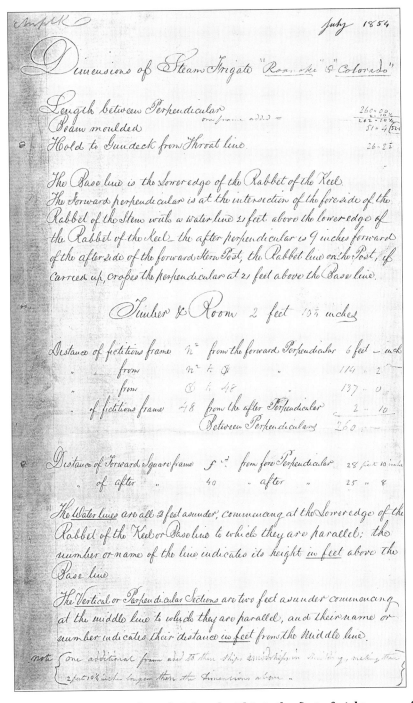

The dimensions of the *Roanoke* and *Colorado*. This is the first of eight pages of very detailed dimensions for the ships. It is not clear whether these are building instructions or as-built dimensions. The ships were laid down in May, and these dimensions were written down two months later. *National Archives illustration*

and pencil. The former is in the beautiful and distinctive flourishing style that was common in the nineteenth century. The first page is headed, in ink, "Dimensions of Steam Frigate" and then in pencil "Roanoke" & "Colorado." The pencil addition is in a different and hurried hand. The body of the document is, for the most part, neat, with incomplete sentences in ink followed by pencil notations, for example: "Berth deck beam molding" and then in pencil –"1' 1½"." "Height under Gun deck beam," followed by – "5' 9"." These are probably equivalent to forms with blanks to be filled in. The ships were laid down in May 1854, and these dimensions were not recorded until July. Preconstruction specifications would have been prepared long before the ships were laid down. I am convinced that someone wrote down the actual dimensions of the ships in the blanks on the prepared pages, during or after construction.

Drawings of the *Virginia* are also on file at the National Archives. These are not originals, but copies, as explained in the following statement from the Archives Records Administration: "Among the Records of the Bureau of Ships, Record Group 19, Dash plan file are two blueprints, dated 1891, of Porter Plans. Plan 3-4-20 is the basis of the 174932 copy. Legibility of this plan is not good, which may explain the later copy. Plan 76-2-45 is another blueprint copy of a Porter plan of the gun deck. We have no further information on the location of the original plans."[1]

Early in my search for original material I came across Mariners' Museum publication #4, a little book written in 1937 by S. B. Besse titled *C.S. Virginia—With Data and References for a Scale Model*. This book has four small half-tone illustrations, one of a three-view plan of the *Virginia*, a gun deck plan, and two others that show an armor shield configuration. The armor plan drawings are for an ironclad with a flat casement fore and aft, not curved like the *Virginia*. There are two possible explanations for the last two drawings: They are either very early plans for the *Virginia* based on Porter's original concept, which did not have a curved casement, or they are plans for a totally different ship. The *Virginia* was the only ship Porter ever built with a curved casement. All of his later ironclad designs had casements that were flat all around. I have not found any drawings that show an accurate armor plan for the *Virginia*.

These four drawings seem to have gone underground after 1937. The museum reprinted a revised edition of the Besse book in 1996, but the old armor plate drawings were not included. I received the following information from Assistant Archivist Gregg Cina at the Mariners' Museum: "Further to your inquiry concerning the two armored shield drawings featured in the [1937] Besse publication, these are not owned by The Mariners' Museum. The images featured in said publication are Photostats of the originals that were loaned to the Museum in 1930's. To the best of my knowledge, these drawings now belong to a private collector."

When the Mariners' Museum reprinted the Besse book in 1996, they also had drawings of Besse's insert sheets of the *Virginia* and *Monitor* plans revised by Alan Frazer and George Matson. These *Virginia* plans, along with plans produced by Edward Petrucci in 1984 for the Blue Jacket ship model company, plans drawn by Thomas Walkowiak in 1988 that are reproduced in *Rise of the Ironclads*, and illustrative plans done by Fred Freeman in his book *Duel of the Ironclads*, are probably the most accurate small-scale drawings. Freeman's book has some nice color renderings and quite detailed plan illustrations, but he unfortunately did not include a bibliography or any notes on his references.[2]

Unexpected things do turn up from time to time, and in July 2002 part of the missing plan mystery was solved. In the July 22 *Virginian-Pilot,* Paul Clancy described two Porter drawings that the Mariners' Museum had recently purchased from the Porter family. Clancy wrote: "One drawing shows Porter's idea for a 'boxy floating steam battery bomb proof for harbor defense' that he presented to confederate officials on June 1, 1861." This date is fascinating, since on June 1 Mallory was en route between Montgomery and Richmond. He and Brooke didn't discuss ironclads until June 3, and Brooke didn't start any drawings until around June 10. Clancy continued: "The second drawing shows the concept as it would work on the *Virginia.*"[3]

Paul Clancy also mentioned four other Porter drawings that were offered for sale at the same time the museum acquired those two. These drawings were owned by a private party, and at that time no one could tell me what the drawings showed or the name of the person who had them. There is a tantalizing piece of evidence in J. W. Porter's 1892 book on Norfolk County (p. 357): "The plans upon which he [John Luke] converted the Merrimac into an ironclad were his own, and were fully matured, delineated and calculated before he ever saw Mr. Brooke. No better proof can be adduced of this than the original drawings of the *three boats*, which are still in existence." Nothing else is said on the subject. What drawings, what three boats? Are these the four drawings Clancy mentioned as being in private hands, or are they something lost and not yet rediscovered? Clancy wrote that the drawings the museum acquired were rolled up in a florist's box under a bed in the Porter residence. We can only wonder what other treasures may have been under the bed.

The "boxy floating steam battery bomb proof" was probably not going to help me, but "the concept as it would work on the *Virginia*" showed promise. The museum offers photocopies of these drawings for sale, so I immediately ordered a set. Eureka, I found the original gun deck plan! When I compared the book illustrations, the photocopy I bought from the museum, and the plans I obtained from the National Archives, I discovered that they were almost identical. The details in the tracings from the archives are a precise match to the museum drawings.

These were obviously the drawings that were copied from the original Porter plans in 1891 by someone named W. G. Hughes, two years before John Porter died. I cannot find any explanation of why this was done some thirty years after the fact. As mentioned before, the Hughes copy (# 3-4-20) at the National Archives is in bad condition, and W. E. Allen made a tracing of the Hughes tracing (Plan #174932) in 1932, during the Great Depression, when the government was finding busywork for unemployed actors, artists, draftsmen, ditchdiggers, and everyone else who could be employed to get the country out of its despair. This second drawing could have been a product of that program. Here is the title block from the second tracing:

BUREAU OF SHIPS
Bu. C. &R. No. 174932
TRACED 1932 BY W. E. ALLEN FROM B. P. OF TRACED
FROM COPY BY W. G. HUGHES 1891.
Bu. C. & R. No. 3-4-20

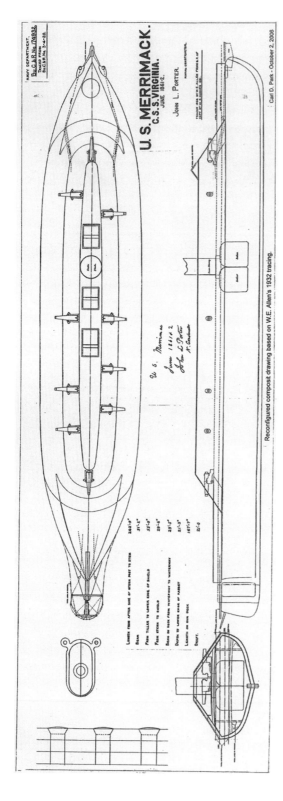

Reconfigured composit drawing based on W.E. Allen's 1932 tracing.

Carl O. Park - October 2, 2005

Porter's *Virginia* plan. This is an enhanced and reconfigured copy of Porter's plan that was copied by W. C. Hughes in 1891 and again by W. E. Allen in 1932. The lines have been strengthened to make them stand out, and items in the drawing have been rearranged to fit the area allotted. The original plan and tracings are two feet by seven feet, and the lines had become too faint if reduced to fit on a page of this size. The text on the left and in the center of this drawing was on Porter's original and traced by Hughes. Allen added the text on the right when he made his tracing. Age took a toll on the Hughes copy, and over time it disintegrated. When it was falling apart and could no longer be touched, the remains were removed from the archives' files and destroyed. The archives' 1932 tracing has been misplaced and, at the time of this writing, could not be located. The information shown on this drawing is from a full-size copy of the Allen plan that the author purchased from the Archives in 1997. *National Archives illustration*

This tracing has a border with decorative corners that I was sure were not on the original drawing. When these drawings were being traced, Porter's signature and some notes were copied in his handwriting. They also indicate where Porter used pencil lines instead of ink, one of the most interesting of which is the iron conical "pilothouse" at the front of the casement. In Porter's writings, he said that there were to be pilothouses fore and aft, but the drawing, and the finished ship, had only one.

The three primary views of the ship—starboard profile, deck, and cross section—are drawn to a scale of 1" = 5', which is reversed on the plan (5' = 1"). There are notations giving dimensions, but point-to-point measurements are given in only three places, and these are shown in pencil. There are two detail drawings to the left of the ship plan drawings. One is of a gun port shutter lying on its side, drawn to a slightly larger scale than the ship plans, but no exact scale is noted. Because no section drawing is shown, there is no way to determine the shutter's thickness. To the left of it is a section drawing, which may be to actual size, of what appear to be bolts going through three thicknesses of the armor plate. The plating measures one inch thick, and the bolts are one and a quarter inches in diameter. In a letter Brooke sent to Catesby Jones in 1874, he mentions one and three-eighth inch bolt holes. Porter's title block on this drawing gives meaningless dates:

> U. S. Merrimac
> June 1861 & 2
> John L. Porter
> N. Constructor

The key to the time when the drawing was made lies in two letters: the Brooke letter pointing out Porter's omissions and Porter's letter to his son-in-law, Rev. J. S. Moore. If Brooke had given the date when his last complaint was issued, we would know that this drawing was made after that date. As it is, we know only that the drawing was made well after the ship was being constructed and probably before the pilothouse, shown in pencil, was put on the casement. The letter Porter wrote to Moore is dated November 4, 1861, in which he drew a sketch of the *Virginia* and gave a detailed description. The sketch and the description reflect Brooke's recommended changes. This evidence shows that the drawing was made after the last change was adopted and before November 1861. Based on this information, we may regard the drawing as a work in progress or an as-built rather than an original conceptual drawing. The gun deck drawing in the archive (No. 76-2-4) is a copy of the original W. G. Hughes tracing from 1891. It is in better condition than the other drawing, which is probably why it wasn't copied in 1932.

I contacted the Mariners' Museum to get more detailed information about the original missing Porter drawing that showed the three views. I received the following response:

> As it turns out, we own only three Porter drawings. When Paul Clancy wrote his article, we were in possession of six, but only for review. We ended up purchasing the two Paul wrote about, along with a *third one* earlier this year. The other three were returned to the dealer who was selling them.
>
> The plans for the floating, steam battery were most likely based upon Porter's earlier schemes in the 1840s. The vessel depicted resembles a small casemate ironclad, with a screw propeller. Supposedly, they were to be towed to the mouths of rivers and inlets

where they would fight a defensive battle against the Federals when attacked. They would barely be able to move under their own power, with engines just powerful enough to reposition them, if nothing else. The date of June 1, 1861 is scrawled at the top, in pencil, along with Porter's signature.

Apparently, Porter's family still owned many of Porter's drawings and papers until just a while ago. They're still living in Portsmouth, but I'm afraid we do not have a contact for them. The museum has dealt with the family's agent.[4]

It might be possible that these drawings are the same ones J. W. Porter said his father presented to the Confederate authorities in 1861.

The original drawing that shows the three view plans was still lost. On August 6, 2003, the last piece of the puzzle fell into place: "The Mariners' Museum is pleased to announce the acquisition of the construction drawing of the famous ironclad CSS *Virginia* (formerly the USS *Merrimack*)." The announcement goes on to say, in part: "Erasure marks reveal evidence of how the stern pilothouse was removed at the insistence of Brooke. The drawing also shows the *Virginia*'s ram, which was added as advocated by Brooke. Other noted changes include the bow and stern pivot gun ports, a redesign of the port shutters, hatches, armor added for steering chains and a bulkhead for a submerged bow. The construction drawing includes Porter's signature, notes, and three views of the CSS *Virginia*. The construction drawing was acquired from a private collector who made it available for purchase by The Mariners' Museum."[5] On August 2 the *Virginian-Pilot* carried a story by Sonja Barisic that cleared up the mystery: "Don Tharp, a collector of Americana and Virginia military items who lives in Fauquier County, acquired the drawing from the Porter family a few years ago. He said he decided to sell because he thought it would enhance the museum's planned USS *Monitor* Center."[6]

When I examined both the original gun deck plan and the three-view drawing, it became obvious that, if this was the plan W. G. Hughes had copied in 1891, he had omitted minor details that he may have assumed to be superfluous but that would have been of great help to me. Details of the three- by six-foot three-view plan wouldn't be visible on a copy in a book.

As far as any hope of accuracy is concerned, we are basically restricted to the Porter drawings and the tracings made from them. At this time, only six original Porter drawings can be accounted for: the four that the Mariners' Museum owns and the two armor plan drawings that are privately owned and on loan to the Mariners' Museum. The Porter family may still have some drawings, but there is no public information about how many or their subject matter. The Mariners' Museum is the only place where the public can see any of the original drawings, which the ravages of time have turned to shades of brown.

THE PICTURES

One of the most popular subjects for Civil War–era publishers and illustrators was the battle between the *Monitor* and the *Merrimack*. Immediately after the engagement, the pictorial newspapers of the period carried illustrations and detailed "eyewitness" accounts. Because few, if any, of the reporters were actually on the scene, we cannot consider these

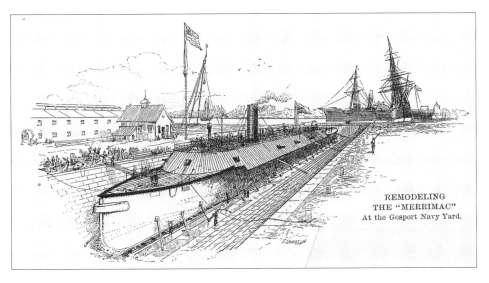

REMODELING
THE "MERRIMAC"
At the Gosport Navy Yard.

"Remodeling the 'Merrimac'." This Davidson drawing, made nineteen years after the war, is one of the popular illustrations shown in numerous books and articles about the *Virginia*. B. A. Richardson's 1905 painting of the *Virginia* in dry dock, which has also been frequently reproduced, is based on this drawing. *The Century War Book*

illustrations and accounts as historical fact. It took weeks, sometimes years, for the real eyewitness accounts to be published and for the illustrators to transform these accounts into detailed drawings and woodcuts. As always, the accounts and illustrations varied among individuals. The only accurate depiction would have been a photograph. On July 9, 1862, photographer James Gibson went on board the *Monitor* and took a remarkable series of photographs, both single frame and stereoscopic, of the ship and its crew. Because of these pictures, copies of which are available through the National Archives, the contemporary detailed plans, the survey of the sunken ship itself, and the retrieval of artifacts from the wreck, we have an excellent record of how the *Monitor* was constructed. Like most things Confederate, not a single photograph of the *Virginia* has ever been found, and there is no evidence of one ever having been taken. Apparently, very few photographers worked in the South until there was nothing left to take pictures of but defeated generals and architectural ruins.

In the Century Company's classic publication, *Battles and Leaders of the Civil War*, and in practically every article or book ever printed about the *Virginia*, is a reproduction of *Remodeling the "Merrimac,"* a woodcut engraving adapted from renowned Civil War naval illustrator Julian O. Davidson's drawing. The engraving shows the *Virginia*, just prior to completion, sitting in the dry dock at the Gosport Navy Yard. A reader's first assumption would be that this is the first illustration ever made of the ship. Davidson was an accomplished illustrator who is best known for dramatic naval battle scenes. His drawing of the Gosport Navy Yard on fire and the *Merrimack* consumed in flames is a classic example of his work. His original drawing *Remodeling the "Merrimac"* was a 6⅞- by- 10-inch pen-and-ink sketch. There are no artist's notes or thumbnail sketches to indicate

"The Encounter at Short Range." This dramatic illustration is how J. O. Davidson imagined the battle would have looked. Considering how little information about the *Virginia* he had to work with, his errors can be excused. *The Century War Book*

how he obtained or developed any reference material he used in making this drawing. Another popular Davidson illustration of the period is *The Encounter at Short Range*, which shows the *Monitor* firing at the stern of the *Virginia*. This inaccurate drawing shows the *Virginia* with protruding bolts as large as those of the *Monitor*, square gun ports, boat davits, and the smokestack completely shot away. We don't know where Davidson found his reference material, but we do know that he never saw the *Virginia* in or out of dry dock: in 1862 he was a nine-year-old schoolboy in Nyack, New York.[7] Not a single drawing, engraving, or painting done in the nineteenth century by Davidson, or any other artist, can be relied upon for accuracy in showing the *Virginia*.

Another drawing of the *Virginia* that demands attention is an engraving that appears in *Battles and Leaders of the Civil War* and numerous other publications. It carries the deceptive caption "The "Merrimac" From a sketch made the day before the fight" and is attributed to Lt. B. L. Blackford, who is supposed to have made the sketch based on a "description" given to him by friends who worked at the yard. That had to be the mother of all descriptions because the drawing is almost to scale and is more detailed in some respects than Porter's drawing. There are only a few minor differences. The drawing appears to be reversed. It is of the port side of the ship, but the gun ports are in position for those on the starboard. There is a galley smokestack directly behind the pilothouse and a ventilator in front of the smokestack. It shows the handrails, awning supports, and furled awnings and also details of the ship that were underwater, such as the propeller and ram. In all likelihood, draftsmen at the Navy yard made the drawing

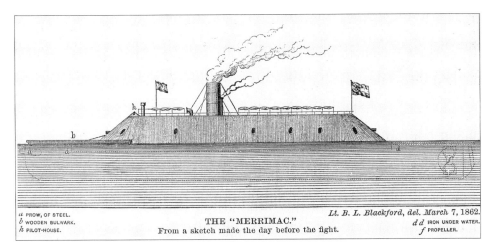

THE "MERRIMAC."
From a sketch made the day before the fight.

a PROW, OF STEEL.
b WOODEN BULWARK.
h PILOT-HOUSE.

Lt. B. L. Blackford, del. March 7, 1862.
d d IRON UNDER WATER.
f PROPELLER.

Lieutenant Blackford's sketch of the *Virginia*. This drawing is far too detailed to have been created from the verbal description Lt. B. L. Blackford claimed he received from friends who worked in the shipyard. *The Century War Book*

and gave it to Blackford. This was clearly classified information, so, to protect his sources, the "sketch from a description" story was told. I have not been able to find any information about Blackford or his interest in the *Virginia*, and of course, no one has a clue as to where the original sketch is.

Another contemporary sketch is attributed to Edward Johnston, who was born in Ireland and served as an assistant engineer on the CSS *Baltic* and CSS *Atlanta*. Apparently Johnston was in the vicinity of Hampton Roads in March 1862 and made a sketch. Johnston was taken prisoner in 1863 and sent to Fort Warren in Boston harbor, where he later died. Sometime after the war, Johnston's sketch, or a copy of it, found its way to England and is now in the Admiralty Papers at the British National Archives (Paper 1/5819:P.184). In script across the bottom of the sketch there is the following legend: "Confederate Steamer 'Virginia' as she appeared in Hampton Roads March 9th 1862— From a sketch by Edward I. Johnston 1st Asst. Engineer C.S.N." "From a sketch by" indicates that someone other than Johnston wrote the legend because the word "from" can be construed as meaning it is not Johnston's original sketch but a copy. The sketch shows the port side of the ship above the waterline. Unlike the Blackford sketch, it has the gun ports in the correct placement, but a strange-looking galley stack is behind the pilot-house and a ventilator behind the smokestack. It shows two boats on chocks on the port side of the casement, a gun on the top deck at the stern (probably a howitzer), and one-piece chain-operated gun port shutters. An inverted L-shaped device attached to the top deck in front of the smokestack appears to be holding signal flags. Handrails and an awning stanchion are similar to Blackford's. We know that the one-piece gun port shutters are pure fiction and that the March 9 date is incorrect. On that date, the *Virginia* was badly battle damaged. Because both Blackford and Johnston actually saw the *Virginia*, part of what is shown in these sketches is probably correct. But which part?

One of the best plan-and-profile drawings I have found comes from the Weider History Group in Sharon Hills, Pennsylvania. This is a fifteen-by-twenty-two-inch print of a

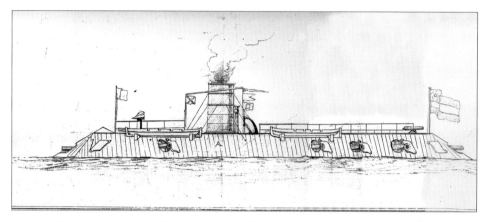

Seaman Johnston's sketch of the *Virginia*. The date on the sketch, March 9, 1862, is incorrect. The *Virginia* had considerable battle damage that day, and the details shown do not agree with any of the other descriptions of the ship that we have. Johnston's strange-looking galley chimney is actually placed in an appropriate location, which is not the case with the more conventional chimney shown in the Blackford sketch—another mixture of fact and fiction. *The British National Archives illustration*

rendering by Joseph B. Hinds that has very few errors. There is a flagstaff flying a blue flag and standing directly in front of the forward pivot gun on the bow that would not have been there. The forward flagstaff, on the top deck, is flying some sort of pennant rather than Buchanan's red flag. The six gun port shutters are top-hinged, and there is a minor problem with the scale of the pilot's house. There are a couple of things that are intriguing, but unfortunately there is no documentation that tells how Mr. Hinds decided that they should be included. He shows four "air intakes," two on each side, on the casement wall just below the smokestack. I have never seen any reference to air intakes and doubt that the armor would have been compromised in this manner. There may have been cleats or a ladder of some sort to provide access to the ship's boats near there. There is a "signal lamp" on a pole just behind the pilot house. I have never seen any reference to this, either, and have doubts about how an oil lamp on a pole could have been used for signaling. Aside from these minor issues, however, this is a better than average depiction of the *Virginia*.

I have found several cutaway drawings that show internal details of the *Virginia:* the plan style drawing by Fred Freeman mentioned earlier, a perspective rendering by Tony Bryan that appears in both *Duel of the Ironclads* and *Confederate Ironclads 1861–65*,[8] and James Gurney's *National Geographic* rendering (March 2006, pp. 140 and 141). All of these are attractive to look at, but all have errors.

There are also some plan drawings for sale that were made in 1986. These two sheets of pure fiction should be ignored.[9] Movie producers have made two efforts to depict exterior and interior views of the *Virginia*. One is a History Channel *Great Ships* video titled "The Ironclads." They failed in the set design of the exterior and interior scenes, and the entire sequence devoted to the *Virginia* is absurd. It states and shows scenes of the *Virginia* as covered with railroad rails and the guns and crew's uniforms are inaccurate. Unfortunately, this mess is shown in history classes at schools.[10] The second is a work of fiction titled *Ironclads*. Although the sets are not perfect, they are more accurate than those in the documentary.[11] For reference and research purposes, however, both films should be avoided.

Beautifully made models of the *Virginia* are displayed in museums across the country. Model ship kits, both wood and plastic, provide a nice overall exterior appearance of the ship. Attractively rendered pictures hang on museum walls and appear in reputable publications. The artists and model builders who executed these works did not have accurate, detailed information about the ship. At this point, we should assume that there are errors in these works and that many of the details presented in *Virginia* literature, models, and paintings are only someone's best guess.

THE PIECES

The most reliable source of information about any large artifact is a piece of the subject itself. Unfortunately for historians, the remains of the *Virginia* were a source to be mined rather than preserved. The wreckage was a scrap dealer's delight, full of iron, brass, copper, timber, and other wonderful things that could be sold. The smoke of battle had hardly cleared when the scavengers appeared. Word soon reached Washington about what was happening, and on May 24, 1862, orders were sent stating that no salvage operations were to be allowed. On May 27, 1862, Gideon Welles sent the following letter: "Flag Officer L. M. Goldsborough, Commanding N. A. Blockade Squn. Hampton Roads, Va. Sir: The order of May 24th applies to all vessels belonging to the U.S. Navy and was given because it was rumored at the Department that parties under contract with some unauthorized person were about to go to work upon the steamer *Merrimac*. That vessel and all others borne upon the U.S. Naval Register are under your charge and must be protected."[12] The "unauthorized person" Welles was referring to was Brig. Gen. John E. Wool, who had been given command of the Department of Virginia instead of the overall command of the army he wanted. George McClellan was promoted to major general over Wool's head, at which Wool rebelled and announced that he would take no orders from McClellan. He took charge in Virginia and began running things as he pleased,[13] including entering into a contract with a salvage firm to raise the *Virginia*. When the Navy's order to cease and desist reached him, he took the following position: "This vessel does not belong to the navy. She being entirely remodeled and iron clad at the time of her destruction. If there should be any timbres remaining that would be serviceable to the navy, they will be turned over to the navy. I have therefore to register that you will not again interfere with the raising of the wreck."[14]

Neither Washington nor Commo. Louis M. Goldsborough accepted this argument, and on June 4 Welles authorized Goldsborough to stop Wool's salvage attempts: "Sir: I have received your letter of the 2nd instant and enclosures. Your course is approved. The *Merrimack* is a Naval vessel and is borne on the books of our Navy. Major General Dix being in command at Fortress Monroe, it is presumed that there will be no further difficulty. Major General Wool had no authority to contract for raising the Merrimac and his agent must not disturb her."[15]

Not only had Brigadier General Wool made waves at the Navy Department but he had also caused problems at the War Department. On his own initiative, he reoccupied Norfolk and Portsmouth, where he began interfering with McClellan's Peninsular Campaign plans. On June 1 the army took drastic steps—he was promoted to major general! The good news was that he was taken out of Virginia. After being assigned to several different posts in rapid succession, he got the message and retired from the army in July 1863.[16]

The Navy Department returned to the subject of salvage on October 25, 1864, when a salvage contract for both the CSS *Virginia* and the USS *Congress* was written. The heading of the document reads: "Sketch of Agreement for removing the wrecks of the 'Congress' & 'Merrimack'—Underdown & Co." In addition to salvage instructions, the contract stipulates that "any bodies or remains of the dead in and around the wrecks shall be suitably interred at the expense of the party of the first part," which would be Underdown & Co.[17] There is no record of exactly what Underdown & Co. did, but they did not complete the job as stipulated in the contract, which required that the *Virginia* was to "be completely wrecked and wholly removed, and the channel cleared of her." The next mention of any dealings between Underdown and the Navy appears in an old Bureau of Construction and Repairs record book that lists, somewhat haphazardly, sales of *Virginia* scrap to various concerns.[18] The first entry shows: "Dec. 8, 1865 Old junk to Messrs. Underdown & Co. $1474.11." The agreement between Underdown and the Navy stipulated that the scrap was to be delivered to the Gosport Navy Yard, where it would be sold at public auction, and that the Navy would pay Underdown 50 percent of the funds obtained from sales of *Congress* scrap and 75 percent for *Virginia* scrap. Apparently, Underdown & Co. was placing the winning bids on the scrap it had salvaged. At this point, the picture becomes less clear. It appears that Capt. A. D. Underdown was not the only salvager working on the *Virginia* wreck. The next entry was not made in the bureau record book until May 28, 1867: "Articles sold at auction to Brown, Maltby & Co. {Other purchasers not given. This day's sales included large quantities of wrought iron, which was armor of the MERRIMAC.}" In a Web site article, Jeff Johnston mentions that the firm of Brown, Maltby & Co. salvaged some of the machinery and the two Martin boilers.[19] It is not the practice today, for obvious reasons, to allow two competitive contractors to work a wreck site at the same time, but apparently in the nineteenth century the Navy had no objections. The next bureau record entry is for June 20, 1867: "Sale of copper and 20 tons wrought iron, purchaser not given." About this time, Brown, Maltby & Co. appear to fade from the scene. In Johnston's article, he mentions that when Brown, Maltby's salvage operations were completed, they "exploded two large powder charges under the stern area of the wreck in effort to clear the hulk from the river channel." The bureau's next sales entry is for December 24, 1867: "Sale of 15,166 lbs. wrought iron to Mr. Underdown {also a part of the wreck MERRIMACK}." An article in the *Norfolk Virginian* in January 1868 reported: "Captain D. A. Underdown had recovered the CSS *Virginia*'s 13,000 pound iron ram and delivered it to the Ship Chandlery of Sanders & Brown on Wide Water Street in Norfolk."[20] Because all items salvaged had to go through the Navy shipyard, the ram, which did not weigh 13,000 pounds, was probably part of the 15,166 pounds of material Underdown had purchased in December. An article in the *Virginian* of February 4, 1868, tells how Underdown had used the tugs *Orlando* and *Pilot* to salvage a section of the *Virginia*'s drive shaft and other machinery.[21] On March 9 the bureau record shows: "Sale of wrought iron, copper, composition, (brass) shaft, etc, to D. A. Underdown," obviously the shaft that he had recovered in February. The *Virginian* report said that the shaft was to be cut up for scrap, but there are no records to show if this was ever done. In April, Underdown purchased 36,705 pounds of cast iron and 69,654 pounds of wrought iron. In May he bought an unspecified amount of cast iron, and on September 5, 1868, he made his final purchase of 201,794 pounds of wrought iron for $4,227. At this point, Underdown must have decided that the work was complete, for he also detonated explosive charges under the wreck to clear the channel.

In 1867 only two salvage firms appeared to be involved in the *Virginia* project, but others later participated. On January 8, 1869, the Navy entered into a salvage agreement with Lewis Baer & Co., and on January 13, the bureau record shows that "Lewis Baer & Bro." [*sic*] purchased an unspecified amount of "iron, Copper, etc.," and that's the last we hear of Baer. A contract was negotiated with Bangs & Dawson on September 15, 1869, but no purchase records are shown for this firm. On November 4, 1870, the firm of Asserson & Hebrew came on board. By this time, the "mine" seems to have just about played out. On December 30, 1870, Asserson & Hebrew sent a letter to the commandant at the Navy yard to complain that the thirty tons of wrought iron they had recovered was worth less than the cost of its recovery. Because they, and not the Navy, had to pay for the cost of advertising the sale, they asked "in view of which we would respectfully beg you to have it advertised in one paper only." There is a footnote at the bottom of the title page of the Asserson & Hebrew contract: "The Comdt. Of Norfolk Yard, under date of May 18th 1871, informs the Bureau that the wreck of the Merrimac is completely removed." The bureau record shows that on January 17, 1871, E. J. Griffith bought 102,883 pounds of wrought iron, and James Pearson & Co. bought 127,120 pounds on May 24, 1871. Here the official Navy record appears to end. I have found no other contracts or Bureau of Construction and Repairs records that mention *Virginia* salvage operations.

The final three contracts that the navy negotiated, from January 1869 to November 1870, all had seven things in common: They stipulated that the wreck of the ship was to be completely removed from the waters of the Elizabeth River and from the waters between the river and Fort Monroe. The contractor's work would be supervised by a person appointed by the Navy. The work was to commence without delay, and a date was given for its completion. All salvage material was to be delivered to the Norfolk Navy Yard. The materials would be advertised for sale and would be sold at public auction to the highest bidder. The salvager would be paid 90 percent of the sum received, with 20 percent to be held until the work was complete. If the work was not satisfactorily completed, the Navy would take possession of any unsold material. Because additional contracts had to be let, obviously the first contracts were not completed to the Navy's satisfaction. The final contract with Asserson & Hebrew required a thousand-dollar performance bond,[22] which explains the footnote at the bottom of their contract stating that the work was satisfactorily completed.

From this point, the official Navy record's trail goes cold. Everything else I have found concerning the *Virginia* salvage comes from newspapers and other authors' statements. The Navy must have considered the work of Asserson & Hebrew to have been completed the project satisfactorily because they were paid for their work. If the sole intent was to clear the area of navigation hazards, the work was not done satisfactorily. Some parts of the *Virginia* remained to be recovered, and she was still a navigational hazard. On October 7, 1874, the *Norfolk Virginian* reported: "The Old *Merrimac*—Operations against the wreck of the famous iron clad *Merrimac* or *Virginia,* sunk just above Craney Island, have been recommended, and the wrecking firm of B. & J. Baker & Co., has the matter in hand. There have been many bites made at this cherry, but we imagine that a clean sweep will be made this time, as the firm is not in the habit of doing things by halves."[23] The Baker firm mentioned in the article was the same company hired in 1861 to raise the *Merrimack* and get her into the Navy yard dry dock where she was converted. There are no detailed records of exactly what was salvaged. The *Virginian* did report on October 22, 1874, that the schooner *Planet Mars* had delivered a section of the *Virginia's* propeller shaft to the Navy yard. The Bakers also recovered an unspecified quantity of copper bolts and piping that was sold to John O'Conner Jr., a Portsmouth junk dealer. O'Conner sold the metal to a Philadelphia firm that melted it down to make souvenirs.[24] Apparently the *Norfolk Virginian* was premature in asserting that the Baker firm was "not in the habit of doing things by halves." In the spring of 1875, the project was turned over to yet another salvager, Capt. William West, whose work was obviously slow and time consuming. On July 28 a newspaper story mentioned that West had "recovered 2 cannon and some metal."[25] The next detailed account appeared in June 2, 1876, when the *Virginian* published an article titled "The Remains of the Celebrated Ironclad Merrimac":

> The remaining timbers of the once formidable floating battery, having been successfully raised by diver West, were towed up Tuesday to the Navy Yard dock with pontoons and lighters attached, with which she draws 24½ ft. of water. The diver has certainly been indefatigable in his efforts to raise the sunken wreck, and his efforts have been crowned with success, having cleared the navigation of the most dangerous obstacle. Although in a pecuniary point of view, it may not be so advantageous to him. The pontoons have been pumped out and the hulk will be taken into dry dock for examination today. The bottom timbers are for the most part of live oak, and all the wood suitable for manufacturing into canes will be utilized for that purpose, and as but little of it is suitable, parties should not delay in sending their orders to 52 Roanoke Avenue.
>
> All day yesterday, the Navy Yard was crowded with parties curious to look at the remains of the once famous vessel, and a good opportunity will now be offered for doing so while the hulk is in dry dock.

A lot of what I learned about *Virginia* artifacts had little to do with the ship's construction but is historically interesting. The "canes" in the article refer to a fund-raising project undertaken by the ladies of St. Mary's Catholic Church in Norfolk, who acquired some of the timbers and had Mr. J. M. Freeman make them into walking canes.[26] Mr. J. L. Wright presented one such cane on behalf of the people of Virginia to Jefferson Davis while he was in prison at Fort Monroe. The Norfolk firm of W. P. Tilley & Co. acquired live oak timbers that also became souvenir canes. Uncounted numbers of *Merrimack/Virginia* canes are now scattered all over the country. In a letter of November 1916, E. V. Wright of the United Confederate Veterans wrote concerning *Virginia* scrap, "Most of the iron was rolled into small S shapes and sold as souvenirs largely during the Jamestown Exposition, which was held" April 26 to December 1, 1907.[27] The Old Domino Iron and Nail Works of Richmond made Jamestown Exposition tokens and souvenir horseshoes from *Virginia* scrap. Even Tredegar got in on the action with more souvenir horseshoes. I have never found any information that explains what horseshoes had to do with either the *Virginia* or the Jamestown bicentennial. Some wags say that all of the wood and metal souvenirs ever produced from *Virginia* scrap would be enough material to build two *Virginia*s. Let the buyer beware!

People who saw the hulk of the *Merrimack* in dry dock said that it was only about two-thirds of the total hull but did not mention whether it was fore or aft. After Tattnall had the *Virginia* run aground, Catesby Jones was assigned the task of supervising the laying of fuses to the forward and aft magazines and shell lockers. Getting the two magazine areas to explode simultaneously would probably have depended more on luck than skill, and it didn't happen. Apparently one magazine area had exploded first, which probably blew away that end of the ship, and then water rushed in and squelched the fires still burning. Part of the remaining old *Merrimack* hull settled into the mud of the Craney Island flats, and the rest slipped into the channel proper. Most of the remaining timber, either fore or aft, that protruded above the waterline would have burned away, a situation that would have concealed a dangerous navigational hazard.

Unfortunately, this final salvage record is sketchy. Any detailed salvage records that ever existed at the Navy yard have been lost or remain undiscovered. Any usable wood that was salvageable was removed, and the rest was burned so that the copper, brass, and iron bolts could be salvaged.[28] By the end of June 1876, the saga of the *Merrimack* had come full circle. All that remained of the steamer USS *Merrimack*'s hull was a pile of ashes alongside the place where the CSS *Virginia* had been built, Dry Dock #1 in the Portsmouth Navy Yard.

In museums around the South, parts and pieces of the *Virginia* are on display. Some of these artifacts might be invaluable clues as to how the whole ship might have looked when it was assembled. The key point here is that the museum be respected and accredited. Having worked in a history museum, I know the academic and political problems associated with unsolicited acquisitions. The generous museum patron who believes he is bestowing a gift of great-granddaddy's—most cherished possession—a beaded rifle scabbard that belonged to Geronimo but actually turns out to be a 1930s Western movie prop—can require a diplomacy that would challenge Disraeli. Items in most private collections, such as the cannonball from the *Monitor* that is used as a doorstop in the judge's office at the courthouse, are to be avoided unless they are accompanied by irrefutable documentation. I have, however, located several genuine pieces of the *Virginia* that, because of their location, may be perfect reference sources.

The largest pieces of the *Virginia* that are still intact are at the Museum of the Confederacy in Richmond, Virginia, which was founded in 1896. An excerpt from two letters I received from the museum gives the particulars:

> In addition to the pieces mentioned in your letter [anchor, bell, and drive shaft], we own a number of artifacts associated with the *Virginia* and her crew. Some of these include several pieces of her armor plating, one of her flags, the anchor chain from the USS *Cumberland,* a cane made from her wood, a fuse from one of her shells, uniform pieces from several of her crew, swords from several of her officers, binoculars carried by an officer, several models of the *Virginia*, one by a member of her crew.
>
> After the war for a number of years, the site of the wreck was marked with a buoy, sometimes known as the Merrimac buoy. From the wreck, the drive shaft was obtained

right after the war by a Richmond business concern, Haxall Crenshaw Co., and secured by the Museum from that firm in 1898. The anchor was raised in 1907 and procured in the 1930's from a dredging company. A bell was obtained by the Museum in early 1970's.[29]

We will examine the bell saga in detail next. There is no way to know if the driveshaft that Haxall Crenshaw had was the one found by Underdown or B & J Baker. The Haxall company had acquired the shaft from a James C. Smith, but there are no records to show how or when Smith acquired it.[30] In 1899, the shaft's authenticity was certified by H. Ashton Ramsay, who before the war had served two years as an assistant engineer on the *Merrimack* and was the chief engineer on the *Virginia*.

THE *VIRGINIA* BELL

Although a ship's bell has no bearing on the construction of a ship, the story of the *Virginia*'s bell is worth telling. In-depth research on the location of the *Virginia*'s ship's bell soon shows too many bells in existence. I found references to a bell at the Museum of the Confederacy in Richmond, one at the Hampton Roads Naval Museum in Norfolk, and a third at the Chrysler Museum of Art in Norfolk. I started sending letters and e-mail messages and soon solved part of the riddle: A broken bell on display at the Hampton Roads Naval Museum is there on loan and is actually the property of the Chrysler Museum of Art.[31] The provenance of this artifact is a fascinating story. The bell was said to have been recovered from the *Virginia* wreck in 1875, when William West was engaged in what turned out to be the final salvage effort. If the requirements of the salvage contracts were followed, West would have taken the bell, along with other salvaged material, to the Navy yard to be inventoried and then advertised for sale at public auction. Apparently, West bought the bell to present to Father J. T. Brady at St. Paul's Church in Portsmouth. The *Virginia* bell was hung in St. Paul's bell tower beneath the regular church bell. The Portsmouth fire of 1907 destroyed the church and its bell and broke the *Virginia* bell vertically in half. The parishioners gathered up the remains of the bells, along with other scrap metal, and sent the lot to Baltimore to be recast into a new church bell. At this point, the heroine of the story, Mrs. Loulie Trugien, enters the picture. Believing that the damaged *Virginia* bell was an important part of Southern history that should be preserved, she arrived at the foundry in Baltimore before the broken *Virginia* bell had gone into the melting pot, purchased what was left of it for its value as scrap metal, and returned it to Norfolk. When she died, she left the broken bell to her brother-in-law, W. C. Brooks, who in turn willed it to his daughter, Mrs. G. A. Sawyer. Here the story gets murkier. The acquisition records at the Chrysler Museum, formerly the Norfolk Museum of Art, show that the half-bell section was donated to them in 1953 by Mrs. W. E. Darden in memory of her father, Mr. W. C. Brooks. Records from the Mariners' Museum show that Brooks left the bell to "his daughter, Mrs. G. A. Sawyer." It may be that Mrs. Darden and Mrs. Sawyer are the same person.

Further information from the Mariners' Museum may shed some light on the multiple bells. A newspaper clipping from a scrapbook Mrs. Sawyer once owned mentions that a replica of the *Virginia* bell had been cast in Baltimore.[32] This bell had nothing to do with the *Virginia* except that some of the scrap metal from the original may have been in it. Accurate replicas are the bane of every historian's existence, because over the passage of time, they have a nasty habit of becoming "originals." The Baltimore foundry could have made a pattern from original bell parts on hand and then made as many copies as they liked.

The story of the bell at the Museum of the Confederacy, which is intact with no breaks, fire, or battle damage, is not as detailed as the one at the Chrysler Museum. "The bell was acquired in 1971. It was 'presumed' to have been taken from the USS *Merrimack* and was purchased in 1865 by Cleveland & Co., of Baltimore, then transferred to James Kane of Gittings, MD, who had it used as a glorified dinner bell. From him it made its way into the hands of the donor."[33] None of the salvage records I have seen mention Cleveland & Co., and I don't know who they were or where or when this bell was found. Moreover, there were two *Virginias,* the original and the *Virginia II* from the James River Squadron.

A recent development in the bell story came from *National Geographic* magazine (March 2006). An article by Joel K. Bourne Jr. titled "Iron VS. Oak: The Day the Wooden Navy Died," about the Battle of Hampton Roads, includes the section "Found: The *Merrimack*'s Lost Bell." One photograph shows the entire side of a battered bell and another a section of the bell that shows the ship's name (misspelled) in raised letters. Once again, the provenance of this bell is sketchy. It belonged to the Pearsell family, and about seventeen years ago, a family friend, James Bernnan, tracked the bell back through several previous owners and finally to a Philadelphia veterans' post, where a former member, "Apache Jack" Nixon, onetime Indian fighter and Buffalo Bill's Wild West Show veteran, had put the bell on display. The bell is assumed to be a souvenir brought back by some Union soldier after the Civil War. Both U.S. and British experts agree that the bell fits the descriptions of those used on Civil War vessels. It is believed that the badly damaged bronze bell, bent and cracked, was exposed to extreme heat, which would certainly have been true if the bell had been on the *Virginia* that last night off Craney Island or on the *Merrimack* the day she was burned at the Navy Yard. In the summer of 2005, Mark Wertheimer, head curator of the Naval History Center in Washington, D.C., authenticated the bell as being from the *Merrimack.* The Pearsells have donated the bell to the Navy, and it will soon be displayed at the U.S. Navy Museum. But this doesn't clear up the mystery of the "*Virginia* bells." Was this a bell found by a Union soldier on a Portsmouth yard scrap heap, where it was tossed after being destroyed in the *Merrimack* fire in 1861? Is the bell at the Hampton Roads Naval Museum the bell that was on the *Virginia* when she was destroyed? It could have been blown clear in the explosion and later recovered, only to be destroyed in the church fire. In fact, there could be more than one authentic bell, one from the wreck of the *Merrimack* and another from the wreck of the *Virginia.*

THE ANCHORS

The possible recovery of one of the *Virginia*'s three anchors gives a slightly different twist to our story. The law states that a lost U.S. naval vessel or aircraft remains the property of the Navy, no matter where in the world it is found or who finds it. In recent years, scuba

Possibly an anchor from the *Virginia*. This anchor on display at the Museum of the Confederacy was discovered in 1907 in the Elizabeth River near the site of the buoy that marked the wreckage site of the *Virginia*. The museum purchased the anchor from a dredging company in the 1930s. *The Museum of the Confederacy photo, Richmond, Virginia*

divers have been prosecuted for taking souvenirs off sunken ships and aircraft in the South Pacific. But when it comes to dredging operations, the waters get murky, both literally and figuratively. Usually dredging operations occur to deepen a waterway or clear it of hazards to navigation. A private firm can be hired by the federal or local government to carry out dredging operations, or the work can be done by the Army Corps of Engineers. This is not a salvage operation, and there are no naval supervisors or archeologists around to inspect or certify the authenticity of anything of interest that might come to the surface. Historically it was a case of finders keepers. Correspondence I have from the Museum of the Confederacy states: "After the war, for a number of years, the site of the *Virginia* wreck was marked with a buoy, sometimes known as the *Merrimac* buoy. The shaft we have came from the Haxall Crenshaw Co. in 1899. The Haxall Co. acquired it from one James C. Smith. Our records don't note who had it before Smith. The anchor was raised in 1907 and purchased in the 1930's from a dredging company." If the anchor at the Museum of the Confederacy was found near Craney Island, there should be a second one near where the first was found, but apparently no one has ever come across it.

Another interesting bit of anchor legend comes from the *Southern Historical Society Papers* (volume 34, 1907):

Norfolk, Va., January 25: As a result of her mud anchor getting afoul of something in Hampton Roads yesterday, a fishing schooner was the innocent cause of the discovery of the lost anchor and chain of the Confederate armor clad "Merrimac" or "Virginia." The stock in the anchor is black walnut. Live oak was generally used, but this material ran out during the war, and other kinds of wood had to be used. The stock [is] of two pieces, shaped in the canter to fit around the shank, between the shoulders, and the two pieces are held together by stout iron bands. The shank is fourteen feet long and a foot thick. The stock is two feet through the middle, and was originally fourteen feet long, but part of one arm is gone. It is stated that the Jamestown Department of History and Education will endeavor to obtain the anchor for exhibition.

The statement about the stock being made of black walnut is not what we would like to hear. In 1862 the Portsmouth yard had literally tons of live oak. If the author of this article was correct in stating that the stock should have been live oak but was walnut, the anchor would be post-1862. If the article had said that the anchor was found near Craney Island, that would be excellent evidence that it was the *Virginia* anchor. To simply know that the anchor was found somewhere in Hampton Roads is not much help. But there was a *Virginia* anchor with a piece of chain attached that was shot away on March 8 somewhere in Hampton Roads. Could that be what the schooner found?

Besse's *CS Ironclad Virginia* shows a picture of an Admiralty pattern anchor with an iron stock, though "(whether [a] wooden or iron stock is not stated)." The anchor at the Museum of the Confederacy is configured to take a wooden stock. There is no explanation for Besse's decision to show an anchor with a metal stock in his book. Model kit manufacturers and people making scale drawings of the ship have locked in on Besse's illustration, and that is the kind of anchor provided in kits and shown in illustrations. If the anchor at the Museum of the Confederacy was dredged up at the old *Merrimac* buoy site, it is probably the original, and the anchors provided in kits and shown on drawings are incorrect.

We know very little about how the *Virginia* anchors were handled. The forward deck was submerged with a breakwater between the deck proper and the anchor chain and anchor. There were no catheads or other devices to assist in bringing the anchor on board, so it would have been impractical, if not impossible, for a crew knee-deep in water to have lifted the anchor and brought it on board. The anchors had to be left in the water beside the prow. Further evidence for this is the fact that when the anchor chain was severed, it recoiled violently, flew into the casement next to the forward pivot gun, and injured a seaman. There had to be tremendous strain on the chain for this to have happened. However, towing the anchors beside the ship would certainly have a detrimental effect on speed and maneuverability. None of the construction drawings shows a capstan or any other device for lifting the anchor, so we will probably never know just how that was done.

THE ARMOR PLATE

The most important artifacts for visualizing the external structure of the ship are the pieces of armor plate that have been recovered. Both Porter and Brooke describe the basic plates in enough detail for museum curators to recognize them, for the most part, on sight. Most are eight inches wide and one inch thick for the first produced, and two inches thick for the final production run. The lengths can vary, depending on where they were placed on the ship or whether they had been damaged. The bolt-holes that were made at the Tredegar Iron Works were either punched or drilled, and those made at the shipyard were all drilled. The punching and drilling processes would have left distinctive patterns on both the external surface of a plate and the inside of the hole. If a piece was not too deteriorated from rust and corrosion, it might be possible to determine whether it was punched or drilled, and from which side. If authenticity is in doubt, the final determination has to be made through metallurgical analysis. There are still two problems in determining if a piece of armor was used on the *Virginia*, even if all of these tests prove positive. During the early stages of production, numerous tests were conducted at Tredegar to determine the best method of punching the holes in the plates. Any test pieces that were not melted down can be identical to a piece actually used on the *Virginia*, but the placement of the holes would be misleading and meaningless. The second problem deals with the armament test conducted by Brooke and Catesby Jones on Jamestown Island. To determine the proper thickness and angle for the casement's sides, cannons were fired against iron and wood targets designed to simulate the casement. The battered iron samples from these experiments would have been carefully examined and analyzed and, unfortunately, might have been preserved. They would be a perfect match, even including "battle damage," to the plates that were on the *Virginia*. Once again, documentation becomes paramount. There must be a paper trail from the salvage company that took the piece out of the water, to the person or organization who had it after that, and then to the museum. Without this provenance, we can determine only that a piece of metal fitting the *Virginia*'s specifications was produced by Tredegar. It could have been discarded in Richmond or Norfolk, used in a punching test, used as a target, damaged and discarded during construction, removed from the *Virginia* after the battle, or salvaged from the wreck. Of these six possibilities, only the last two are of any real value in analyzing the construction methods used. We will examine the armor plate configuration in detail when we analyze the design and construction of the *Virginia*'s casement.

THE *VIRGINIA* RAMS

In addition to the actual pieces of iron and wood that have come to light over the years, other tantalizing tidbits of information have appeared from time to time. In the archives at the Mariners' Museum in Newport News is a small photograph, 3½ by 2¾ inches, that shows a strange-looking piece of iron lying on a brick walk or road beside an old, rather dilapidated building. On the back of the photograph is the following notation: "Ram said to have been taken from the bow of C.S.S. VIRGINIA (MERRIMAC) Now located at The Jones Hard Ware Co. Baltimore, Md. Presented by Grace I. Miller Baltimore, Md 5/18/37." This picture and the bit of information accompanying it started me on a treasure hunt. Was it possible that the Virginia's ram was still in existence? That this was only half of a ram was obvious in the photo. First, I tried to see whether the hunk of metal shown came close to matching the descriptions of the ram. Porter makes several references to it:

C.S.S. VIRGINIA (MERRIMAC) Story of Her Construction, Battles, Etc.: The ram was put on at my suggestion. Very little was known about them at the time, and for want of something better to make one out of, we used cast iron; it was fitted to the bow and stem head and bolted strongly to both.

A Short History of Myself: The idea of a ram was a new one, and had not been talked of much by anyone until the steamer was nearly completed. For my part, I did not rely much on the idea, but to please all, I continued to do so as ordered. For want of money, I had to put on a cast iron one and had the Cumberland been struck a blow at right angles, it would have stood very well. But the Merrimack struck a glancing blow and although it broke through the Cumberland, it also caught the ram and broke it off.

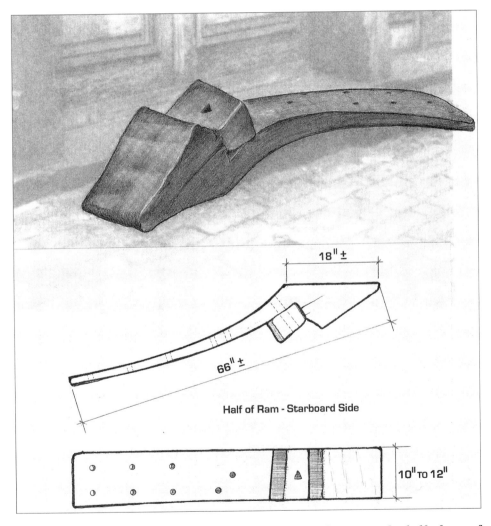

Is this part of the *Virginia*'s ram? This strange-looking device may be half of one of *Virginia*'s rams. In 1937 it was at the Jones Hardware Co. in Baltimore. Its present-day whereabouts are unknown. *Drawn by author*

Events in Norfolk County: When the beak was put on her Mr. Porter was apprehensive that, as the ship was not built originally with a view of making a ram of her, it would not be safe to do so, but Captain Buchanan decided to take the risk, and sink the Cumberland without materially injuring his own ship.

Her iron beak, or prow, broke off. This was originally made wedge shaped, projected about two feet from the ship, and was slanted on top.

First it was Porter's bright idea, and then a little later, he tells us that he was putting it on under duress. Porter's vacillation was not that unusual, as we have seen before. According to other information, Mallory wanted the ram in the first place, and Brooke concurred. Rams had been an efficient weapon on the old galleys but were impractical on a sailing ship. With steam power, it once again became practical to put a ram on a ship that could be aimed and charged at its target.

On May 17, 1906, former steam engineer Ashton Ramsey, who then lived in Baltimore, described the ram in a letter he wrote to J. W. Morrison in Brooklyn:

Replying to your inquiry in regard to the Merrimack, at the time this vessel rammed the Cumberland in Hampton Roads, March 62, her ram consisted of cast iron, the casting weighed about a ton [other references say 1,500 lb.] which was built into the wooden prow of the vessel. It was triangular in shape, about 6" wide at the extreme end, and extended back about 3 or 4 ft. embracing the wooden stem through which it was secured by bolts passing through the flared sides of the casing.

This ram, and the method of securing it, proved very temporary, as it was broken off at the time of the collision with the Cumberland.

Another brief firsthand description comes to us through John S. Wise's autobiography. Wise's father, Confederate general Henry Wise and former governor of Virginia, was a frequent visitor to the Navy yard while the *Virginia* was being constructed. Fifteen-year-old John often tagged along and was fascinated with the huge, strange ship. John said that his father was critical of several of the *Virginia*'s design features: "He repeatedly expressed the opinion that she was being built to draw too much water, and that her beak or ramming prow was improperly constructed in this, that it was horizontal on the top and sloped upward on the bottom, where it should have been horizontal on the bottom and made to slope downward to a point."[34]

These descriptions of the ram, and J. Anderson's description that we examined earlier, are a mixed bag. As best as can be determined, it protruded some eighteen or twenty-four inches forward from the bow and weighed about one ton. Establishing any legitimacy for the ram shown in the picture would require arriving at approximate dimensions and weight based on what was shown. In comparing the bricks in the walkway with the doors, windows, and columns on the building in the background, I saw that the bricks were larger than the standard variety. I finally decided that a brick that was twelve inches long by four inches wide would provide a logical scale to work from, and I made a scale drawing accordingly. From the drawing, I calculated the cubic inches in the half of the ram shown to be 2,562. By doubling this number and multiplying by 0.277 (the weight in pounds of a cubic inch of iron), I arrived at a weight of 709.67 pounds for that piece. A total weight of 1,420 pounds was close enough to make the ram section shown in the photo a candidate for the original.

The general design of this thing is quite odd. It is actually two separate pieces: the long section with the large barb on the end and a hundred-pound chunk of iron attached with a triangular key behind the barb. From the photo it is not possible to determine if the entire ram was made in one piece, like a wishbone, that broke in half on impact, or if it was originally fabricated with starboard and port sides. Regardless of how it was originally made, Porter would have attached a large barbed spear point to the bow of the *Virginia*.

Any experience with arrows or fishhooks can tell you that anything with a barbed end is designed to penetrate something and then not come out. I doubt that Porter would have attached something to the *Virginia* that would impale itself in a wooden hull and stick fast. If this was the actual design, it is obvious why the *Virginia's* bow was trapped in the side of the *Cumberland*. If the ram had been a little larger and better constructed, it could have pulled the *Virginia* down with the *Cumberland*.

By this point, I felt there was enough circumstantial evidence to warrant more research. To prove that this was a piece of the *Virginia's* ram, I would have to find out when and where the ram was found, who found it, and what they did with it after recovering it. Artifacts like the ram are usually found by accident during dredging operations or as a result of salvage or archeological work. Because there was a good chance that the ram had gone down with the *Cumberland*, I looked for evidence there.

I obtained a copy of a letter written by C. I. Willard in 1931 that describes the accidental discovery of the *Cumberland's* anchor chain. Sometime around 1910, the British steamer *Queen Willimena* came into Hampton Roads and fouled her anchor in the wreck of the *Cumberland*. In retrieving their anchor, the crew brought up the *Cumberland's* anchor chain, which is now on display at the Museum of the Confederacy.[35] I couldn't find any other references that might indicate an accidental discovery, so I investigated dredging operations. The Norfolk division of the Army Corps of Engineers had records of private dredging companies they hired to work around Craney Island and also near the approximate location of the *Cumberland's* wreck, but nothing was mentioned in the records about anything having been recovered.[36] Next came the Navy's salvage records for the *Cumberland*, which are brief and somewhat amusing:

> *U.S. Flagship Minnesota,*
> *Norfolk, Va. June 3, 1862*
> *Hon. Gideon Welles, Secretary of the Navy,*
> *Washington, D. C.*

Sir:
> *As it is of the intention of the Department to contract for raising the wrecks in these waters, and those of Newport News, I beg leave to suggest that, in my judgment, it would be better to begin with the Cumberland, which vessel I think, ought to be attended to as early as practicable. The person who came to me with a note from the department, was directed by me to make a preliminary examination of the Cumberland, and then report results, and also making propositions for raising her, but after spending only a short time along side of her, he I am informed, started off for Washington, and this without contacting me, and I have not heard from him since.*
> *I am, very respectfully, your obedient servant,*

> *L. M. Goldsborough,*
> *Flag-Officer, &c.*

The contractor who vanished from the scene without bothering with Goldsborough was Thomas Wells. Disappearing acts became Wells's standard method of operation. The next entry in the record is a letter from the Navy Department to Wells.

> *Navy Department*
> *Bureau of Construction, &c., June 23, 1862*
> *Thomas F. Wells, Esq.,*
> *Station A,*
> *New York P. O.*

Sir,

> *I am instructed by the Honorable Secretary of the Navy to inform you that he will accept your offer to raise the sunken vessels of the U.S. Navy in the waters extending from Fortress Monroe to and including the vicinity of Norfolk and Gosport Navy Yard, clearing the channel and removing all obstructions under the general conditions of your letter of the 22nd of May 1862.*
> *That is, for removing the Cumberland and delivering her whole, with all she has on board at the Gosport Navy Yard, the sum of 8,000 dollars will be paid.*
> *The remaining vessels that in the opinion of the department require to be wrecked will be removed in that way on a salvage of 45%.*

The letter then goes on to stipulate the general conditions as required in the salvage contracts mentioned earlier. The work was to commence immediately and be completed in twelve months, and a performance bond of $50,000 was to be posted. We don't hear anything about Wells again until October:

> *U.S. Flagship Minnesota,*
> *Off Newport News, Va., October 10, 1862*
> *John Lenthhall, Esq.,*
> *Chief of Bureau of Construction*

Sir:

> *In reply to yours of the 7th instant received yesterday, I have to report that nothing visible has been done at Newport News by Mr. Wells, the contractor, for raising the Cumberland and other vessels in the vicinity under his contract of July 17 last.*
> *I learn from Commodore Livingston that a party, of which he presumed Mr. Wells was one, visited Norfolk Navy Yard about a month ago, brought with them diving apparatus, examined the wrecks near the yard, remained there two days and then departed, informing Commodore Livingston that they would soon return, since which time he has neither heard of or seen them.*

> *S. P. Lee*
> *Acting Rear Admiral*

Wells had disappeared again. He reappeared in late November:

> *U.S.S. New Ironsides,*
> *Off Newport News, Va.*
> *November 21, 1862*
> *Hon. Gideon Welles*
> *Secretary of the Navy.*

Sir:
The contractors for raising the Cumberland, have commenced operations this morning.
In the absence of Admiral Lee, I have thought it my duty to remind the department that there is a great deal of private property, on board the ill-fated vessel, belonging to the officers who were attached to her; and I believe a considerable sum of money belonging to the Government.

T. Turner,
Captain and Senior Officer Present

Obviously, things did not go as planned. Wells was supposed to have started work in July, but nothing was done until near the end of November. He was running out of time before he started. At this point, he ceased operations and disappeared permanently, as the next letter in the series will testify:

Offices of Charles B. Pratt & Co.
Submarine Navigators and Wreckers
All kinds of Submarine Operations executed with dispatch
Worchester, Mass. Nov. 15th 1864
Hon. Gideon Welles
Secretary of the Navy

Sir,
Will you invite us when you are willing to give us to raise the valuable parts and contents of the Cumberland [illegible] at Newport News? We are now so situated that we can do any work for the Government in our line with the utmost dispatch. Hoping to hear from you.
We are Respectfully your [illegible],

Charles B. Pratt & Co.

For all practical purposes, this letter, written in an almost unintelligible hand, was the end of the salvage records. Nothing indicates that the government ever responded to the letter from Pratt & Co. The next document is from the twentieth century:

Mr. James F. Cooper, A. D. G.,
National Command, Union Veterans' Union.
827 East Third Street
South Boston, Mass
March 6, 1914

Dear Sir:
Replying to your letter of the 9th ultimo concerning the U.S.S. CUMBERLAND. I have to inform you that all efforts of contractors to raise the vessel were unavailing, and she rests where she sank in Hampton Roads.
I note with pleasure your kind words about my Flag Day address in Boston, and am gratified to hear that it proved of interest to you and your comrades of the Kearsarge Naval Veterans' Command.

Sincerely yours,
Truman H. Newberry
Secretary of the Navy[37]

In the 1980s scuba divers came across the wreckage of the *Cumberland* and the USS *Florida* and began some clandestine salvage operations. The fruits of their labors—inkwells, pipes, bottles, and the like—started showing up in antique shops, where they were brazenly labeled as artifacts from Civil War shipwrecks. Naval justice was swift. The profit-minded "archeologists" were prosecuted, and their loot confiscated and turned over to Hampton Roads Naval Museum for proper preservation and display. And so end both the official and unofficial salvage operations on the *Cumberland*.

I had exhausted the records, so I decided to look for the *Virginia* ram's trail in Baltimore. I wrote to the Baltimore and Maryland historical societies to ask for any information about Grace Miller, the Jones Hardware Co., or the ram itself. I soon learned that there was an hourly charge of forty dollars to get an answer to my questions. My *Virginia* ram search could take hours, if not days, of research time, so I decided to leave that research project to someone else!

This was not exactly the end of the *Virginia* ram story, however, because the *Virginia* had two rams. All or part of the original probably was lost somewhere on March 8, in the *Cumberland* or in Hampton Roads, so it would have needed a replacement. In January 1906 J. M. Morrison of New York, in trying to find information about the *Virginia* ram, wrote to Archer Anderson at the Tredegar Iron Works. Much of the correspondence that resulted from Morrison's inquiry is in the files of the Mariners' Museum archives and makes fascinating reading, including Archer's response to Morrison:

Tredegar Iron Works
Richmond, Va., Jany. 30th 1906

Dear Sir:
    Your letter of the 27th inst. was duly received.
    I will try to find the number of the Scientific American Supplement.
    Our Engineer, Mr. E. R. Archer, remembers the ram of the Virginia-Merrimac, and has made the enclosed sketch of it.

Yours Truly,
Archer Anderson

Archer's sketch was a bolt out of the blue. I had never seen or heard of anything quite like it. As shown on the tracing of Archer's sketch, it was a huge, fifteen-foot, sharp, pointed lance, with three-foot by six-foot side plates to be fastened to the prow of the ship. This was certainly not what was on the *Virginia* on March 8, 1862. Morrison must have been perplexed as well, since he wrote back in May to request more information. That letter was answered by Archer:

Tredegar Iron Works
Richmond, Va., May 9th, 1906

My dear Sir;
    As to the size and shape of the first ram that was made for the "Virginia" at these works a sketch of which was sent to you, made from recollection. Another ram may have been put in place of the first one which was broken in the collision with one of the vessels off Newport News. I would suggest that for further information you would write to

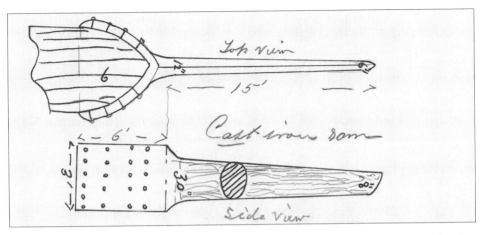

The Tredegar ram. We don't know who designed this odd-looking "harpoon" or what became of it (if it ever got to Portsmouth). It is highly unlikely that it would have been attached to the *Virginia* in this form. *Author's tracing from a photocopy of Archer's sketch*

H. Ashton Ramsey [Ramsay], Baltimore, Md. who was chief Engineer of the Virginia during the whole time the Virginia was in commission. He may give you a full description of the ram and injury done when the attack was made etc or you may write to Col. John M. Brook [sic], Lexington, Va. who designed the Virginia. It has been a long time ago since the writer had anything to do in connection with this subject and my memory may be at fault, but I think not. I was Assistant Engineer at these works when the ram was cast.

Yours truly. (E. R. Archer)
Engineer

We were told by Porter that the original ram was made by the blacksmiths at the Navy yard. It is obvious from all of the preceding information that when Archer writes about the first ram made for the *Virginia*, he had to be referring to the first one cast at the yard, which he sketched, and not the first attached to the *Virginia*. Morrison took Archer's advice and contacted H. Ashton Ramsay. Ramsay responded on May 17, presenting some interesting new information, as well as new confusion:

American Bridge Company of New York
Baltimore, MD., May 17, 1906

Dear Sir:
Replying to yours of the 15th inst., which has been handed to me by the Postmaster. You will note I am still in the land of the living, and Contracting Manager for the American Bridge Co. of N. Y.
Replying to your inquiry in regards to the Merrimac, at the time this vessel rammed the Cumberland at Hampton Roads, March 62, her ram consisted of cast iron, the casting weighing about a ton, which was built into the prow of the vessel. [Here again we run into the comment about "casting." As already pointed out, the original ram described by Porter was forged, not cast.] It was triangular in shape, about 6" wide at the extreme end,

and extended back about 3 or 4 ft. embracing the wooden stem through which it was se-
cured by bolts passing through the flared sides of the casting. [This description is in basic
agreement with those made by Porter and the others closely involved. He neglected to
state how far it protruded from the stem.]

    This ram, and the method of securing it, proved very temporary, as it was broken at
the time of the collision with the Cumberland. Later, after the fight with the Monitor, a
much more effectual prow was forged of wrought iron, and extended well back into the
vessel some 6 or 8 ft., to which it was thoroughly bolted, but there was never an opportu-
nity to use the new ram, for the reason the Monitor withdrew and refused to engage the
Merrimac on her second advent into Hampton Roads. [Ramsay's description could fit
Archer's sketch except that he said it was forged, not cast. Ramsay then goes on to give a
somewhat inaccurate description of the casement before giving his version of the "leak"
that did, or didn't, happen.]

    Some of the reports concerning the engagement of the Merrimac with the Cumber-
land and Monitor mention that the ship was leaking badly after her encounter with the
Monitor, on account of the cast iron prow before described having been broken off, but as
a matter of fact, no considerable amount of water came into the vessel. [This is a direct
contradiction to statements made by Catesby Jones.] There were water tight collision
bulk-heads, both in the forward and after ends of the vessel, and so little water came into
the hold, that it was only necessary to use one of the bilge pumps, and this worked slowly.

This is the only reference I have seen about watertight compartments in the *Virginia.*
Such compartments were a novel idea and first gained notoriety in the case of the Titanic.
It is most unusual that Porter or someone else wouldn't have mentioned them.

    Ramsay went on to give a very brief description of the two battles and the destruc-
tion of the ship but doesn't offer any more startling information. I have found no information to suggest that the strange-looking ram cast by Tredegar was ever attached to the
Virginia. The British seaman Anderson was probably the last person to give a written
account of the ship, but his description of the ram had to be heresay and not something
he saw. With the *Virginia* afloat, the ram would have been several feet underwater and
impossible for him to inspect and describe with such clarity. That brings another question to mind. How much did Anderson actually see, and how much was simply described
to him? Anderson used the information he had acquired to gain free passage back to
England so he could pass this military intelligence along to the British Admiralty.

    The descriptions of the *Virginia's* original ram all bear similarities but nothing that is
indisputable. The second ram certainly existed and probably was found by D. A. Underdown. According to the *Norfolk Virginian,* Underdown "recovered the CSS *Virginia's*
13,000 pound iron ram" in 1868. As mentioned earlier, Underdown probably found a
ram of about two thousand pounds that was soon broken up and melted down as scrap.

    I had exhausted the search for pictures, plans, and pieces, and it was time for me to
try to determine how everything came together and how the *Virginia* was assembled.

PART III

Building the *Virginia*

Chapter Eight

Iron for the Ironclads

According to John Brooke, he and William P. Williamson went to the Tredegar Iron Works immediately after the meeting of June 24, 1861, to discuss the possibility of procuring a marine steam engine for the proposed ironclad. There are no recorded accounts of this meeting or of the hundreds of other visits that Brooke would make to Tredegar. All we know is that, on this occasion, they were told that it would take months for an engine to be designed and built to meet their particular specifications. At this point the concept of building a new vessel from the keel up began to fade. The next time the Tredegar name comes up in the *Virginia* story is in connection with armor plate and cannons. Although it is seldom pointed out in any of the letters, diaries, or newspaper accounts, the *Virginia,* as we know it, would never have come into existence if it had not been for the Tredegar Iron Works.

It is a common misconception that the South was bankrupt in manufacturing capabilities at the start of the war. If the war could be concluded in a short period of time, there were ample natural resources and manufacturing capability available, particularly from Europe and Tennessee, Kentucky, and Virginia. The gods of war hadn't planned a brief one, however. The Union's blockade would take Europe out of the picture, Kentucky was at a stalemate, and the mines, railways, and factories of Tennessee were soon in Union hands. The task of doing the nearly impossible would fall on smaller sources of raw material and manufacturing scattered around the South, in particular in Virginia and the Tredegar Iron Works.

Tredegar was neither new nor small in the overall national manufacturing picture. The stock company came into existence on February 27, 1837, and in just twenty-four years was the fourth largest iron fabricating facility in the United States.[1] The three larger facilities—Montour Ironworks, Cambria Ironworks, and the Phoenix Iron Co.—were all located in Pennsylvania, surrounded by their natural resources and tied into the industrial North by an efficient rail and canal network. By 1861 Richmond was the manufacturing center of the South, with machine shops, forges, and rolling mills employing more than 1,500 free and slave laborers. Tredegar was by far the largest facility, with 800 employees. It filled a five-acre site between the James River and the Kanawha Canal, with the tracks of the Richmond and Petersburg Railroad near its east end.

Tredegar came by its name in a roundabout way. In 1837 the first process to be carried out there was rolling iron. The rolling mill that was used was designed and built by a young Welsh engineer who had been trained at the renowned ironworks in Tredegar, Wales. Apparently the owners thought that was a good omen and picked Tredegar as the name. The young company had barely started when the panic and depression of 1837 threatened its existence. For three years the stockholders struggled to find markets for their products to keep the little company afloat. In March 1841 the directors hired a twenty-eight-year-old ex-Army officer to become the firm's commercial agent and, they hoped, the savior of the firm. The southern railroad system was floundering, and Tredegar's primary market for iron had dried up. The new commercial agent's prime assignment was direct and to the point: find new markets, sell iron. This new employee was Joseph Reid Anderson.

The youngest of nine children, Anderson was born on a modest farm near Fincastle, Virginia, on March 16, 1813, the same year as John Luke Porter. Life on a farm in the Blue Ridge country had contributed to his good health, and he was intelligent, serious-minded, and ambitious. Joseph's father, William, was a veteran of the Revolution and the War of 1812. He had served in the state legislature and been a presiding judge of the county court and the state commissioner in charge of James River improvements. He raised his Presbyterian family with a strong hand and valued education. Joseph's mother, Anna Thomas, was descended from Maryland Episcopalian planter stock and taught her children obedience, thrift, and honor at an early age. Though prominent and respected in the community, William Anderson was far from wealthy. In 1832 a family friend had described William as being financially "barely in a condition of rural independence."[2] Despite monetary handicaps, two of William's sons became lawyers, and a third a doctor.

Young Joseph was a good student who decided to attend West Point and begin a military career. The family's first two attempts to get him an appointment failed, but in January 1832 the appointment finally came through. At the academy, Joseph was liked by his classmates, excelled in infantry tactics, and was first in his class in artillery. By graduation in 1836, he was fourth in a class of forty-nine and held the highest command rank, cadet captain. Despite his successful four years at the academy, his interest in things military began to wane because of his underlying burning ambition. He soon realized that, in a time of war, a soldier might obtain fame but never fortune. In a letter to his brother, he wrote, "Those who are not born to fortune should take every step to a view to its practical benefits." Apparently he did not realize at the time that his West Point education could open doors in the future. He reconciled himself to beginning his adult life as an Army officer. In July 1836 he became a second lieutenant in the 3rd Artillery but was immediately transferred to the Corps of Engineers and sent to Fort Monroe. There was no demand for artillerymen in the civilian world, but in the mid-1800s there were unlimited opportunities for engineers. He settled down in bachelors' quarters at Old Point Comfort and continued his government-sponsored education in engineering. The post offered another unexpected opportunity. He soon discovered seventeen-year-old Sally Archer, the pretty daughter of the post surgeon, Dr. Robert Archer. In the spring of 1837 Joseph and Sally were married.

In September the opportunity Lieutenant Anderson had hoped for came his way. He resigned his commission and became an assistant state engineer to supervise the construction of the turnpike between Staunton and Winchester, Virginia. While at West

Point, he had seen that prosperity in the North was made possible by the network of canals, railroads, and turnpikes that moved raw materials and finished products. He wanted the same for Virginia, and he joined organizations and met men who could make it happen. A convention of industrial movers from all over the South met in Norfolk in 1838 to discuss the southern commercial movement. Anderson had been appointed as the delegate to represent Staunton at the convention. He also became active in the Whig Party and met more influential people in the state at a Whig convention in Richmond. He was rubbing elbows with the owners of the Tredegar Iron Works at these conventions, and they soon began to take more than a casual interest in this energetic and well-spoken young man. He had heard about the financial difficulties the company was having and decided to apply for the job of financial agent. His knowledge of the iron business was quite limited, but he knew he worked well with people and could be persuasive. Most important, there was more money to be made in sales than in supervising turnpike construction. The new venture was risky but offered three substantial rewards: a 5 percent commission on sales, a bonus of 2.5 percent of the company's debt if he retired it, and a house to live in.[3] He and Sally had friends in Richmond, which would make relocating enjoyable for them and their new son.

In his new position he ignored the struggling railroad market and went after federal government contracts. By 1843 he had sold the government $90,000 worth of iron. He remembered his West Point training and decided to become an expert in the manufacture of artillery. He persuaded the Tredegar owners to invest in new furnaces, lathes, cranes, and the other heavy equipment required to make cannons. This would be a learning process that included both successes and failures. One hundred cannons were cast for the Navy Department, but, unfortunately, five of the final forty guns failed during testing, and the Navy refused delivery of all forty. Joseph tried unsuccessfully to persuade the Navy to accept the passed guns, but they flatly refused. He immediately began searching for the cause of the failures. He discovered that by using only Cloverdale and Grace pig iron, produced by his brother, and Black Heath coal from mines near Richmond, he could cast perfect guns.[4]

Naturally management was nervous about the failures and began to interfere with Anderson's business and technical decisions. He knew that the company could not be successfully run by committee, and in November 1843 he made another bold step by entering into a contract with the Tredegar owners to lease the entire facility for five years at $8,000 per year. Joseph's brothers John and Francis had become quite successful in the smelting business before Joseph had joined Tredegar, and John lent him the money he needed to start out on his own. John and Francis would supply the high-quality iron required to make first-rate ordnance, and Joseph would find the market.

The 1840s and 1850s were a time of complex business transactions involving acquisition and partnership arrangements. In 1856 he was able to buy Tredegar outright and became responsible for all business and manufacturing decisions. Anderson formed partnerships with other manufacturers to strengthen the company's production and financial position. In addition to Tredegar, he acquired the Armory rolling mill that adjoined the Tredegar property. On March 29 the Richmond *Dispatch* announced the formation of the firm of Anderson and Company. His empire was expanding, and every move he made increased production and profitability. He was making artillery pieces, train wheels and axles, locomotives, and steam engines. The carpentry shop made parts and pieces for sawmills and sugar mills and assembled freight cars. The complex became the prime supplier of metal manufactured goods and machinery throughout the South and began making inroads into northern markets. Between 1844 and 1860 they made 881 pieces of artillery for the federal government, built the revenue cutter *Polk,* and made the engines and boilers for two ships being built at the Portsmouth shipyard, the *Roanoke* and the *Colorado,* sister ships of the *Merrimack*.

Having the final say on how things were to be done would not necessarily simplify Joseph's life. Nothing was ever simple in the antebellum South where manufacturing and transportation were concerned. Northern industry had a seemingly endless supply of cheap manual labor arriving from Europe daily. Highly skilled mechanics and craftsmen were eager for work. Raw materials were practically underfoot, and good transportation was in abundance and growing yearly. The materials Tredegar needed came from distant places and could take an inordinate length of time getting there. Labor was an ongoing battle in the home of the free and the slave. As strange as it may seem, slave manual labor could be expensive. The Northern capitalists paid their immigrant laborers starvation wages. If a man or a child died, it was no loss to the employer because he hadn't bought them in the first place, he didn't pay for doctors or provide food, clothing, and shelter, and there were ten more wretched souls standing in line to fill any vacancy. On the other hand, a Southern slave was, in the thinking of the time, just as valuable as a good mule. For the owner to protect his investment the slave had to be fed, clothed, and given medical attention.

The majority of highly skilled craftsmen, all whites, were trained and employed in the North, and it took a lot of money to lure these men south. Racial bigotry was not a sectional phenomenon in young America. The skilled laborer, whether he was from the North or the South, was jealous of his pay and his knowledge. There was a highly regimented apprentice system in place for hiring and training skilled mechanics and artisans. Trade secrets and the ways of doing things were handed down from generation to generation, and tradition and trade societies made sure it stayed that way. Teaching a Negro a trade secret or how to read and write was prohibited by law. Anderson had to buy, feed, clothe, house, and care for his slaves, but he could not teach them to become more productive as skilled laborers. Any job that was physically exhausting, required no skill, or might be considered demeaning was classified as "nigger work," and white men were not asked to do it in this labor caste system. Joseph Anderson had the same opinion of some of these rules as John Porter when he had allowed his daughter to teach a slave to read. Porter's transgressions went unnoticed, but Anderson went public with his and caused a firestorm.

In pre–Civil War America, the manufacture of high-grade iron was a little bit of science and a lot of artisanship. The raw pig iron was cooked out of the ore in furnaces where the proper amounts and quality of the raw materials were slightly different from furnace to furnace. The quality of the charcoal was a key factor, and Joseph's brothers made sure they used the very best in smelting the ore that he would use to make cannons. Even the best pig iron had a high carbon content that made it too brittle to shape and bend. Driving out this impurity required a process that might be compared to kneading bread dough, only here the dough was "baked" before it was kneaded. Pig ingots were melted in a specially designed furnace where a skilled laborer called a puddler stirred and worked this white-hot, hellish dough with a long, hooked rod. There was no science here, just experience and skill. The puddler had to handle the stir rod so it would not melt and become a part of the mix as he transformed the shapeless blob into an iron ball. Because pig iron weighs 450 pounds per cubic foot, this work required great strength and was physically exhausting, while at the same time demanding close attention to detail. Color was all-important as the pliable mass began to cool and stabilize. The puddler had to know the exact moment when the color told him that the job was done. It went from white to yellow and then, on the puddler's signal, it was pulled from the furnace and pounded flat with huge tilt hammers. It was kept hot while it went through squeezers and back and forth through rollers until it became an elongated muck bar free of most contaminants. The cooled bar was then cut into pieces that were bundled and again heated to a point when the pieces were about to fuse. This hot mass of metal was then run through heavy rollers until it was a uniform iron bar ready to be worked into some finished product. The rolling equipment that was used could make plates only up to eight inches wide. All of these activities were played by ear; there were no written instructions or formulas.

The skilled puddlers, heaters, and rollers had barely tolerated the slave labor that Anderson began bringing into the mill in 1842 to assist on some occasions and do the menial labor. The white employees had tolerated the slaves in the most menial work at the squeezers and puddle rollers, but blacks were not allowed to work with the puddlers. As Anderson continued to bring more slaves into the mill, tensions grew, and on May 22, 1847, many of the skilled workers from the puddling furnaces informed Anderson that they were going to strike unless the slaves were pulled from the facility. While they were at it, the puddlers and heaters also decided to demand an increase in pay. On May 26 in order to squelch rumors that they were planning violence, they issued a proclamation stating that there would be none and the only reason there was a problem in the first place was because of Anderson's "wishing to employ and instruct colored people in our stead in the said Tredegar Iron Works." Their primary objective was "to prohibit the employment of colored people in the said works." That same day Anderson wrote a letter of his own "to my *late* workers at the Tredegar Works." He claimed he had never intended to use Negro puddlers or fire any efficient employees. But that was then, and things had changed, he said. There had been a strike, the employees had all been fired, and he would have to have Negroes in all positions throughout that department. Any ex-workers who rented houses from him were to vacate their homes as soon as possible, and obviously the question of a pay increase was moot. If the former employees had hoped for public support, their hopes were quickly dashed. They had stirred up a hornet's nest that had nothing to do with their personal grievances but was a challenge to the total Southern economy. The Richmond *Times and Compiler* stated the case quite simply on May 28: "The principle is advocated, for the first time we believe in a slave-holding state, that the employer may be prevented from making use of his slaves. The principle strikes at the root of all the rights and privileges of the master, and if acknowledged, or permitted to gain a foothold, will soon wholly destroy the value of property." Newspapers throughout the South took up the clarion cry. The Northern abolitionist press took a different position, that the antiblack attitude of southern white workers made them revolt at the idea of working alongside men they considered as being of a degraded race. The Southern papers howled back that race had nothing to do with it; it was about the rights of a property owner and basic economics. That was precisely what Anderson claimed when he filed suit against the strikers for offering an illegal argument to exclude slaves from his factory. It was an attack on his property.

By now the ex-workers were in a panic. They pleaded innocent of knowingly taking any illegal action or doing anything against the law, and they expressed regret for the entire affair. The case was dismissed, but Anderson had clearly won. The workers who struck were not rehired, the remaining white workers were meek and compliant, and by 1848 slaves were joining the rolling mill hands and blacksmiths in the ranks of the skilled. Anderson was placing slaves only in crafts where long-term training or the ability to read or do mathematical calculations was not required. The only thing they could not do in the areas where they were assigned was become a boss. By 1860 almost 10 percent of the Tredegar workforce was slave.[5] Other Southern industries were facing the same labor problems, and soon, for practicality and profit, the old prohibition against teaching a slave a trade was being overlooked. Slave labor was becoming just as important to industry as it was to the plantation system. Some of the slaves were owned by Tredegar. Others were owned by Anderson and leased to Tredegar, and still others were leased yearly from other owners. This increased slave population became an economic advantage on two fronts. It was more economical to buy huge quantities of food and clothing at wholesale prices, and as their skills increased, production and profits went up. Anderson housed his industrial army, for those who wished it, in dormitories. Some were given room and board money and lived away from the facility. There were also military-type mess halls and a hospital. The slaves worked a specified numbers of hours six days a week and then could earn money for themselves by working overtime. From the end of the workday until starting time the next morning, they could come and go as they pleased so many of them made extra money doing odd jobs around town. They all got two weeks' vacation at Christmas. The most important thing they lacked was freedom.

Just prior to the war, word spread in the North that top wages were being paid for skilled labor in the South, and there were soon more expert mechanics in the Richmond area than there were jobs. As soon as the first shots were fired, all of that changed, and the tide swept back north. The foundry workers threatened to quit if they did not get a wage increase. Anderson had no choice. Orders were pouring in for cannons and munitions, and the demands of the off-and-on railroad industry were on again. He had to give the workers what they demanded. To add to the troubles, money was tight. The bankers seemed to have a more realistic view of the terrible end than anyone else. His creditors could not borrow money to pay their bills, and he had trouble finding the funds to stay in production. In the days before the Confederate government was organized to the point where they were selling worthless bonds and printing imaginary money, there were times when Tredegar teetered on the edge of bankruptcy.

The next blow to Anderson and Company came immediately after Fort Sumter was fired upon. Highly skilled workers began joining the military. Even though they were eventually declared exempt from military service, patriotic fervor early in the war caused a serious loss of skilled artisans in all technical industries throughout the South. Anderson's most skilled cannon rifler joined the Army in the spring of 1861 and became somewhat of a mystery, which we will examine later. An entire force of blacksmiths, who were building iron gun carriages, joined en masse. The civilian population's attitude made this rush to enlist more acute as the war wore on. Any healthy-looking male not in uniform, regardless of his skill or contribution to the war effort, was often publicly embarrassed and accused of being a coward. Southern pride outweighed logic.

The Tredegar Iron Works was obviously going to be the engine that supplied the vast majority of metal products the war would demand. An ironclad warship would require a lot of metal produced to exacting specifications. It would become John Brooke's responsibility to determine what kind of armor plating would be required, get it produced, and then get the parts and pieces delivered to the shipyard. Anderson's responsibility was to quickly obtain the raw metal that would be required for these plates and the multitude of other orders that were pouring in. With the assistance of Gen. Thomas "Stonewall" Jackson, the Baltimore and Ohio Railroad became an unwilling contributor to the *Virginia* project. In the summer and fall of 1861 Jackson's troops ripped up all of B&O's tracks in northern Virginia. Usable rails were sent south to become part of the Confederate railway system, and damaged rails went to Tredegar, where they were melted down to became part of the *Virginia*'s one- and two-inch armor.

The first assumption, not based on any research or facts, was that three layers of one-inch iron plating would be sufficient to form the armor shielding. Because Tredegar's maximum plate width was eight inches, that dimension was predetermined. The first order to Tredegar for manufacturing the plates was submitted accordingly. This specification for the plates' thickness also had more to do with production capabilities than with the final requirements. Tredegar had punch presses that were used to make spike holes in the thousands of rail chairs (iron plates used to join two rails to a crosstie) that they produced. The armor plates would also require numerous holes punched in various locations, so the chair punch would do the work nicely. At this point they had the cart before the horse, and Mallory wisely decided to do some testing. On August 12 he issued orders "to test the iron plates now being prepared at the Tredegar Works, in the best manner to determine what their power of resistance to shot and shell will be when placed on the *Merrimac* according to the plan adopted."[6]

By this time, John Brooke was annoyed and angered by the Southern press. Stories about the *Merrimack* made good copy and also provided excellent intelligence for the enemy. The *Mobile Register* had blithely described progress on the ship's construction and declared that it would break the blockade, sink the Union Navy, and destroy Northern coastal cities. It was just this sort of publicity that set the wheels in motion on August 3 for the U.S. Congress to start the preliminary assessments that led to the design and construction of the *Monitor*. For security purposes, Brooke selected secluded Jamestown Island as the site for his testing.

Lt. Catesby ap Roger Jones.
The Century War Book

His old friend, Lt. Catesby ap Roger Jones (the "ap" being a Welsh idiom meaning "son of"), was in command of the Jamestown Island Battery, which guarded the James River approach to Richmond.

Sixteen workmen with materials were transported to the island to build a huge twenty-foot by twenty-foot target inclined at 36 degrees that replicated the side of the Virginia's shield. The target had three overlaying one-inch iron plates, but we don't know the exact arrangement of these plates. In three days the project was completed, and the workmen were taken back to Richmond. The secret test began by firing an eight-inch Columbiad with a ten-pound charge at a distance of three hundred yards at the target. Shells did little or no damage, but solid shot broke plates and impacted the underlying pine to a depth of four or five inches. It was obvious that point-blank shots from close range could be disastrous and that the iron plates would have to be thicker. Here Brooke mentioned pine as the lumber directly beneath the iron plating; in the final configuration, two layers of four-inch-thick oak planks were directly below the plating. Not only did Brooke change the specifications for the iron but the structure of the wooden casement was modified because of the firing test. In his letter to Porter on April 3, 1862, he said that he recommended "the application of four inches of oak outside under the iron."

The request to increase the plate thickness to two inches presented a problem for Tredegar. The chair punch could not penetrate a two-inch plate. Here again, we run into procedural discrepancies. According to Brooke, the foreman of the rolling mill, at the risk of breaking the machine, began making modifications in the punch and finally succeeded in cold punching two-inch plates. In a letter to Catesby Jones, written years after the fact, Brooke said that "the plates were fastened by one and three eighth inch bolts secured by iron nuts and washers. The plates were eight inches wide. The first made were one inch thick, which was as thick as we could then punch cold iron. We succeeded soon in punching two inches, and the remaining plates, more than two thirds, were two inches thick."

According to historians Kathleen Bruce and Charles Drew, the holes were to be drilled, not punched.[7] There were questions of not only how to make the holes but also where to make them. In September, Anderson and Company complained that cost had increased by some 20 percent because of the change in the thickness of the plates and that they "had had to change the position of the holes in some plates three or four times and were awaiting a decision on further modifications."[8]

For these changes to be made, there must have been a constant flow of drawings or full-size templates going between the shipyard and Tredegar. The problem would have been intensified because the holes had to mesh on the vertical and horizontal plates; in the case of the earlier one-inch plates, there had to be three sets of matching holes. No wonder John Porter said that "arrangements are of the most intricate manner, and have caused me many sleepless nights."

According to Robert Elliott, in his book *Ironclad of the Roanoke,* someone solved the alignment problem, probably Peter Smith, by placing two-inch-thick pieces of wood between each of the courses of horizontal plates. Bolt-holes were drilled in the vertical plates to be in line with the wood, creating a straight line of holes that were equally spaced. Chief Constructor Porter inspected the *Roanoke* as she was being built, so he knew what had been done, but there is no written evidence that he ever used this approach on his future designs. Enlargements of the photos of captured Confederate ironclads might shed some light on the subject.

From September until February 1862 the rolling mill was devoted almost exclusively to the production of *Virginia* armor, with the final lot delivered on February 12. For some reason that was never explained, plates were made with both eight-inch and seven-inch widths. Where and how large were the holes that were either punched or drilled? Once again, there are minor discrepancies. Brooke says that the bolts were 1⅜ inches. A detail on the left side of Porter's three-view drawing indicates that there were 1¼-inch bolts on four-inch centers. A piece of one-inch armor plate that the Museum of the Confederacy has in its collection has a 1⁵⁄₁₆-inch hole. To settle the question of hole size, I contacted museums, without success, in hope of locating one of the bolts used to attach the armor. None of the authors who had access to the Tredegar sales books has mentioned any bolts. Correspondence from the Atlantic Iron Works in Portsmouth mentions brass fittings, iron bolts, and washers that were sold to the Navy but mentions no sizes. We do know that during construction some holes were drilled and punched in the plates at the shipyard. There are no records to show what size holes were made or the thickness of the metal, although it is possible that the holes and bolts were of various sizes. The metal punch that was used for this work was still in use many years after the war. The Porter drawing shows that the outside plates were to be countersunk to take the bolt head.

The concept of cold punching one-inch-plus holes on four-inch centers through two inches of iron plate in 1862 is hard to imagine. This would be a neat trick even with modern technology. The pressure being applied to the iron plates every four inches would have caused small stress fractures that would have compromised the integrity of all the plates. Close examination of the plates that are still in existence might settle this question. If the plates were punched, there should be vertical striations on the inside of the holes. If they were drilled, there should be horizontal drill bit marks inside the hole. Microscopic and X-ray examination could tell us a lot.

Early in October Brooke and Catesby Jones completed the firing test. The two layers of two-inch plates were successful. Shot could smash the outer layer and crack the inner but could not penetrate the wood. Because of these experiments and the changes they brought about, Porter's final design drawings of the casement could not have been completed before mid-October.

In addition to the armor plates, Tredegar also was requested to produce some cannons and cast the shutters for the gun ports and probably the cone-shaped pilothouse that Porter designed. The conical pilothouse was obviously an afterthought because it appears on Porter's drawings only as a rough pencil sketch. Porter originally planned to have pilothouses at both ends of the ship. As you move forward or aft on the upper or spar deck of the *Virginia*, the overall width of the deck becomes smaller as the casement rounds out at the ends. By the time you reach the point that is the center of Porter's pilothouse, the overall width has gone from fourteen feet to ten feet. J. W. Porter said that on his father's first drawings of the *Virginia*, which he had in his possession, "the pilot houses were to be about four feet high, with straight sides and circular at the top and bottom." He described the revised design: "Mr. Porter subsequently had two cast iron conical shaped pilot houses made and *put one on each end*. These were cast hollow in the middle and about twelve inches thick, with four loop holes for observation."[9]

As you might expect, John Brooke was highly critical of Porter's design: "Porter has placed upon the shield at *the forward end* of the opening a sort of look-out-house a hollow core of iron. . . . It will I think break into fragments if struck by a shot. He has also closed the aperture so that now there will be great difficulty in repelling a boat attack."[10]

I can find no account, other than J. W. Porter's statement, that there was ever a second pilothouse put on the *Virginia* before or after the battle. The subject of this pilothouse will be discussed in greater detail when we examine the actual construction of the casement.

The Tredegar Iron Works. This photograph, attributed to Mathew Brady, was taken in 1865. (Alexander Gardner was also taking pictures of the Tredegar during this period.) The building at the extreme left, by the James River, was the blacksmith shop and brass foundry. The large building with the arched doorway and large smokestack was the "new" gun foundry, and the gun mill and machine shops are located just behind it. The two-story building with the two chimneys at the extreme right housed the company offices. The building with a large smokestack behind the office building was the original gun foundry. The brick foundation ruins, seen in the foreground at the right, were part of the Richmond & Petersburg Railroad's platforms and other structures. The bridge in the foreground crosses over to Brown Island (or Neilson's Island), where the Confederate ammunition laboratories were located. The entire Tredegar complex was destroyed by fire in 1952. *National Archives photo*

All we know about the gun port shutters must be gleaned from Porter's drawing. If any of the shutters were ever salvaged, there are no records of it. Porter drew only a front view of the shutters, so some assumptions will be necessary as to their actual construction. We do know that there was some sort of delay at Tredegar, but no explanation is ever given. All of the shutters were either not delivered to Portsmouth before the battle or were delivered too late to be installed. Six shutters, made at Tredegar or at the yard, were attached to the fore and aft ports and the four quarter gun ports before the battle. As we examine the construction of the casement, we will look more closely at the design and structure of the shutters.

The Tredegar Iron Works was the backbone of Confederate iron manufacturing throughout the war. Mallory kept them busy making armor plates and other parts for ironclads, and they were casting guns for both the Army and Navy. When the war ended, they made a successful transition back to peacetime production. New rail lines were being built all over the country, and Tredegar became one of the main suppliers of iron products for several lines. The panic of 1873 put them in a weakened financial position and almost took the firm under. By the late 1800s steel became the mainstay of industry, and Anderson didn't have the money to buy equipment for the transition. Tredegar's market shrank from national to local. When Joseph Anderson died in 1892, the company was once again profitable but operating on a much smaller scale. In 1952 the old plant was gutted in a huge fire. Without Joseph Anderson and the Tredegar Iron Works, there would probably have never been a CSS *Virginia*.

Chapter Nine

The Guns

The story of the CSS *Virginia*'s guns would once again involve Joseph Anderson and John Brooke in pivotal roles. Brooke's involvement might be considered a happenstance that resulted from a bad business decision Anderson had made several years before. To understand how this all came about, we need to go back to the mid-nineteenth century and examine some aspects of the development of Civil War ordnance.

For hundreds of years, casting cannons, like most pre–Civil War manufacturing, involved a great deal of art and little science. The earliest cannon casters had a rudimentary and instinctive understanding of what to do when designing a large gun, but they had no clear understanding of the mathematics and physics involved. As they made ever larger guns, this trial-and-error method of design became deadly for the gun crew and any bystanders. A flaw in the design or in the manufacturing process could cause the gun to explode. That is precisely what happened on board the new screw steamer *Princeton* on February 28, 1844, when a huge gun called the "Peacemaker" exploded during a demonstration. The blast killed five people, including Secretary of State A. P. Upshur and Secretary of the Navy Thomas Gilmer.[1]

Early scientific study was concerned with the projectile rather than the gun, and it centered on two questions: What happened inside the barrel when the powder ignited and the shot started down the barrel? What happened when the shot was in flight? In 1537 Niccolo Tartaglia, "the Father of Ballistics," published a treatise on the subject, the main emphasis of which was the projectile in flight.[2] By the early eighteenth century, Newton's principles of gravity and plane geometry had begun to take the guesswork out of gunnery. The French and British conducted numerous experiments with guns, powder, and shot. They discovered that a heavy projectile would travel farther than a light one when fired with the same weight of charge. An Englishman, Benjamin Robins, conducted experiments with guns to examine the effects of varying powder weights, windage (the space between the projectile and tube wall), and barrel lengths. In the United States, the Army Ordnance Department took the lead in experimentation and innovation. Army Chief of Ordnance Lt. Col. George Bomford devised a clever Rube Goldberg–type experiment to determine the pressure exerted along the interior of a barrel as a projectile moved toward the muzzle. He had holes drilled at regular intervals along a cannon barrel. Pistol barrels were then fastened into the holes, each loaded with a bullet. Opposite each barrel he placed an instrument called a ballistic pendulum. When the cannon was fired, the bullets shot out of the pistol barrels and struck the base of the pendulums. As each pendulum swung away from the force of the pistol ball, it registered its highest point of deflection on a card and scribe device mounted above the pivot point.[3] Not only did Bomford prove what most artillerists already assumed, but he also had a mathematical projection curve to show how the pressure in the breech was at its highest at the moment of firing and then decreased as the projectile moved down the barrel. His curve made it possible to determine the correct thickness of metal required from breech to muzzle. In 1844 the Army began making 8- and 9-inch guns based on Bomford's calculations. These guns kept the longitudinal steps along the barrels at the breech as before, but now the position and thickness of the metal was based on some science and not entirely on guesswork.[4]

Inexplicably, the Navy lagged far behind the Army in ordnance technology. The Army had the infantry, cavalry, and artillery to bring to bear on the enemy, but a naval ship depended wholly on its cannons for both offense and defense. The first step in correcting the Navy's ordnance shortcomings came about through circumstance, when on January 12, 1847, Lt. John A. Dahlgren reported for duty at the Bureau of Ordnance and Hydrography at the Washington Navy Yard. The "Father of Naval Ordnance" wanted to be at sea, but he made the best of the situation by learning everything there was to know about naval ordnance so he could "fit myself more fully for sea service."[5] He quickly learned two things: there was little new to be learned there, and someone had to correct that situation. Dahlgren set out to bring naval ordnance up to date but was hampered by petty internal politics and the Navy's resistance to change. In time, he overcame the obstacles and introduced new methods of testing the guns, mapped out and set up a firing range on the Potomac, and began designing guns and gun carriages. During testing on the firing range, Dahlgren determined that in order to increase the momentum and range of shot or shell, he had to increase its weight, and in order to increase the projectile's weight, he had to increase the size of the gun. Heavy guns like the ill-fated Peacemaker and the coastal columbiads were becoming too cumbersome and heavy to manage on a ship. During this time he began to formulate the concept of the "soda-bottle shape." This new, smooth configuration would provide the bulk and strength needed at the breech and chase and yet require the least amount of metal. In 1850 he submitted the design for the first 9-inch gun. After that was built and proved successful, Dahlgren wanted to move on to something bigger—the shell instead of the cannon. He determined that the heaviest shell that could be efficiently handled at sea would weigh about 135 pounds. A 135-pound shell would require an 11-inch bore, and an 11-inch bore in a soda bottle–shaped gun would result in a gun weighing about 16,000 pounds.[6]

The hidebound Navy dug in its heels at the suggestion of replacing its beloved 32-pounders with this strange-looking device. The breakthrough finally came with the reconfiguration of the old *Franklin* but not in the way Dahlgren had hoped. The specifications for the refurbished ship called for twenty-eight 9-inch Dahlgrens on the gun deck, twenty old-design 8-inch shell guns on the spar deck, and one Dahlgren pivot gun aft and two forward. He didn't get the 11s, but in December 1854 the Navy placed orders with the Tredegar and Fort Pitt foundries for fifty 9-inch Dahlgrens. Seven 10s and

John A. Dahlgren and the Dahlgren gun. Matthew Brady took this picture of Dahlgren, standing beside a 50-pound Dahlgren rifle on the deck of the USS *Pawnee*, on Friday, April 21, 1865, just one week after Lincoln was assassinated. *Library of Congress photo*

seven 11s were ordered from both the Alger and Parrott foundries. But all did not go smoothly. There were metal failures and inconsistencies in guns from some of the foundries. Both Anderson and Dahlgren realized that one of the most critical steps in the casting operation was the cooling process. If a tube cooled too rapidly, a microscopic crystallization could form between the hotter and cooler areas in the iron, which would result in a weakened spot that in time could break and result in a Peacemaker-type disaster. At Tredegar great care was taken in controlling the slow cooling process, and none of their guns failed.

Dahlgren's principal antagonist during this time of attempted change was actually his boss, Commo. Charles Morris. Morris was a hero of the War of 1812 and the chief of the Bureau of Ordnance and Hydrography, and he seemed to believe that he could best serve his country by maintaining the status quo. He rejected Dahlgren's quality-control proposals, testing procedures, and recommendations for changes in gun-casting methods. On January 27, 1856, the old commodore died, and three days later Secretary of the Navy Dobbin offered the job as head of the bureau to Dahlgren, who turned it down. He wanted to make revolutionary changes in numerous naval ordnance practices, but as bureau head he would probably become bogged down in paperwork and politics. When his old friend Joseph Smith was made temporary head of the bureau, he immediately gave Dahlgren carte blanche to implement every program and change he had recommended. With his recent promotion to commander, and with the backing of Joseph Smith, Stephen Mallory, and other progressive thinkers, John A. Dahlgren was now in a position to make the changes he had longed for. He soon sent out young officers, nicknamed "smart young fellers," to oversee and inspect every operation in the manufacture of his guns at the various foundries. He immediately initiated one of his pet projects, the standardization of naval gunnery procedures on every U.S. ship. A manual was written, and young lieutenants were trained as gunnery officers to go on board the new steam frigates and train and drill the gun crews in the proper and uniform handling of the Dahlgren and other guns. Dahlgren picked a young man who had served under him at the testing range on the Potomac, Catesby ap Roger Jones, to be the gunnery officer on the new *Merrimack*.[7]

While Dahlgren was struggling with Morris to make changes in naval ordnance, Army Lt. Thomas Jackson Rodman was about to totally change the method of casting artillery pieces. Rodman, born in Indiana in 1815, was a West Pointer from the class of 1841. After graduation, he immediately entered the Army Ordnance Department and in time, like Dahlgren, became an expert in gun manufacture and testing. Rodman also knew the inherent problems of cooling gun castings but found a radical solution that would cause manufacturers like Anderson great consternation—the foundry owners were no more in favor of radical change than Commodore Morris had been. To fully appreciate what Rodman proposed, we need to examine an earlier period in artillery history.

In central Europe, around the start of the fourteenth century, metal or wooden tubes, constructed the way a cooper would build an elongated barrel, became the first cannons. Casting guns was soon seen as more practical, and in 1326 the city-state of Florence ordered a number of metal cannons to be cast for its defense.[8] These early guns were all made of brass an outgrowth of artists' methods of casting bronze statues. About 1550 iron guns began to appear, but they were more difficult to cast, and brass remained the material of choice. By the end of the eighteenth century, the manufacturing process had been refined and pretty much standardized in Europe. The materials and methods of casting used in the Royal British Gun Foundry in 1793 were described and illustrated in a manuscript by Isaac Landman, Professor of Artillery and Fortification at the Royal Military Academy in Woolwick.

In an abridged version of Landman's description, the first step was to make a pattern, a full-size replica, of the gun. The pattern was laid up on a long tapered wooden spindle that had a smaller diameter than the finished gun would have. The spindle was greased and then wrapped tight with a thick string "untwisted, and such as it comes from the hand of the spinner before making cordage."[9] After the spindle was wrapped, it was then covered and formed into the finished shape of the gun by applying a clay composite material in successive layers. This modeling material was made from a mixture of one part brown clay, one part well-aged horse manure, and one half-part white sand. This was mixed with water for two or three hours and then made into two consistencies, a soft doughlike form for the base coat and thick soupy liquid for finishing. As the workmen applied the clay to the pattern, it was turned, as if in a lathe, with a wooden scribe on one side to form the desired shape. The pattern was then slowly cured over a low fire of wood, peat, or charcoal. After hardening, the details, such as dolphins, handles, or decorations, were applied by artisans using wax. Next a mold was made from brown clay, white sand, and a little wadding (finely shredded rags) or cow hair mixed with water. Successive layers of this mixture were applied to the model until they had a thickness of several inches. This mixture, when cured, was considerably harder than the material used to make the pattern. The mold was then bound with metal hoops every four or five inches along its length, then covered with another layer of the brown mold composite and cured over a low fire. The spindle that formed the core of the model was lightly tapped at the protruding end and pulled until it broke free of the interior of the mold and was then withdrawn. Next a fire was lit inside the model. The fire caused the remaining material that formed the finished shape of the pattern to crack and flake away and for the wax to melt. The inside of the mold was then thoroughly cleaned with long brushes and covered with a slurry of white ashes. The finished mold was placed vertically into a casting pit. Two or three days before the pour, the mold was heated with an internal fire until it was white hot. At this point, the mold was open on both ends so a cascabel (back part of the gun tube) mold was made in basically the same manner as the gun mold and attached to its rear. The assembled mold—as a rule, several molds—was heated red hot and then two or three days later placed upright in a casting pit. The pit was filled with earth until only the top ends of the molds were exposed. At this point, the gun's bore was formed by inserting and suspending a long core rod in the center of the barrel. This rod had been wrapped in twine and covered with clay in the same manner as the original pattern.[10]

The next step was pouring the molten brass. The pit was alongside the furnace, and the metal was allowed to flow from the tap hole, at the furnace base, through channels made in the earth around the molds and into an opening, called a horn, on the side of the molds. The metal was never poured into the opening at the top of the mold, which was left unimpeded so the gases and heat could escape. The molds were allowed to cool for a day or two. Then the core rod was removed, and the molds were dug out of the pit and broken away from the bronze gun inside. To remove imperfections on the inside, the bore was drilled smooth by large horse-powered drills and then polished. The exterior of the gun was cleaned and polished, and the vent hole was drilled and tapped to take a copper vent tube. The gun was then ready for testing.

Over time there were some changes in method and materials, but until the Civil War era, most of the basic principles described by Landman remained in use. As the Industrial Revolution took hold, larger and more powerful lathes and drilling machines, powered by steam, came into use. By the time of the Civil War, the step of inserting a core rod was discontinued. Guns were solid cast, using two-part sand molds, and then the bore was drilled out mechanically.

Dahlgren and others realized that part of the cracking problem with the big guns was that the breech of the gun was so much larger than the chase that the metal would obviously cool unevenly. Dahlgren advocated an expensive and time-consuming change, casting the guns almost like a cylinder and then cutting away the excess on a lathe. But even this cumbersome process was not entirely satisfactory, which is where Thomas Rodman enters the picture. Rodman reasoned that, given the big guns' configuration, if they were cooling unevenly from the outside in, it would be better if they cooled from the inside out. He took the process full circle and went back to the old concept of a core rod, but not the type of rod used in the past. His rod was revolutionary, a kind of elongated water-cooled radiator. A hollow tube, closed at the bottom, formed the bore, and inside that tube was a smaller tube open on both ends. Water was pumped, under pressure, into the small tube. It flowed to the bottom and then was forced back up through the outside tube, picking up heat as it went, and then out the top. Coals surrounded the outside of the mold to ensure that the gun cooled from the inside out.[11] In the mid-1850s Rodman was so adamant about the superiority of his method that he traded his patent rights to Charles Knap of the Fort Pitt foundry for Knap's services in casting guns with the Rodman method so he could conduct a test. Identical guns were cast using his method and the solid cast system. In the firing test, he concluded that his new method produced superior guns. He and Anderson were now in opposite camps. Each tried to convince the government that his method was best.

The fall of 1859 was a dark period for Joseph Anderson at Tredegar. He worried about the long-range effects John Brown's October attack at Harpers Ferry might have on business and national politics. Ordnance orders were lagging, and the ever-struggling Southern railroads and their slow payment of bills had left him short of funds. A bright spot came the first of November when the Army Ordnance Bureau placed an order for $20,000 worth of 8-inch columbiads. But two weeks later, any optimism he might have mustered was dashed. After a series of tests, Rodman had convinced Secretary of War John B. Floyd that his casting method was best. Tredegar received a letter from the War Department stating that the 8-inch columbiads, and any future guns they would cast, must be produced using the Rodman method. Each gun foundry in the country making heavy ordnance for the government received a similar letter.[12] Each foundry owner, with the exception of Charles Knap, was thunderstruck; this change would require expensive new equipment, hours of conversion work, and retraining of workers. On December 1 Anderson wrote to Floyd, his old friend and fellow Virginian, protesting the change. He pointed out how, in 1854 and 1855, the Fort Pitt foundry, then using the old casting method, had failed to make a single acceptable gun out of an order of fifty-five. Tredegar had then been given the order and successfully produced all fifty-five guns. Fort Pitt simply couldn't produce guns of the high quality made by Tredegar, no matter what casting method they used. He also claimed that in the past Knap had attempted to drive him out of business and that this new ploy was a further attempt to that end. He concluded, "All I have to say now is that I beg for God's sake that you will see that I have a fair chance and I pledge myself to satisfy you that I ought not be forced into this thing."[13] On December 12 Anderson received a letter telling him that the order for casting by the Rodman method would stand.

To facilitate the change, the Ordnance Department agreed to pay Knap a 20 percent royalty for each gun produced by other foundries using the patented process, and Captain Rodman would visit each foundry, personally supervise the installation of equipment, and give instructions in its use. To avoid giving the Fort Pitt foundry any perceived advantages, the government agreed to pay the same price for each gun made by all of the foundries involved. By February the other foundry owners gave in. They concluded that, based on certified test results, the Rodman method did produce a superior gun. Each cast required less metal, and the finishing time was dramatically shortened. More guns could be produced in less time, and adopting the new system made economic sense. Anderson stood alone in continuing to resist. The Ordnance Department informed him that he would cast federal guns by the Rodman method or not at all.

With war clouds gathering, Anderson was to suffer an even deeper blow. The Southern states were strengthening their militias and needed guns. The request for bids went out, and Anderson lost to Northern foundries. By this time Anderson and his brothers in the smelting business contemplated giving up the ordnance work, but just as Joseph was about to dismantle the ordnance shops, the U.S. Navy made what would turn out to be a terrible mistake. The Army, the Navy, and the Southern states were ordering guns at such a rate that demand may have started to outstrip supply. The Navy needed more guns, and John Dahlgren had not concurred that the Rodman columbiads were better than the Dahlgrens produced by Tredegar. Besides, he now had his "smart young fellers" inspecting every step of cannon production, and all guns had to pass his test. For reasons not fully explained, the government relented, and Tredegar unexpectedly received an order for nine 9-inch shell guns, solid cast, that would keep the foundry busy until November 25, 1860. Unintentionally the U.S. Navy had saved the future Confederacy's most important ordnance works from disassembly. It later became quite clear that Joseph Anderson had made a monumentally bad business decision in refusing to adopt the Rodman casting method, and his stubbornness would make the South compete on an uneven playing field in cannon production. The 9-inch shell guns were the last cannons Tredegar would ever produce for the U.S. government, but for many months the foundry continued to provide the Union forces with shot and shell. This strange situation continued until the war actually started; companies in both the North and South were shipping war matériel back and forth across the Mason Dixon Line that would soon come back to kill their own people.

In the summer of 1860 Anderson and Company felt bullish again. An expansion and remodeling program began. The engine finishing shop was expanded, new tools were purchased for manufacturing boxcars, improvements were made in the iron, brass, and car wheel foundries, and a large steam hammer was installed in the blacksmith shop. A large waterwheel and new belt drive system were installed. As the November election drew near, optimism began to fade. New orders dwindled, the railroads couldn't meet their obligations again, and money became scarce. Banks, both North and South, became pessimistic about the country's financial future, and interest rates climbed. By the election, Tredegar once again teetered on the verge of bankruptcy. On December 7, 1860, Anderson and Company was forced to take out a $100,000 loan at the highest rates and deliver a deed of trust to the lenders for the property, buildings, and machinery. The first payments would fall due in March and April,[14] so they had a four-month window in which to turn the company's fortunes around. Lincoln's election was the catalyst that put Old Dixie on the road to self-destruction and momentarily saved Tredegar. On December 14, 1860, Tredegar shipped the Navy's nine Dahlgren guns. Five went to Brooklyn, and four went, in a roundabout way via the Gosport Navy Yard, to the Confederacy.

At the beginning of 1861, orders started coming in from the Southern states: six guns for Georgia, two columbiads for Alabama, and a huge order for munitions from South Carolina. Requests for information about capacity and prices came in from Virginia, North Carolina, Kentucky, Tennessee, Florida, Louisiana, Mississippi, and South Carolina.[15] Anderson and Company's financial crisis had ended, and a national crisis of unimaginable proportions had begun. On January 17 Tredegar received an urgent telegram from Charleston, South Carolina. How soon could large quantities of 8- and 10-inch shot and shell be shipped? Was there any cannon powder available in Richmond? They wired back that they had 250 8- and 10-inch shot and 450 8-inch shells. There were a thousand kegs of cannon powder in town, and they would start loading everything onto railroad cars in the morning. A second telegram ordered seven 10-inch mortars and large quantities of shells to be manufactured and shipped as soon as possible. Tredegar went into wartime production, working day and night, and by January 24 special trains loaded with munitions were leaving for Charleston almost every day. By February 9 the first 10-inch mortar was shipped. On February 24 Anderson went to Charleston on one of the munitions trains to meet with Governor Pickens. Before leaving Charleston, Joseph rowed over to Fort Sumter to visit his old West Point artillery instructor, the fort's commander, Maj. Robert Anderson. Although the major knew why his old pupil was in Charleston, he greeted him cordially and invited him to stay for dinner.[16] This meeting was probably one of the first of this kind. Throughout the war old comrades in arms, now wearing blue and gray, met on battlefields, in hospitals, or as prisoners of war and sat talking of pleasant memories from times long past.

For a while during this strange and strained transition period between peace and war, Tredegar was working for both North and South. Anderson needed money desperately and did not have the luxury of turning down profitable federal munitions orders. More orders for munitions and artillery poured in from the Southern states. Unlike the struggling Southern railroads, the states paid promptly. With the formal establishment of the Confederate States of America in February, Tredegar had a new paying customer ready and able to tax its manufacturing capabilities to the limit. Anderson and Company could now meet the March loan payment and even make a profit. On April 1, 1861, Anderson met with Secretary Mallory in Montgomery and discussed the ways and means by which Tredegar could meet the new Navy's needs. On the fourth Mallory placed the Navy's first order, ten cannons with boat carriages and ammunition.[17]

At 4:30 AM on April 12 the roar of a Tredegar-built 10-inch mortar shattered the morning quiet, and the cometlike tail of a Tredegar shell arched across the predawn sky over Charleston harbor. An explosive flash above the ramparts of Fort Sumter signaled the beginning of the American Civil War. Anderson had not been a strong supporter of secession, but now that the deed was done, he turned hawkish and pressed Governor Letcher to abandon the Union and take Virginia into the southern camp. He organized a demonstration to press the point and led three thousand Richmond citizens in a march

Joseph R. Anderson. Mathew Brady persuaded Robert E. Lee and other Confederate generals to put on their old uniforms to have their pictures taken, and Anderson was no exception. He served for less than a year in 1861–62 as a brigadier general and was more valuable to the cause on the home front than on any battlefield. *Library of Congress photo*

to support secession. Lincoln's call for 75,000 Army volunteers tipped the scales, and on April 17 Virginia became a Confederate state. The gun foundry and ammunition shops were in full wartime production, and for a while, the burden of producing heavy guns for the entire Confederacy would fall on Tredegar. For the moment, the Navy had more cannons than they could use. When the Union forces abandoned the Portsmouth yard, they had left the cannons behind. Even knowing that the equipment was on hand to redrill vents, the Union soldiers still took the time to spike some of the 1,202 guns. Everything the *Virginia* would require in the way of armament, with the exception of rifled guns, was there.[18] Only guns were in short supply. A few weeks into the war, the supply of vital materials from the North that Tredegar had depended on were exhausted. They ran out of copper to make bronze and had no steel to make machine tools, no sheet zinc, and no lead. There were no new files, so old ones were recut, and nuts for bolts were laboriously made by hand. Most serious of all was the lack of firebrick to line the furnaces. The brick they found in the South was inferior, not being able to withstand the heat of the furnaces and crumbling in a few days instead of lasting for months. To add to the problems, Joseph Anderson decided in August that he wanted to be a soldier and began pestering the War Department to give him a commission. Davis and Lee were much opposed to the idea. They knew that he was vital to the cause right where he was and not on some battlefield. He insisted that his partners could run everything without his help and that his presence was probably superfluous. On September 3, 1861, he won the argument, became Brigadier General Anderson, and soon departed for coastal defense duty in North Carolina. His partners did not prove to be as efficient as he had supposed, however, and in less than a year the general was back in command of Tredegar.[19]

As orders poured in to Tredegar for more and more cannons, Joseph Anderson's decision to refuse to make guns in the Rodman manner came back to haunt him. There was no way he could produce guns as fast or as cheaply as they were being produced in the North. He was still casting solid guns with excess metal that had to be removed on a lathe, as Dahlgren had specified, and then the bore laboriously drilled out. In addition to this problem, there was a sudden demand for heavy rifled Navy cannons. Tredegar had produced some rifled field cannons in the past but nothing on a large scale. Until the Civil War, cannons built for the Navy were smooth bore. Dahlgren didn't even start testing rifling in his guns until May 1862, and even then, because of his love affair with his soda-bottle smooth bore, he was not convinced that his 11-incher wasn't just as potent as the new rifled British Whitworth.[20]

There was nothing new about the theory of rifling. During the Revolution, the minutemen, armed with hand-crafted rifles, picked off helpless British soldiers, armed with Brown Bess muskets, at long range. Rifling grooves scribed into a bore made a fired projectile spin as it went down the barrel and while in flight. That spin caused the bullet to go farther and straighter and hit with more impact. A fight between a man with a musket and one with a rifle was not a fair fight. Many Union naval captains with a ship full of smooth bores were terrified at the prospect of going up against heavy long-range rifled cannons. Stephen Mallory was of the same opinion as those captains, and he didn't intend to allow his small Navy to be outgunned. In the late summer of 1861, about the same time that Brooke was coming to grips with the *Virginia*'s armor requirements, Mallory assigned him the development of a rifled cannon. Brooke later wrote: "by order of the Secretary I designed two rifled cannon of seven inch caliber for the *Merrimac*—one of them had been cast and is now nearly bored." The first two guns were ordered into production on September 21, and Brooke had to consider some very specific factors. First and foremost, Tredegar had to be able to produce the gun en masse; it had to contain the minimum amount of metal, require minimal manufacturing time, and be safe and economical. A

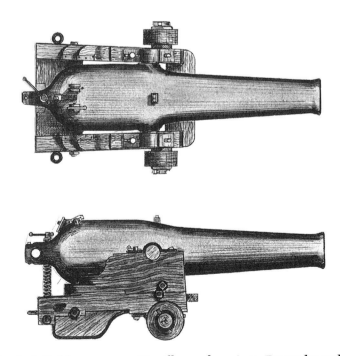

Nine-inch Dahlgren gun on Marsilly naval carriage. *Drawn by author*

reworked Dahlgren would not be the answer; it had to be something totally new—almost. As it turned out, Brooke's problem had already been solved by Robert Parrott.

Robert Parker Parrott, born in New Hampshire in 1804, graduated third in his class from the U.S. Military Academy in 1824. He was commissioned a second lieutenant in the 3rd Artillery, where he served a short time before returning to the academy for four years as an instructor. He worked his way up through the ranks, and by 1836 he was briefly a captain of ordnance at the Washington Navy Yard. In October he resigned his commission to become superintendent of the West Point Foundry.

The foundry, just across the Hudson River from the military academy, was one of Joseph Anderson's major competitors for ordnance work.[21] Unlike Anderson, Parrott accepted the Rodman method of casting in 1859, and the facility was soon turning out guns. Parrott developed a plan to even further increase production and reduce cost. He had a tube cast that had very little taper toward the muzzle and no reinforcement enlargement whatsoever around the breech. An iron bar, about sixty inches long and four inches square, was heated white hot and coiled in a spiral around a mandrel that was the same size as the tube. The coil was then welded with a large trip-hammer. The finished product was a cylinder open on the ends, about eighteen inches long, with a wall that was a little less than four inches thick. The finished cylinder was again heated to make it expand and then slipped over the back of the tube at the breech.[22] The tube was then turned horizontally on rollers and cooled with jets of water. As the cylinder turned and cooled, it contracted uniformly around the breech. There was nothing new about banding a gun, begun in the Middle Ages, but Parrott's turning and cooling method was entirely new, and for this he was awarded a patent. The completed unit was finished on a lathe and then rifled. The total cost to produce a 10-pound rifle was $187. A gun produced using the old method would have cost twice as much. By war's end, hundreds had been produced, ranging in size from 10-pounders to 300-pounders. As a result of John Brown's raid, the state of Virginia was in the market for cannons and requested the West Point Foundry to send a sample of its work. The first 10-pounder manufactured in 1860 was sent to the Virginia Military Academy, where it was tested and found quite satisfactory by Professor of Artillery Thomas J. (Stonewall) Jackson.[23]

Tredegar didn't have the equipment to duplicate Parrott's manufacturing process, so Brooke had to find a way to get the same results with a different approach. His first design was a 7-incher. It had a distance of approximately twenty-two inches from the cascabel to the trunnion. From there, it tapered to eleven inches at the muzzle face. It slightly resembled a Dahlgren and had a cascabel that was a direct copy, probably taken from one of the patterns used when Tredegar was casting Dahlgrens. Because he couldn't duplicate the Parrott cylindrical reinforcement, he settled on a series of five 6-inch-by-2-inch bands that a blacksmith could heat and wrap individually around the breech area. Because the reinforcement bands were relatively small in width and depth, a skilled blacksmith could pound away at a red-hot band until a uniform bond was created between band and tube. The end joints in the bands were welded together in a staggered fashion, so no two end welds would align. We can assume that the tubes were machined, drilled out, and rifled before the bands were attached because the first guns shipped for the *Virginia* went as do-it-yourself kits. The tubes and bands were shipped separately, and then blacksmiths at the Portsmouth yard attached the bands. Brooke rifles became

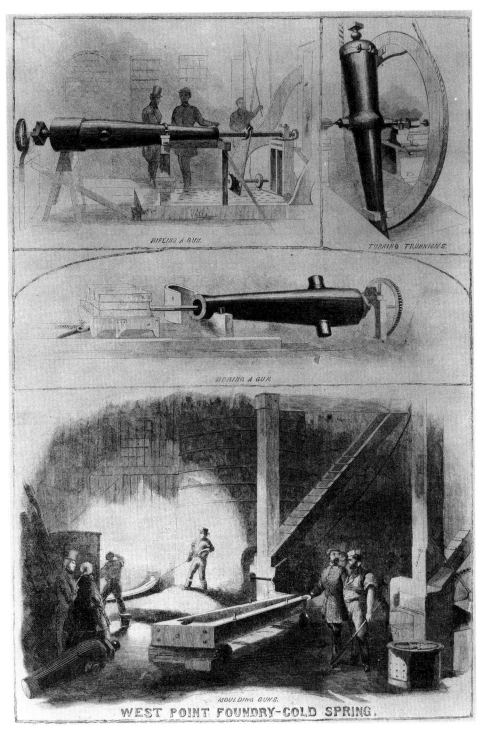

RIFLING A GUN.

TURNING TRUNNIONS.

BORING A GUN.

MOULDING GUNS.

WEST POINT FOUNDRY-COLD SPRING.

The West Point Foundry. In this reverse depiction of Parrott's manufacturing process, the last picture shows a gun being cast, and the first shows a gun with the reinforcing cylinder attached to the breach. *National Archives illustration*

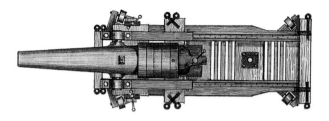

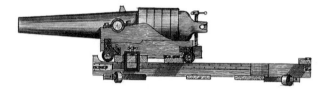

Seven-inch Brooke rifle on swivel mount. *Drawn by author*

the standard for the Army and Navy and were made in 6¼-inch, 7-inch, 10-inch, and 11-inch models. There were also some 10- and 11-inch smooth bores. For increased reinforcement, Secretary Mallory had guns manufactured after October 28, 1862, double banded; some were even triple banded.

John Brooke is credited with having "invented" the gun that bears his name, but that may be a stretch. With his depth-sounding device and safe boat hook, he had made something new that could be patented, but there was nothing unique about the exterior appearance of Brooke's gun. It was banded, but that couldn't be done as efficiently at Tredegar as Parrott was doing it at West Point. It depended on the skill of blacksmiths, pounding with hammers, that blacksmiths had been doing for thousands of years. Whether or not it was a true invention, it was a boon to the South. The relatively uniform thickness of the tube reduced the cooling time, and the banding provided the necessary strength. The one thing about Brooke's gun that was unique was the "triangular rifling."

On first examination Tredegar seemed to have made only smooth-bore guns before Brooke designed his gun in the late summer of 1861. Dahlgren didn't start considering rifled guns until about the same time Brooke did, so Tredegar would not have rifled any of his guns. The columbiads were all smooth bore, so this brings us back to the mystery of that skilled rifler who left Tredegar to join the Army in the spring of 1861. What had he been rifling? I can find no mention of rifled guns at Tredegar prior to the Brooke guns. The only evidence that rifled guns were being made is that mysterious mention of the rifler who went off to war. Whatever the case may be, the machinist who did the rifling work on Brooke's gun was quite skillful and had good equipment because the rifling is unique and complex. The general practice in rifling was to scribe a series of equally spaced spiral grooves down the inside of the barrel. The rifling groove was usually rectangular, but it could be V-shaped or half round. In a piece of wood, it would be called a mortise. The depth and width of the rifling grooves in these old cannons can range anywhere from a sixteenth of an inch up to a quarter of an inch or more, depending on the gun's caliber. The distance straight across a gun at the barrel face from land to land (the

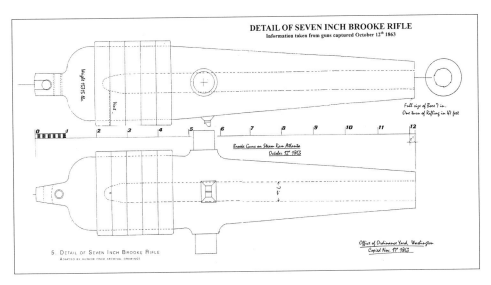

DETAIL OF SEVEN INCH BROOKE RIFLE
Information taken from guns captured October 12th 1863

5. DETAIL OF SEVEN INCH BROOKE RIFLE
ADAPTED BY AUTHOR FROM ARCHIVAL DRAWINGS

Detail of 7-inch Brooke rifle. The original drawing was made at the Washington Navy Yard on November 17, 1863, with information taken from guns captured October 12, 1863. *Adapted by the author from an archival drawing*

flat surface on the inside of the barrel) is the caliber. Brooke's gun was a complete departure from this method. Looking down the tube, you would see the pattern of a 7-inch ratchet with only seven teeth. What would have been a rifling groove had only one wall. At what would have been the bottom of the groove, the land swept up in a gentle arc to connect with the top of the next groove. This pattern was repeated seven times. In the 6¼-inch rifle, the spiral would have completed a turn in 45 feet, and in 47 feet in the 7-inch model. Scale drawings of the 6¼- and 7-inch guns were made from captured guns at the Ordnance Department at the Washington Navy Yard in October and November 1863.

I have never seen any Confederate drawings of the guns, and I can't find any of Brooke's notes or calculations that arrived at this design. Not only did he do something unusual in his rifling pattern but also, because of it, he had to design a different type of projectile to work in the gun. His rifling method and projectiles could probably have been patented, but there is no record that he made an application. To understand how this worked, it is necessary, once again, to look into ordnance history.

In the early days, loading handheld weapons with powder and shot could be a simple process relying on gravity. Powder was poured down the muzzle from a powder horn, and a ball was rammed in on top of it. A cannon, horizontal to the ground, was more of a problem. The powder had to be contained in a bag that could be rammed down the barrel, and then the cannonball was rammed home to rest against the powder bag. The French improved on this process by making the powder and ball a packaged unit. They attached the cannonball to a disk of wood with the same diameter as the ball, the *sabot*, which translates to "a shoe carved from a single piece of wood." The powder bag was then attached to the bottom of the sabot. This combination of shot and powder could then be rammed home in one operation. When spherical shells came into use, the sabot took on a secondary function. It kept the leading surface of the ball, where the time fuse was placed, facing forward as the shot passed down the barrel. When the ball left the barrel, the muzzle flash ignited the fuse. The same principle applied when percussion fuses were used. When cylindrical bolts and shells were introduced, the sabot kept its name but actually became the rear part of the projectile that was molded into the metal. When rifling was used, the sabot took on another function. When a rifled gun was fired, material had to be forced into the rifling grooves so the projectile would spin. Obviously, cast iron bolts and shells were too hard to do this, so sabots made of softer metal were attached to the base of the projectile. The force of the propelling charge pushed the sabot edges into the grooves to produce the spin. Because of the unusual configuration of Brooke's rifling pattern, the gun needed a copper sabot with a surface that conformed to the gun's rifling.[24] Rifling presented a new problem that caused much emphasis on reinforcing the guns at their breech. In a smooth bore, the windage (the minute space between the projectile and the wall of the tube) allowed some gas to escape around the sides of the shot and thus reduced the overall internal pressure. When a sabot expanded into the rifling grooves in a rifled gun, the windage at the base of the shot could be reduced to zero. The breech reinforcement on a smooth bore that would be adequate with a given powder charge could be inadequate in a rifled gun of the same size. This is why the reinforced guns of the Brooke and Parrott pattern were superior to Dahlgren's old "soda bottle" approach. Some of Brooke's first guns were actually reworked casts of Dahlgren guns that were bored and rifled to 7 inches and then banded at the breech.

Although many experts say that Brooke's guns and projectiles were the best made during the war, they were not enough to stem the tide. The Northern foundries using the Rodman method could turn out more guns and make them at lower cost than the Southern manufacturers. In the next four years, Tredegar would produce hundreds of Brooke guns for both the Army and Navy. The first two they made, along with armor plates for the *Virginia*, were ready for shipment to Portsmouth, but the fact that Confederate war matériel was ready didn't necessarily mean that it was going anywhere. The Southern railway system would become a factor at this point as once again inefficiency and obsolescence plagued the South. While things were going well on the battlefield, Old Dixie began to lose on the home front, and the fight had barely begun.

Chapter Ten

The Long Road to Portsmouth

In 1607 an exploring party from Jamestown sailed up the James River to the point where the deep water ends and the shoals and shallow water begin. That place would become the site for the city of Richmond. From that day until this, boats and ships have plied the ninety miles of the James between Richmond and Hampton Roads. Antebellum Richmond was one of the South's most important seaports. West of Richmond, the James River and Kanawha Canal brought agricultural products, raw materials, and passengers into the city from the Appalachian foothills. From there, riverboats and ships took over and moved goods and people to the sea. Steamships and packets with daily and weekly scheduled runs connected Richmond with the coastal cities. Travel from Boston south or from St. Augustine north was primarily by boat. No one would take "the cars" (as rail travel was referred to) up and down the Atlantic coast or on to Richmond if there was an alternative. Richmond's important waterways formed two boundaries of the Tredegar property, the canal on the north and the river on the south. Because of the plant's strategic location, Joseph Anderson owned a small fleet of barges, brigs, and sloops that were used to bring in raw materials and to ship finished products.[1]

Other than travel over plank or unpaved roads, the next most important way to move people and goods in and out of Richmond was by rail. In 1861, five railroads came into Richmond—almost.[2] To protect their interests, the city drayage companies in Virginia lobbied the state legislature to pass a protective tariff. In the Old Dominion, it was against the law for a railroad to have tracks on any city streets without the elected city authorities' permission, and permission was never given if it meant that two lines could meet. All of the railroad tracks of one line came to an abrupt stop a mile or so from any connecting line. Without liverymen, there could be no cross-town traffic for passengers or freight. The Richmond, Fredericksburg & Potomac railroad came in from the north down Broad Street to Fifth Street, which was within about half a mile of the Virginia Central, which also came in from the north as it followed Shockoe Creek to Broad and Seventeenth streets. The Richmond & York River came in from the east and terminated on the east side of town between Rocketts and Chimorazo Hill. The Richmond & Danville came from the west, followed the south bank of the James, and then crossed the river to the depot at Mayo's Bridge and Fifteenth Street. The Richmond & Petersburg came from the

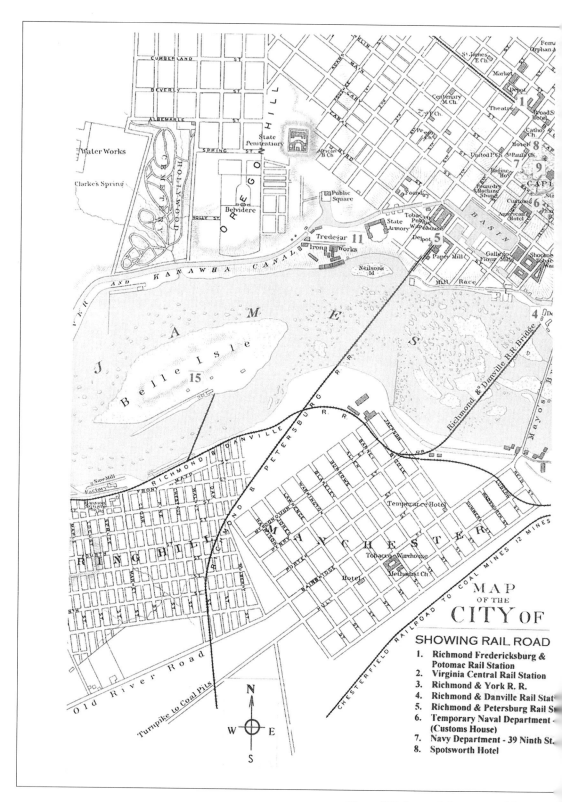

Map of Richmond showing rail lines an

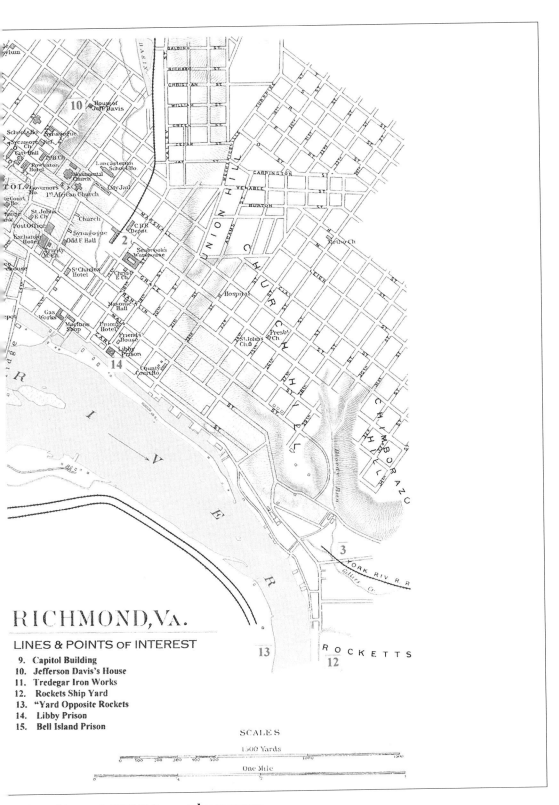

RICHMOND, Va.

LINES & POINTS of INTEREST

9. Capitol Building
10. Jefferson Davis's House
11. Tredegar Iron Works
12. Rockets Ship Yard
13. "Yard Opposite Rockets
14. Libby Prison
15. Bell Island Prison

SCALES

1500 Yards

One Mile

points of interest. 1858 U.S. coastal survey map

south and crossed the James to the depot at Eighth and Bird Streets. The Tredegar Iron Works was within a quarter of a mile of the Iron Richmond & Petersburg tracks.[3]

A Virginia Central train coming into Richmond with a passenger bound for Norfolk would off-load at the Seventeenth and Broad Streets Depot. From there, the passenger would take a carriage to the Richmond & Petersburg Depot, if a train was leaving that day or, if not, to a hotel to stay overnight and catch a train out the next day. This process would be repeated at every major rail juncture. For freight headed for Norfolk, the process was agonizingly slow. A freight train unloaded its cargo north of the station in Richmond onto a platform or onto the ground. There, sometime during that or the next day, a work gang of slaves loaded the shipment into a wagon or wagons that took it across town to the Richmond & Petersburg freight area, where more slaves would unload it and put it by the track. On that day or the next, more slaves loaded it onto a train, where it would travel to Petersburg. At Petersburg this agonizing process of off-loading, loading, off-loading, and loading again was repeated because trains were not allowed to pass through Petersburg either. Railroads were independent fiefdoms that had no interest in any other line's schedules; a quick connection between trains was by accident, not intent.

Standardization was another concept that hadn't quite matured in 1861. Confusion on the railroads reigned supreme, in everything from the time of day to the distance in inches between the iron rails. Every city, town, hamlet, and railroad decided for itself what time of day it would be, calculated on the sun at high noon; consequently, as someone traveled from town to town going east or west or even north and south, the time could be different in every town he passed through. As rail traffic increased, collisions and accidents between trains running on different times and schedules were inevitable. Whichever train got to a rail junction first claimed the right-of-way. This confusion didn't come to an end in the United States and Canada until 1883, when laws were passed to standardize railroad time. The general public held out until Congress established the four national standard time zones in 1918.[4]

The next monument to poor planning was rail design and track gauges. Three different gauges (distance between rails) were in use in the Confederacy: 4 feet, 8½ inches, which eventually became the national standard, 5 feet, and 5 feet, 6 inches. The railroads coming into Richmond were 4 feet, 8½ inches, with the exception of the Richmond and Danville, which was 5 feet. This variance in gauges didn't cause as much confusion as you might suppose. In states where the lines of different companies using the same gauge actually connected, the management of one company would not allow its passenger or freight cars to run on the tracks of another line. So although cars of one line could run on the tracks of other lines, the practice of loading and unloading cars at railheads remained a standard, labor-intensive, and time-consuming procedure. In peacetime this ridiculous process was tolerable, but in time of war it became another nail in the Confederate coffin.

By May 1861 the delays at railheads in Virginia had become a national emergency that had to be corrected. It was finally agreed that connecting rails, which would be taken up at the end of the war, could be laid in Richmond and Petersburg but for the use of military traffic only. Passengers and commercial freight would still be forced to use the old process. The grades of the temporary connections between the lines on the high north side of Richmond and those on the river bottom south side were too severe for a fully loaded train to make it up the hill and therefore, despite the best of intentions, the

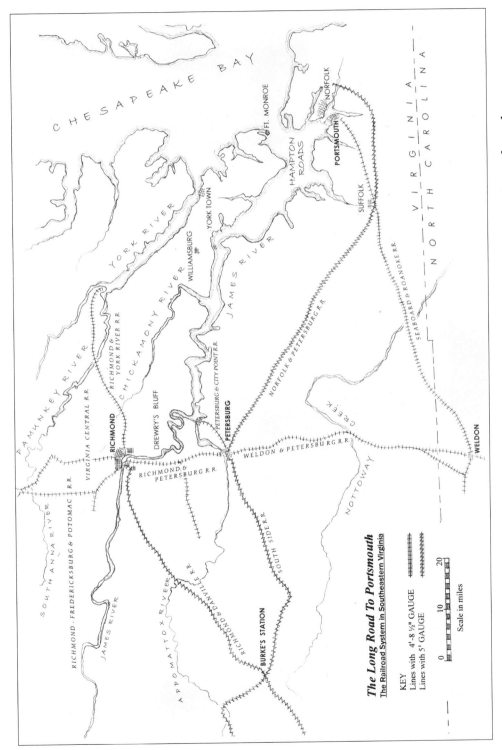

The long road to Portsmouth. Map of the railroad system in southwestern Virginia. *Drawn by author*

connections never proved to be practical. Of course there was no connection at all to the Richmond & Danville's five-foot gauge tracks. The connection on the flat terrain around Petersburg, completed in late August, was more satisfactory.

Squabbles between the companies about the use of one another's rolling stock continued. Because of the national emergency, some of the lines reluctantly agreed to allow limited use of some of their cars by other lines. One company would accuse another of using its cars as warehouses for freight waiting to be shipped or of not returning cars after they had been unloaded. The Norfolk & Petersburg was unhappy because the connecting track in Petersburg crossing their yards interfered with their work and schedules. The Petersburg connection point did nothing to improve east-west traffic between Richmond and Norfolk, where the Richmond & Petersburg 4-foot, 8½ inch gauge met the Norfolk & Petersburg's 5-foot gauge.

There were also people problems. The yardmasters and train dispatchers controlled the loading and unloading, plus the coming and going of all trains. With an average wage of only about sixty dollars a month, these men were interested in supplemental income. Every shipper knew that for his shipments to come and go promptly, these individuals would have to be kept happy.

A large percentage of the laborers on any of the Southern lines were slaves, either owned outright by the company or leased. Not only did they do the manual labor of loading, unloading, and track maintenance but they were also the firemen, brakemen, and, by the end of the war, often the skilled mechanics required to keep the line running. Railroad work was long and hard for blacks and whites, and there were no unions or pension plans. Once again, more and more skilled white laborers chose to become cannon fodder.

The physical conditions of the Southern railroads became a paramount problem. No rails were manufactured in the South during the war and became so scarce that it took a court injunction to prevent the Mexican Gulf Railroad from making a big profit by ripping up its tracks and offering them for sale. Manufacturers like Tredegar, not even equipped to make rails, were overburdened with military orders and in addition struggled to supply the railroads with the most rudimentary of their requirements. There were not enough locomotives or cars, and those available were in constant need of repair or replacement. Deplorable track conditions restricted train speeds to fifteen or twenty miles an hour. Eventually, in many places, trestles and bridges were in such bad condition that a conductor would have to proceed across on foot to make sure that the weight of the train would not cause the structure to collapse.[5]

For the most part these dilapidated ribbons of rust were the arteries that moved the Confederacy's military goods throughout the South. In the fall of 1861 Joseph Anderson selected the Richmond & Petersburg and the Norfolk & Petersburg railroads to take the guns and armor for the *Virginia* to Portsmouth. In hindsight we might wonder why he didn't take a more direct, simpler approach. As pointed out earlier, the James River was a well-traveled highway to the sea, and Anderson owned, or could hire, boats to transport the *Virginia*'s armor via this route. As it was, the plates were loaded onto a wagon at Tredegar for the trip to the Richmond & Petersburg's tracks and off-loaded and reloaded at Petersburg. It would have been just as simple for a wagon to go from Tredegar to Main Street and east to the Rocketts dock. A boat loaded there could have gone directly to the Portsmouth shipyard. If Victor Vifquain, the man who supposedly tried to kidnap

Jefferson Davis, is to be believed, Davis made frequent trips down the James to Portsmouth to see the progress being made on the *Virginia*. He made these trips on an unnamed tug that "runs down in eight hours and comes back in twelve."[6] Jefferson Davis may or may not have made them, but such trips were made daily, and the *Virginia's* armor could also have been on board.

As it was, the *Virginia's* armor was taken by wagon to be loaded onto a Richmond & Petersburg train, running on a 4-foot, 8½-inch track. At Petersburg, it was off-loaded and taken to the Norfolk & Petersburg yard, where the trains ran on a 5-foot track. Near the little town of Suffolk, just west of Portsmouth, the Norfolk & Petersburg crossed the tracks of the Seaboard & Roanoke's 4-foot, 8½-inch tracks that went into Portsmouth. The *Virginia's* armor plates couldn't go directly to Portsmouth but had to go on to the Norfolk railhead in the village of Washington, which was on the south side of the Elizabeth River across from Norfolk. It was then taken by wagon about two miles over to the Navy yard. This was only the beginning of the chaos. In this part of the South, the Army of Northern Virginia ruled supreme. What the Army wanted, the Army got or, if necessary, took. At this particular time, what the Army wanted most was railroad cars. They had a lot of supplies that had to go north. As Army officers were scrambling in the rail yards in and around Petersburg looking for transportation, they kept running across these flatcars loaded down with what appeared to be scrap iron. Obviously this stuff had no military value, so they threw it off along the tracks and took the cars for some important use.

Under Brooke's supervision and insistence, Tredegar had gone into high production of the two-inch plates. By October between seventy and a hundred tons of armor were ready for shipment, but Porter complained that only about two tons had reached the shipyard. Mallory's pleas to the railroad and the Army fell on deaf ears, and they finally decided on a different approach. A transportation agent, William Webb, was appointed to shepherd the Navy's materials from Richmond to Portsmouth.[7] Webb discovered that one of the biggest bottlenecks was the twenty-plus miles between Richmond and Petersburg, so the plates were put on the Richmond & Danville line, with its 5-foot tracks, and traveled southwest from Richmond to Burkeville Station near the village of Burkeville. There the plates were transferred to the five-foot-gauge South Side line for shipment east to Petersburg, where it was transferred to the other five-foot-gauge system, the Norfolk & Petersburg, to go on to Norfolk, where they came to a stop just across the Elizabeth River from the Navy yard. This route added more than ninety miles to the overall trip, and I have never found any information that explains how the transfers were made. Logically, they would have simply switched the cars from one line to the other rather than going through the awkward process of loading and unloading cars at every junction. Whatever process they followed, it didn't prove to be the total solution either.

Webb found new problems causing delays, for which no explanation is given, somewhere on the seventy-mile run between Petersburg and Norfolk, leading to yet another change. Freight from Petersburg was then sent sixty miles south on the 4-foot, 8½-inch gauge Weldon & Petersburg Rail Road to Weldon, North Carolina. From there, it went via the Seaboard & Roanoke, same gauge track, directly to the north side of Portsmouth. This resulted in another sixty-mile addition to the route. The problem was never satisfactorily corrected. For example, Tredegar shipped the 7-inch Brooke rifles on November 12, 1861 but on November 20 Brooke learned that the guns were sitting in Petersburg, while Catesby Jones waited impatiently in Portsmouth to test-fire them.[8] In all Tredegar produced 723 tons of armor plate that was shipped from October until February 12, when the last shipment arrived at the Navy yard.[9]

While all this confusion was going on, the river just kept rolling along. As far as I can tell, no consideration was ever given to the idea of shipping the armor plates, port shutters, or Brooke's rifles down the James River, yet in the spring of 1862, when Norfolk and Portsmouth were about to fall to the Union, large quantities of matériel and machinery were loaded onto boats at the Navy yard and sent up the James to Richmond. How much did this transportation fiasco delay the completion of the *Virginia*? Could she have steamed into Hampton Roads weeks before the *Monitor* arrived? And most important of all, how much would history have been changed?

Chapter Eleven

Building the *Virginia*

CONVERTING THE HULL

According to John L. Porter, on July 11, 1861, Secretary Mallory examined the twenty-seven-foot construction scroll (some accounts say it was seventeen feet long) that he had prepared and taken to Richmond. Mallory approved the drawing and wrote an order to the Navy yard commandant, Commo. French Forrest, to start work on the conversion of the *Merrimack* immediately, "in all respects according to the design and plans of the constructor and engineer, Messrs. Porter and Williams."

The *Merrimack* had been raised by the Baker Wrecking Company on May 30 and had been sitting in the dry dock since then. Porter picks up the story at this point: "Having put the hulk of the burned Steamer *Merrimac* into drydock, I commenced to cutting her down on a straight line from forward to aft—19 feet on the stem and 20 feet on the stern post."[1]

No one has ever given a detailed account of the exact condition of the ship at this point. We know that the attempt to destroy her was poorly done, either by mistake or intent. The petcocks were opened, which allowed her to settle deeper into the water before she was set on fire. If she had simply been burned and not flooded, there would have been nothing left to work with, including the engines. As it was, there were areas where she must have burned down to, and probably into, the beams and planking of the berth deck. Amidships, based on the original *Merrimack's* construction drawings, the berth deck was twenty-one feet three inches above the bottom of the keel. In the finished *Virginia*, the knuckle, where the hull met the casement, was nineteen feet above the keel at the bow and twenty feet at the stern, and the waterline was calculated to be at twenty-one feet. Consequently, there would have been several feet of charred frame sections, planking, fallen beams, and knees that had to be cleared away. The interior of the ship around the engines and boilers would have been filled with soggy burned timbers and other debris. The *Merrimack's* original berth deck would have been above the *Virginia's* knuckle and joined the sides of the casement. Whatever was left of the berth deck had to be demolished. In Porter's description of the work that was done in this part of the ship, he makes a statement that can cause confusion: "The berth deck, fore and aft, magazines and shell rooms were used without any material alteration."[2] Here he probably meant the lower deck, or engine platform, not the berth deck, which had to be demolished to build the casement. The magazines, shell rooms, and so on were not on the berth deck but on the bottom engine platform deck. Another cause of confusion was the fact that Porter's conversion appears to have made part of the *Merrimack's* old orlop deck into part of the *Virginia's* berth deck. For some reason, on his plan he shows this deck in pencil lines, not in ink, and refers to it as having been the berth deck, never the orlop deck.

There was a large opening in the center of the *Merrimack's* orlop deck, approximately 120 feet long, to make headroom for the boilers and engines and to form the space for the forward and aft holds. In the converted *Virginia* there would have been only a very small crawlspace between the orlop and the new exterior decks. Porter mentions that fore and aft sections of the "berth" (orlop) deck below the exterior decks were left in place, and Brooke suggested that ballast tanks might be placed in this space to help bring the *Virginia* down to the desired waterline. This was never done. For all practical purposes, after the *Merrimack's* hulk was cleaned out and the forward and aft exterior decks were in place, there was only one full usable deck left in place, the lower, or engine, deck. This deck had a flat surface twenty-four feet wide amidships and sloped inward fore and aft to conform to the shape of the hull. There were numerous compartments and storage areas on the old *Merrimack's* lower deck, including powder rooms, shell rooms, chain lockers, water tanks, and coal bunkers, that would have been left in place during conversion. The original *Merrimack* drawings show the exact location of these and other compartments. There is not a hint on any of Porter's *Virginia* drawings to indicate how he added to the small twenty-five-foot remaining usable section of the orlop deck to convert it to the *Virginia's* berth deck, nor does he give any information about the cabins and compartments on the converted berth deck. By decking over part of the fore and aft holes, he would have picked up little more than forty feet in the overall length of the deck, which would have given him a space of about twenty-five feet by forty-five feet forward and forty by forty-five feet aft to form the new berth deck. For the berth deck to be functional, companionways on both sides of the boilers and engines would be needed for crew members to get past. From the crew members' written descriptions, we know that there was a captain's cabin plus a galley and mess area, that apparently also served as the surgery. In E. J. Jack's memoirs, he wrote: "I sought my stateroom and there on the floor were two of the men who had been killed,"[3] but this is all we know about any compartments or cabins. Ashton Ramsay's tantalizing statement says there were watertight bulkheads fore and aft, but he gives not a clue as to where they were or how they were constructed.

In many of the postwar pictures, plans, and models of the *Virginia*, there is a galley smoke pipe shown about fifteen feet behind the pilothouse. We know that there was a galley in this general area on the gun deck of the *Merrimack*, but on the *Virginia* plans there is no evidence of where the galley was located. Until some real evidence comes along, the location of the galley, cabins, storage compartments, hatches, and numerous other features on the *Virginia's* berth deck can be nothing more than an educated guess based on the original *Merrimack* drawings and the structure and configuration of other ships of the period.

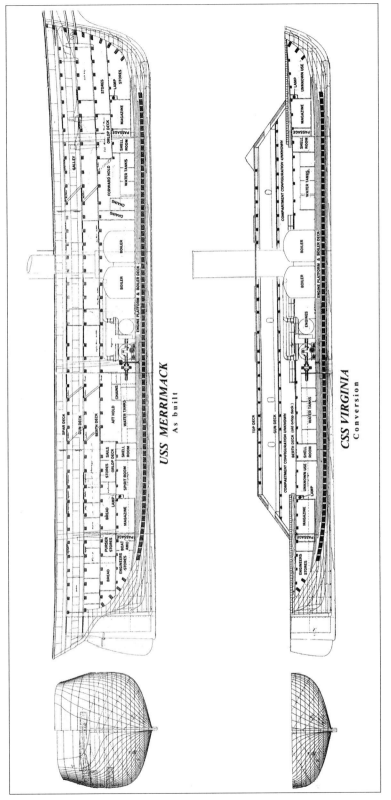

Internal as-built profiles of the *Merrimack* and *Virginia*. Composite by author from archival prints

To make the section drawings through the center of the ship, I used both the original *Merrimack* plans and Porter's plans to check all of my figures. While doing this, I made a discovery that at first I thought was rather startling, but after consideration, it made perfectly good sense. Porter's drawing of the lower portion of the *Virginia's* hull framing bears little resemblance to the *Merrimack's* plans. Porter's drawing shows a stylized depiction of a ship's framing, keel, and keelson, which was really all that was required. No structural changes or work would be done below the boiler and engine deck, so why waste time taking measurements and making detailed drawings in that area? Porter's drawing was adequate for the project at hand, and no one then was concerned with history or the research into the *Virginia's* construction details to be conducted a century later. Nevertheless, the sketchy nature of Porter's plans raised more and more questions. Once again, I returned to the *Wabash*-class half-hull model photo. If the ships of this class were constructed as the model shows, then they were to have sister frames, or futtocks, in all of the spaces, stem to stern, in the lower part of the hull. This arrangement meant that the *Merrimack*-class ships had solid bottoms. The model indicates that these filler frames went up to a point about ten feet above the rabbet line (the upper area of the keel where the external planking and the keel join). Two photos in Wolfram zu Mondfeld's *Historic Ship Models* show a similar type of construction on an Admiralty model of the HMS *Royal Oak*. The entire bilge area of the *Merrimack* would have been solid timber. There were no secondary, or engine, decks in the hold of a typical old sailing ship. In the old ships, the keelson, sister keelsons, and riders were totally exposed. There was a loose limber board on each side of the sister keelsons that permitted access to the open spaces between the frames where bilgewater would accumulate. From here outward, floor-ceiling boards extended out to the point where the heavy timber of the bilge keelson began. In the *Merrimack* there was no space between the frames, and it is not clear if there were ceiling boards on top of the frames. Bilgewater would have accumulated just below the engine platform, which actually sat on the topmost sister keelson, and if there were ceiling boards, they sat on the solid frames.

Before going into any more detail about the dimensions of the ship, interior or exterior, I'll point out the first of the many discrepancies, made by people who were on the scene, in the various descriptions of the *Virginia*. Porter writes that the "depth to the lower edge of the rabbet was twenty-one feet three inches." In scaling Porter's drawing, I saw that this was the distance from the waterline to the *bottom* of the keel and not the rabbet. This error shows up time and again in written descriptions of the ship. When anyone starts making scale drawings based on Porter's drawings, this discrepancy becomes obvious, and the correction is usually made. When Porter describes the frames as cut down on a straight line, they were not necessarily cut with straight, flat tops and left that way. Below the casement structure, the beams—or rafters, as Porter called them—would have had to drop onto the supporting frames. This process will be discussed in detail later.

THE FRAMES

Beginning to understand how the *Virginia* was assembled requires drawing a section plan of the old *Merrimack's* hull and showing how it would join with the *Virginia's* casement. The skeleton of a sailing ship hull like the *Merrimack* has three basic components, akin to the torso of a human skeleton lying on its back, with the keel representing the backbone, to which the ribs, or frames, were attached. The frames were joined by horizontal beams, the human sternum, that held the frames together and carried the deck planks. There were other internal "sternum" beams to further strengthen the ship and support the interior deck planks. After centuries of experimentation, shipbuilders arrived at the most practical way to build and assemble these components. Nothing was simple, and everything was exacting. Only certain kinds of wood could be used for the various components, the wood grain had to go in a given direction, and the pieces had to be joined using various types of bolts and nails made of specific materials to suit specific conditions. William L. Crothers's *The American-Built Clipper Ship* (a must in the library of any serious student or model builder) goes into these subjects in great detail. For our purposes, we need only examine the structure of the *Merrimack*'s frames and beams.

A large ship's frame was a laminated curved member that might have ten to sixteen pieces called futtocks. The pieces were cut and assembled so that the joint between two pieces was always covered by the solid wood of the adjacent futtock. The finished frames were attached to the keel at specified distances on centers and separated from one another by a given distance. In clipper ships, built for speed, the gap between the frames might be the same, or slightly greater, than the width of the frame itself. In warships, built to take a pounding, the gap was less than the frame width.[4] In the USS *Constitution*, "Old Ironsides," the space between her live oak frames was only 1¼ inches.[5] This combination of void and wood was referred to as either "room and space" or, as in the case of the *Roanoke-Colorado* dimensions, "timber & room," timber being the wood and room the open area between (in the former terminology, room referred to the wood and space the gap). This measurement was always taken from the frame centers, and reference marks scribed on the keel showed where the center of each frame was to fall. On the *Colorado* and her sisters, this dimension was shown as "Timber & Room 2 feet 10¼ inches." This is an overall dimension and doesn't give the actual size of the frame or the width of the space. I went back to the *Merrimack*'s profile frame drawing (Bureau of Ships record group 19 #40-11-7K) in order to scale the futtocks and space dimensions. The futtocks were 14 inches, and the space was 6¼ inches, which equaled the 2 feet 10¼ inches shown on the as-built dimensions. This structure of 28-inch timbers and 6¼-inch gaps is what Porter would have to set the casement on. Just below his cut line would have been the ceiling boards on the interior and the heavy oak planking and copper sheathing on the exterior.

THE CASEMENT

The following quotations concern the design and fabrication of the casement. To follow the sequence of construction and analyze the process, I have broken the statements into functional descriptions.

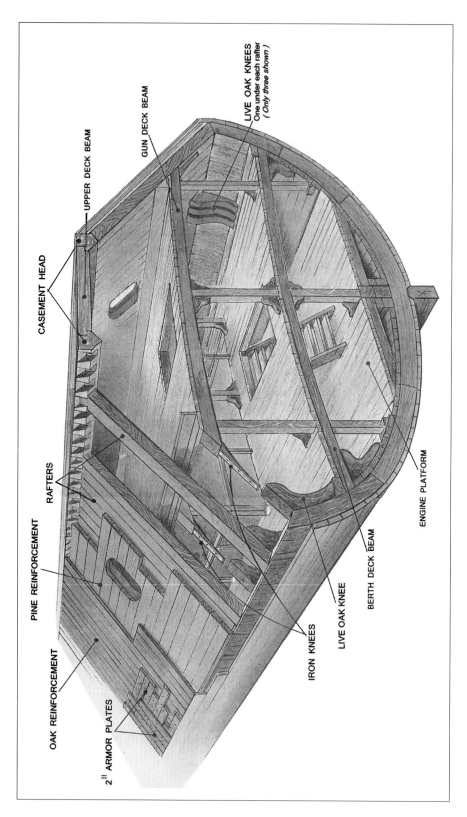

UPPER DECK BEAM

GUN DECK BEAM

LIVE OAK KNEES
One under each rafter
(Only three shown)

CASEMENT HEAD

RAFTERS

PINE REINFORCEMENT

OAK REINFORCEMENT

2^{II} ARMOR PLATES

IRON KNEES

LIVE OAK KNEE

BERTH DECK BEAM

ENGINE PLATFORM

Structural detail. Rendering by author

John L. Porter: Technical notebook and journal kept from 1860 to 1872

1. The shield was joined to the wooden hull side by the use of oak knees running between the old frames and battened to them.
2. The rafters of the shield were white pine and bolted to these knees and also to each other, making this work solid.
3. A molding 16 inches across was placed on the course of yellow pine. It was five inches thick and bolted to the rafters with ¾ inch bolts.
4. All of this was caulked and pitched along with another course of white oak 4 inches thick.
5. This was all done before any of the armor was placed on the shield.
6. The upper shield deck was strongly framed with pine beams.
7. Between these beams at their ends were pieces of oak timber dovetailed to support the end of the rafters.
8. An oak caffing or plank sheer was placed on top of the rafters and also on the beams which served as a bed for the iron grating which covered the entire shield Deck.
9. This deck was made entirely of two inch square bars and crossed, being riveted together.
10. Forward and aft the shield deck, beams were solid and bolted together, on this an iron deck four inches thick was laid. The deck was submerged two feet under water.

John L. Porter: *A Short History of Myself*

1. The shield was 150–180 feet in length and put on an angle of 35 degrees.
2. It was 24 feet on the inclination from the knuckle to the wooden hull, to the deck.
3. A molding 16 inches across was placed [on] the course of yellow pine. It was five inches thick and bolted to the rafters with ¾ inch bolts.
4. All of this was caulked and pitched along with another course of white oak 4 inches thick.

John W. H. Porter: *Events in Norfolk County etc., 1892*

1. The rafters of the shield were yellowy pine *fourteen inches thick*, and were bolted together and were placed at an incline of thirty five degrees (no width given).
   Note: On Porter's plan, the rafters scale to twelve inches thick.

Navy Department official record

1. As soon as she was cut down fore and aft, oak knees worked at an angle of thirty-five degrees were fitted between the original frames and bolted to them.
2. To the beams were bolted yellow pine rafter[s] made solid fore and aft the whole length of the shield, and molded sixteen inches thick.

John M. Brooke: Letter to Catesby Jones, August 1874

1. the heavy timbers of the shield, 12" × 12" which were bolted together
2. and aft course of pine about 8" thick rested upon the heaver timbers of the shield
3. an outer course of oak planks 4" × 12" or 15" laid up and down

Catesby Jones: Service on the "Virginia" (*Merrimac*)

1. The wood was two feet thick; it consisted of oak plank four inches by twelve inches,
    laid up and down next [to] the iron, and two courses of pine; one longitudinally of
    eight inches, the other twelve inches thick.

Henry Ashton Ramsay: Letter to J. H. Morrison, May 1906

The case-ment was built up of timbers squared to 16" placed at an angle, on which, running transversally there were 6" of oak planking and on top of this, 4" thickness of iron
plates made up of two thickness each 2" thick.

Here we find another discrepancy that affects the entire configuration of the ship.
Porter said that the angle of the casement was 35 degrees, and Brooke said that it was
36 degrees. When making scale drawings, I had to use Brooke's 36-degree figure so that
the dimensions given by Porter and others, and the dimensions scaled from Porter's
drawings, would conform.

These brief and frustratingly contradictory descriptions are all we have to tell us
what the parts were made of, what size they were, and how they were assembled. Porter's
only section drawing is nothing more than a simple conceptual line sketch that could
never have been used to give structural details to the carpenters. I didn't give his first
statement, that oak knees were put in the *space between the frames*, much thought on
first reading but found a big problem when I started making drawings. Either I was inter-
preting the statement incorrectly, or it was total nonsense. To understand the problem,
we need to examine, in some detail, the structure and function of ship's knees. As mentioned earlier, a knee is a kind of supporting or stabilizing bracket used to tie two members securely together. In general, a standing knee, or a horizontal knee, has six basic
parts: The *body* is the vertical part that will be attached to a frame. There is an *arm*
extending out from the body that will be attached to a beam, or rafter. The flat part at the
bottom of the body is the *foot,* and the curved end of the arm is called a *toe*. The substance of wood in the concaved arc running between the foot and the toe is called the
bosom. The distance between the point where the body and arm join and the curve of the
bosom is the *throat*. On average, the angle between the body and the arm ranges from
45 to 120 degrees. When a knee has an angle of less than 45 degrees, it is called a hook
knee. Porter's section drawing of the *Virginia* shows hook knees, drawn in pencil, supporting his berth deck beams. Porter described the casement structure as having oak
knees placed *between* the old frames and battened to them. I had never heard of such a
thing, so I started looking for a similar example but couldn't find one. Knees are attached
to members, not slipped between them. For this to have been done, the carpenters
would have had to fabricate 142 custom knees that were 6¼ inches thick with a strange
body that was two feet wide at the throat and with a long arm where the rafters would
rest. There were a lot of standard wooden building components in the shipyard, but
nothing would have been suitable for fabricating these odd parts. It would also have been
terribly time consuming. Porter sketched in some hook knees supporting the berth desk
but doesn't show or mention a wooden knee anywhere else in the ship. Regardless of
what Porter wrote, it is beyond comprehension that knees were ever placed between the
frames. So if this was not the case, what did they do?

Section drawing amidship. *Drawn by author*

There had been concern about weakness in the *Virginia* at the joint between the old hull and the new casement. The 6¼-inch space between the frames appears to have been a worry to Porter. If 142 custom knees had been slipped into these spaces, the problem would have been partly corrected, but because that was not practical, there was a far simpler solution. It would have been necessary only to drive 6¼-inch-wide sister frames that were the same thickness as the main frames, similar to the ones used in the *Merrimack*'s lower hull, into the spaces between the frames. By doing this, the void would have been filled, and they could have put a normal standing knee beneath each of the rafters. This would have been one of the few approaches that make sense. So how did this "knees between the frames" statement ever come into existence?

The answer to that, and to numerous contradictions about the casement structure, might be found in three places. First, in Alan Flanders' book *John L. Porter,* Porter is quoted as saying that "Mr. James Meads, who had resigned his appointment as carpenter in the yard, commenced to cut her down in accordance with my directions, and was active in carrying on the work and assisting me until her completion."

Next, Porter's son, in *Events in Norfolk County Virginia,* writes: "Mr. Porter returned to the Gosport Navy Yard, appointed Mr. James Meads Master Ship carpenter, and commenced work on the vessel in the dry-dock."

It's obvious that Meads was the supervisor of the day-to-day carpentry work on the casement. The next, and possibly most important, clue—once again from Flanders's book—is found in Porter's November 4 letter to his son-in-law, Reverend Moore, which reads in part: "I never was so busy in my life. I have all the work in the Navy Yard to direct, and all the duty of the Bureau of Constructor of the Navy to attend to besides. I have all of the planning of the various gun boats to do which are being built all over the south and I am constantly receiving orders from the Secretary for models, specifications, etc. . . . I have two large gun boats on the stocks now and expect to have two more soon. . . . I have to go to Richmond very frequently to attend to public matters of the department. . . . I have sent plans to Florida, Savannah, Charleston, Memphis, New Orleans and North Carolina where they are building gun boats."

Porter had far too much on his plate to spend time with the nitty-gritty details associated with the daily carpentry work on the *Virginia.* He had made a simple diagram of what he wanted and appointed a master ship's carpenter he obviously trusted to carry out the plan. What may be most significant of all, his descriptions of what was done were not written down until years after the *Virginia* was a casualty of war. James Meads may have been more responsible for the design and fabrication of the individual pieces used in the casement than John Porter.

Although Porter's drawing doesn't show any knees under the rafters, we can be sure that a master ship's carpenter would never drop a solid pine rafter with a weight in excess of six hundred pounds on the top end of a ship's frame and hope that it would stay there. Because Porter's drawing didn't illustrate how anything was attached, I had to go back to my scale drawings to try to find a solution. Here we have to reexamine Porter's statement about the frames being cut down on a straight line at nineteen feet at the bow and twenty feet at the stern. If the frames had actually been cut straight across at this height, the finished ship would not match Porter's drawings or stated dimensions. As the accompanying drawings show, the knuckle would have been higher than desired. I believe this statement should have said that the beams were cut down *so that the finished knuckle* would be nineteen feet at the bow and twenty feet at the stern. The large rafter sections would never have been allowed to "float." There would have been a live oak knee attached under every one of them. Everyone involved with the project was concerned with the ship's vulnerability at the knuckle. Without these knees, a shot against the knuckle could have dislodged a rafter and caused a major problem.

I examined four possible approaches to positioning the rafters on the frames. First, if a straight cut were made from stem to stern, a horizontal and vertical cut on each rafter at this joint would have been necessary: additional work for no good reason. A simpler approach would have been to make a butt joint that required only one vertical cut. To do this, the bottom of the rafter would have been cut to the proper length before installation, and a knee would have been necessary to support the weight. The simplest approach would have been a lap joint. The rafter could have been cut flush with the

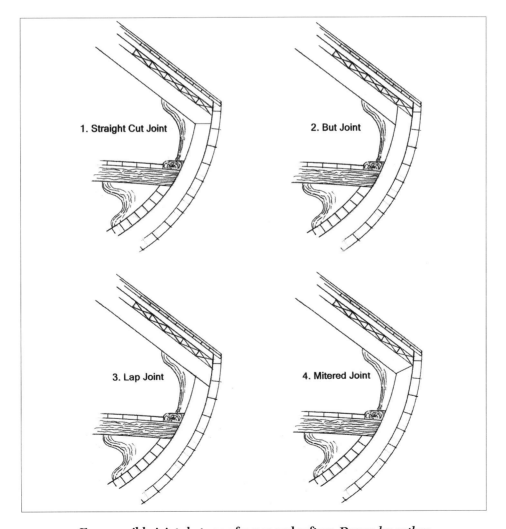

Four possible joints between frames and rafters. *Drawn by author*

frame after it was in place. A mitered joint, cut at 28 degrees, would have been the most professional in appearance and the most compatible with the standards of wood construction at the time. Because the remains of the *Virginia's* hulk were burned to recover the scrap metal, we will probably never know how the attachment was actually made.

LIVE OAK KNEES

We can be sure that a knee was attached to each and every rafter and frame. The live oak knees were a vital part of every large ship. A ship's knee was rather like a large shelf bracket. In dry-land construction, a similar piece was called a corbel and was used to support beams or overhanging balconies. On shipboard, they ran both vertically and horizontally and were placed beneath and beside practically every frame, beam, header, and other places where two pieces of wood might butt join. Live oak was the ship carpenter's steel, used where maximum strength was required. The knees were a marvel of nature's engineering and, like diamonds and pearls, came in a variety of sizes and grades. Men literally worked themselves to death to get them. A member of the beech family, the live oak tree, *Quercus virginiana,* was a key natural resource in the early American shipbuilding industry. An American-built fighting ship of the late eighteenth or early nineteenth century that did not have live oak knees and futtocks would have been considered inferior. For the most part, the trees used by the shipbuilders grew on or near the coasts of Virginia, North and South Carolina, Georgia, and Florida. The trees were monsters—one two or three centuries old could have a girth of thirty feet. They grew from forty to seventy feet tall, with a crown span that could reach 150 feet and provide shade for half an acre of land. These behemoths, festooned in Spanish moss, grew near the coast behind sand dunes, in swamps, in clay along river and creek banks, and in either fresh or brackish water. Branches grew out from the main trunk in twisted and bizarre shapes, with an astonishing cured weight of seventy pounds per cubic foot, North America's heaviest wood. It was these wonderful natural forms that were sought after by the shipbuilders.[6]

Felling and dressing the timber from these trees was an industry unto itself. The men who did the work, called "live oakers," harvested the trees in the tidewater forest during winter, when the sap was down; otherwise, the timber would be too heavy to move. A ship would drop off the cutting crews, their tools, provisions, and oxen on the coast or up a navigable river in the fall. A crew could have eighty or more men, mostly from New England, who were under contract for a season's cutting. There would be choppers and hewers, road cutters, blacksmiths, cooks, teamsters, apprentices, and, overseeing the work, the foreman. The nucleus of the cutting gangs was not the typical lumberjack but experienced ship's carpenters and apprentices. Many of these men could recognize the shapes usable for knees and futtocks while they were still hidden within the twisted and curved branches. After disembarking, they put up a base camp with a kitchen and lean-tos and huts to live in. Then cutters would go into the woods and begin felling trees and roughshaping the pieces with axes and adzes. Others, sometimes assisted by slaves hired from nearby plantations, built rudimentary roads so that ox-drawn log carts could transport the huge rough-hewn timber and logs. These carts had two large seven- or eight-foot wheels and a single heavy axle. The logs were slung beneath the axle, balanced to get the majority of the weight off the ground, and then dragged to the beach or river to await shipment. Blacksmiths were kept busy in the camp, constantly sharpening the cutting tools, repairing equipment, or shoeing the draft animals.[7]

This dangerous and exhausting work went on all through the winter from sunrise to sunset, six days a week. Serious injury went with the work, and their isolation meant that death from infected wounds, broken bones, fever, and disease was commonplace. In many camps, the men were given a rum ration as if they were on a ship. About the only advantage that live oaking had over going to sea was that spring meant a return to civilization. Still, desertion was not uncommon. From a camp within walking distance of plantations or small villages, a deserter might eventually find his way home, but a deserter on a river deep in the forest might lose his way and never be heard from again. When the ship came in the spring, the timber, tools, and surviving men and animals were reloaded for the trip home. Back in the homeport, the men were given their wages, as little as ten dollars a month for the unskilled and as much as a hundred dollars a month for the foreman. By comparison, in the mid-1850s a general in the U.S. Army was paid fifty dollars a month.[8]

The live oak timber was either sold at dockside to shipbuilders or sent to customers who had placed orders for given cuts or quantities the year before. At the shipyard, the timber was stored underwater until it was to be finally shaped because dry live oak was too hard to be worked efficiently. Futtocks, knees, floors, keels, transoms, and other items were shaped while they were wet and then cured. If circumstances permitted, the curing would continue for a year or more.[9] When the Union forces abandoned the Portsmouth yard, they left huge quantities of both used and unused live oak timber and numerous undamaged finished parts. Finding the live oak needed for the *Virginia*'s knees and futtocks would have been no problem.

THE CASEMENT SIDES

My next problem was deciding on a logical width and depth to assign to Porter's rafters. Everyone gives a different dimension for the finished piece. Porter's son stated, "fourteen inches thick it was"; Brooke wrote, "the heavy timbers of the shield, 12" × 12" which were bolted together." Jones arrived at a twelve-inch thickness for the rafters, engineer Ramsay's rafters were "squared to 16 inches," and John Luke Porter doesn't give a rafter dimension at all. However, many years after the fact, he would have provided the dimension quoted by his son. On Porter's drawing, the rafters scale to twelve inches thick, with what appears to be a ceiling of two or three inches backing them up. Brooke objected to the ceiling being installed on the gun deck, and Porter removed it. However, the ceiling could have remained on the hull sides below the point where the frames were cut.

Over the years, Porter may have merged the dimensions of the rafters and the ceiling in his mind and given them as a single unit both above and below the gun deck. Be that as it may, fourteen inches was as close as anything I was going to find straight from a primary source, and because this dimension worked fairly well with other calculations

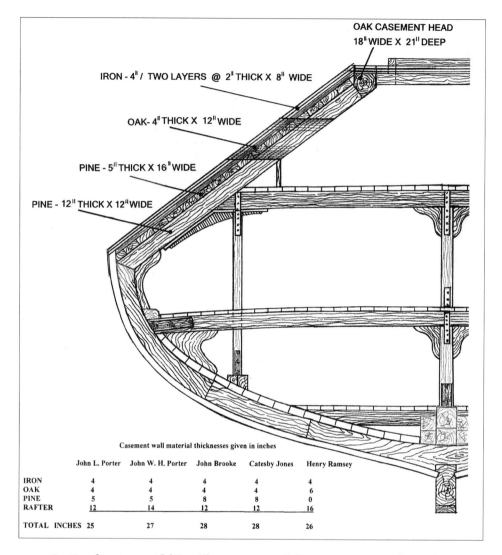

OAK CASEMENT HEAD
18" WIDE X 21" DEEP

IRON - 4" / TWO LAYERS @ 2" THICK X 8" WIDE

OAK- 4" THICK X 12" WIDE

PINE - 5" THICK X 16" WIDE

PINE - 12" THICK X 12" WIDE

Casement wall material thicknesses given in inches

	John L. Porter	John W. H. Porter	John Brooke	Catesby Jones	Henry Ramsey
IRON	4	4	4	4	4
OAK	4	4	4	4	6
PINE	5	5	8	8	0
RAFTER	12	14	12	12	16
TOTAL INCHES	25	27	28	28	26

Section drawing amidship with casement wall dimensions. *Drawn by author*

I had made, I would have to consider it. On the other hand, Brooke had done the "damage control" experiments and had provided the information on the best methods to protect the ship, so his twelve-inch-by-twelve-inch measurement, as well as the scale of Porter's drawing excluding the ceiling boards, couldn't be totally ignored.

At the same time I was trying to find the proper thickness for the rafters, I also had to wrestle with the width problem. Because twelve inches seemed to be a popular number, I decided to check it out. I returned to the same gun port analysis approach I had used to confirm the width of the *Merrimack*'s frames. The width of the *Virginia*'s gun ports scaled out to be exactly two feet, and the distance on centers of the gun ports on the flat surfaces was also in round numbers. From the center port, on the port side of the ship, to the next port back was thirty-five feet; from there to the next was twenty feet. On the starboard side the distance, on centers, from the center port back to the next port center was twenty-five feet, and the next fell at twenty feet. This discovery, along with the fact that the twelve-inch dimension kept popping up, was strong evidence that the finished rafters were twelve inches wide and twelve inches thick. But because Porter said that the rafters were fourteen inches thick and laid at 35 degrees, and Brooke said they were twelve inches laid at 36 degrees, I decided to make one last set of drawings using the various dimensions in different combinations to see which would best conform to Porter's drawings. It quickly became obvious that the 36-degree figure and rafters that were twelve inches thick by twelve inches wide worked best. Porter's drawing, which was made during construction, shows twelve-inch rafters. This is the dimension I have used in all of my calculations and drawings. I should point out here that the twelve-inch-by-twelve-inch dimensions work only on the sides of the casement, where the wall is relatively flat. For the curved ends of the casement, Porter had a new problem to contemplate, which will be explored in detail later.

In the March 19, 1862, article in the *Mercury*, Porter wrote, "Many of the inboard arrangements are of the most intricate character, and caused me many sleepless nights." Porter knew that the gross weight of each of the white pine rafters was almost seven hundred pounds. In a length of ten feet along the side of the ship, there would be seven thousand pounds of outward pressure exerted by the rafters alone on the top of the frames. Porter was going to design a huge layer cake of wood and iron. The ingredients of every square foot of Porter's casement cake were as follows:

> White pine, one cubic foot @ 30 lb per cubic ft = 30 lb
> Yellow pine, 5" × 12" × 12" = 720 cubic inches @ 37 lb per cubic ft = 15.4 lb
> White oak, 4" × 12" × 12" = 576 cubic inches @ 45 lb per cubic ft = 15 lb
> Wrought iron, two layers of 2" stock, 4" × 12" × 12" = 576 cubic inches @ 480 lb per cubic ft = 160 lb[10]
> Miscellaneous bolts and fasteners = 5 lb
> Total per square foot 224.4 lb. There are approximately 320 running feet of flat casement wall, so not counting the curved ends, this portion of the *Virginia* would have had a weight of approximately 71,800 lb, or a little more than 32 tons.

FASTENING THE PIECES

Assembling the mass of the *Virginia*'s casement would be no simple task. The thousands of pieces in wooden ships of this era were held together with metal fasteners called bolts, spikes, and nails and wooden dowels called treenails (pronounced "trunnels"). Treenails could range in diameter from seven-eighths of an inch to an inch and a half, the diameter based on the width of the wood to be penetrated. Their principal use was in attaching external planking and internal ceiling to the frames and beams and to hold pieces of floors, futtocks, and top timbers. Locust was the wood of choice, but other hardwoods were used as well, with the prime requisite that the piece be totally free of knots.[11] Treenails must have been used throughout the old *Merrimack* hull section, but there is no mention of them in any of the descriptions of the *Virginia*'s construction.

The metal fasteners, particularly the bolts, were the principal pieces that held the whole ship together. The bolts were not what we buy at the hardware store today. They were unthreaded round rods with no heads that came in various lengths, diameters, and metals. The name "bolt" is probably derived from Middle English or Old French, meaning "to pass through." Bolts passed through, and held together, every major structural timber on a ship, and if improperly placed or driven, in time they could cause the destruction of the vessel. They were made of three basic materials: iron, copper, and brass. Brass bolts were referred to as "composition." Copper and brass bolts were used in any area where they might be exposed to moisture that could cause corrosion. Brass was the strongest and least expensive of the nonferrous metals. The general practice was to use these materials at any point that fell below the ship's load waterline. If Porter followed this practice, the live oak knees, the lower portion of the pine rafters, and external pine and oak shielding were attached with composition bolts. Everything above the waterline could have been fastened with iron, which gives better "grabbing power" between the wood and metal than composition or copper and certainly would have been preferred in the areas that were going to take artillery pounding.[12] Porter wrote in his journal, "The rafters of the shield were white pine and bolted to the knees and also to each other, making the work solid." As mentioned earlier, the final step in the salvage of the *Virginia* was to burn the old hull timbers to retrieve the bolt metal. Literally hundreds of pounds of bolts, spikes, and nails were encased in every sailing ship.

Two groups of skilled craftsmen did the work of installing treenails, bolts, and spikes. The "hole borers" were responsible for both selecting the locations where the fasteners were to be placed and then drilling the thousands of holes that were required. Using bits and augers of various sizes, the hole borers worked for hours on end to bore the thousands of holes required. Spiral ribbon bits, spoon bits, and nose augers were the tools of choice. The bits were either made in various lengths or attached to extension rods to obtain the required depths. The extension rods had wooden T-handles at the top. The bits could also be attached to wooden braces that would facilitate their turning. The required depth of any given hole could range from a few inches to several feet. After spending years turning braces and twisting T-augers, a hole borer's hands must have been as hard and calloused as tanned leather.

After the holes were drilled, it was a "fastener's" job to drive the bolts, spikes, or treenails home. Fastening was not a matter of brute strength applied with a sledge or mallet. Years of training were required to obtain the greatest efficiency. A bent bolt had to be extracted, and a shattered treenail required the hole borer to bore out the broken piece and repair any damage to the hole. The treenail or bolt therefore had to be struck squarely and with a specific amount of force that could be learned only through trial and error. Treenails had to be cut flush and wedged; bolts were clinched over clinching rings and sometimes countersunk.[13] The work of both the hole borers and fasteners was exacting and, more often than not, done in confined and cramped spaces that added to the difficulty and discomfort.

No record tells us where the bolts were put through the rafters, but someone must have kept a record of the placement because of subsequent work. When the exterior pine and oak layers were applied to the casement rafters, more and more metal bolts or spikes were added to the mix. An X-ray of the *Virginia* after all of the casement timbers were in place would have shown a maze of metal bolts and spikes going in every imaginable direction. When the iron armor plates were attached to the casement sides, this jungle of embedded metal thorns had to be penetrated with 1⅛16-inch spiral ribbon bits. The bane of every hole borer's life was hidden metal. When a bit tore into a piece of iron or brass, the bit was either damaged or ruined, and the hole had to be abandoned and plugged with a treenail. In locating a replacement hole, if the hole borer could not determine the exact direction in which the problem bolt ran, he might strike it again on the next try. Striking hidden bolts might have been one of the causes for the complaint from Tredegar that they "had to change the position of holes in some plates three or four times and were waiting on further modifications."[14]

The bolts that held the armor plates in place were the threaded variety we now use for working with wood and metal. None of the descriptions of the ship ever mentions the size of these bolts. To go through the iron and wood and protrude to accept a washer and nut on the inside, they had to be about twenty-six inches long. Holes in well-preserved existing armor plate measure 1⅛16 inches. Based on this we can establish an average diameter of 1¼ inches for the armor plate bolts.

ASSEMBLING THE PIECES

On reaching this point, through months of research, I had made the best calculations I could in determining the sizes of the pieces that were used, the way they interfaced, and the system that held them together. During this time, I stayed on the lookout for one more factor, which I never found: How were the tons of casement material assembled? Assembling the *Virginia*'s casement was not like standard ship construction. The more I examined it, the more it looked like the structure of a bridge or a barn roof, not a ship. The only practical way to build the casement was to first build a scaffold inside the ship. The scaffold would have to stand on both the new berth deck and engine platform, and it would have two basic functions. First, the upper part would support the oak casement head that ran lengthwise to hold the rafters in place. Porter's description of this part of the ship reveals that "the upper shield deck was strongly framed with pine beams. Between these beams at their ends were pieces of oak timber dovetailed to support the end of the rafters."[15]

The longitudinal casement head members would have dovetail notches cut into them on one-foot centers facing outward. With these pieces resting on the top of the scaffold, the bottom end of the rafter would be placed on the frame. The upper, dovetailed end would drop into the dovetail notch in the casement head. The pine beams to support the upper deck would then be dropped into notches on the inner side of the longitudinal casement head. Unfortunately, there is no mention of the size and number of these beams. This combination of beams and rafters would form the bridge, or roof, to support the two-inch-by-two-inch iron rods that would form the top deck. The center part of the scaffold would have had a platform to support the gun deck beams while they were being fastened to the rafters and the iron knees attached. The illustration that shows how this was done has been greatly simplified for clarity.

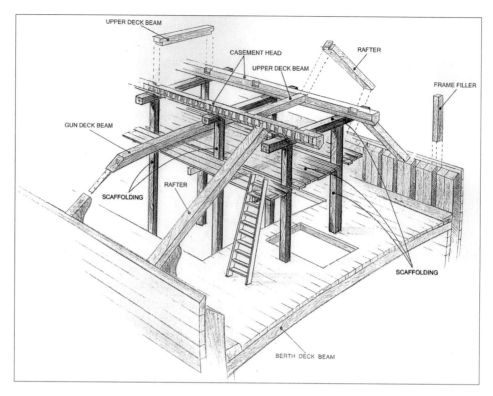

Internal scaffolding. *Drawn by author*

After all rafters and beams were in place, "a molding 16 inches across was placed [horizontally] on the yellow pine. It was five inches thick and bolted to the rafters with ¾" bolts. . . . All of this was calked and pitched along with another [vertical] course of oak 4 inches thick."[16]

FRAMING THE CASEMENT ENDS

At this point, the casement frame on the sides was complete, and the curved ends of the casement could be framed. The sides of the *Merrimack*'s hull bowed outward very slightly along the length amidships where the *Virginia*'s casement was to be placed. This bowing was so slight that it would not cause any significant alterations in the construction methods previously described. When we come to the curved ends of the casement, all simplicity is lost. None of the principals who were involved in the construction of the ship, or any later research, ever mentions this fact. The construction of the curved ends is a three-dimensional puzzle and probably one of the things that kept Porter awake at night.

To visualize what was happening, imagine a huge cone with a twenty-three-foot nine-inch radius at the base. Its sides slope up on a 36-degree angle to the apex at seventeen feet three inches above the base. Now measure twenty-three feet up the sides, and cut off and discard the top. Next, slice the remainder in half vertically. Half will

Top deck structure showing rafter and beam connections. This illustration shows the dovetailed joints that connected the rafters to the beams. Overlaying the rafters is the pine, oak, and iron armor plating. The two-inch-by-two-inch iron bars that formed the top deck rested on the wood cafing that overlaid the beams. The bars were riveted together. *Drawn by author*

become the bow section of the casement, and half the stern. Obviously this geometric shape could never be formed with twelve-inch-by-twelve-inch-by-twenty-three-foot base timbers, or rafters, as Porter called them. The timbers would have to be shaped on all six sides, but there is no clue as to how this was actually done. I have illustrated two possible approaches, and I am sure there are many more. The key was to keep it simple—Porter was under constant pressure to get this monster in the water as soon as possible.

The accompanying drawings show what would have been done on the flat casement sides and illustrate two possible approaches for constructing the curved ends. At a point back about eighteen feet from where the curved casement sides join the knuckle, the sides of the flat casement start to bend in to such a degree that the twelve-inch-by-twelve-inch rafters would no longer fit. Each piece would have to be tapered toward the top end. Up to that point, where the curve casement joins the sides of the hull, the rafters had been resting on the top of the frames and knees, but here the curved end of the casement turns in sharply, and a new foundation is required. Porter wrote, "Forward and aft the shield deck, beams were solid and bolted together, on this an iron deck four inches thick was laid. This deck was submerged two feet under water."[17] As usual, Porter's description is fuzzy, but it's enough information to arrive at a logical conclusion. The solid beam under deck had to start at the point where the curve of the casement and the

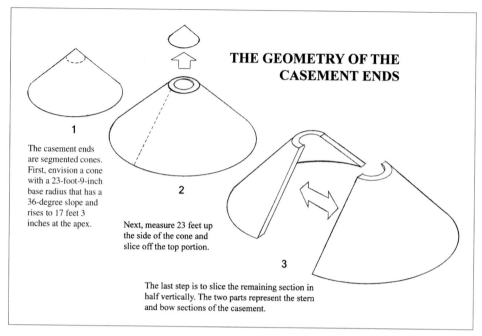

THE GEOMETRY OF THE CASEMENT ENDS

1 The casement ends are segmented cones. First, envision a cone with a 23-foot-9-inch base radius that has a 36-degree slope and rises to 17 feet 3 inches at the apex.

2 Next, measure 23 feet up the side of the cone and slice off the top portion.

3 The last step is to slice the remaining section in half vertically. The two parts represent the stern and bow sections of the casement.

The geometry of the casement ends. *Drawn by author*

Merrimack's hull met. The armor plate was laid on the wooden deck and joined with the armor on the curved casement sides. In addition to this change at the base, the longitudinal oak casement head for the upper deck would also have to curve inward and terminate at a curved end with an external radius of approximately five feet.

The first illustration shows the rafters and additional timbers being installed in a fan pattern. The rafter timbers in the forward part of the casement are all cut to the same size and shape. The base end is twelve inches wide, and the top tapers to approximately four inches wide. Obviously, the dovetail method of attachment to the curved oak casement head would no longer be practical. The timbers would have to rest on the curved oak structure that would also support the forward end of Porter's pilothouse. The second illustration shows a spoke pattern, with rafters of varying shapes and sizes. There would be ten primary rafters at twelve inches by twelve inches and eight secondary rafters made from twelve-by-twelve stock but tapered toward the top ends to fit between the primary rafters. Next, sixteen pointed rafters would have a twelve-by-twelve base, but starting at nine feet from the base, they would begin to taper to a point at their tops. These would fit between the primary and secondary rafters. Last, to fill the remaining gaps, there would be thirty-two wedges with a nine-inch base that would come to a point at about nine feet. The dovetail attachment method could still be used with the primary and secondary rafters with this second approach.

To conform to the original pattern established on the casement flat surfaces, the next layer of material on top of the pine rafters was to be a horizontal course of yellow pine, sixteen inches across by five inches thick. Having managed a cabinet shop and a display company, I have had a lot of experience in bending and shaping various materials, but I had

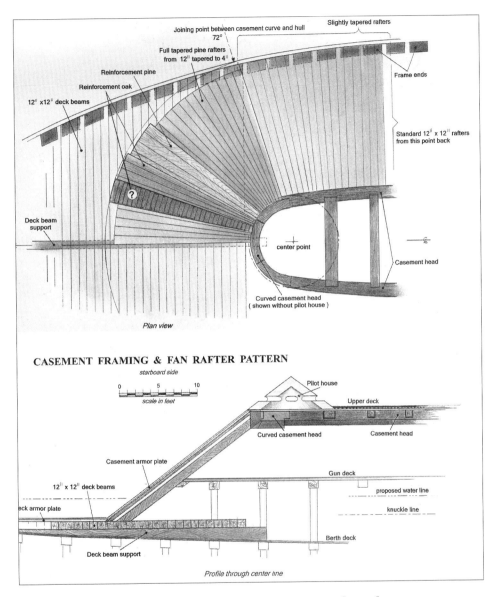

Casement framing and fan pattern. *Drawn by author*

never heard of bending five-inch-thick yellow pine boards into double compound curves. I had no idea how this could have been done so I posed the question to the restorers at the Boston National Historic Park at the Charlestown Navy Yard, the people responsible for maintaining the USS *Constitution*. There is little, if anything, left of the original sides of Old Ironsides. The hull's oak planking deteriorates, and from time to time individual planks have to be replaced. The method the restorers use to replace the planks is almost identical to the method used to initially assemble the ship. A plank has to be cut and shaped to fit a certain area and then steamed and bent in the molding loft. The work is exacting and takes split-second timing. No time can be lost from the moment the plank is

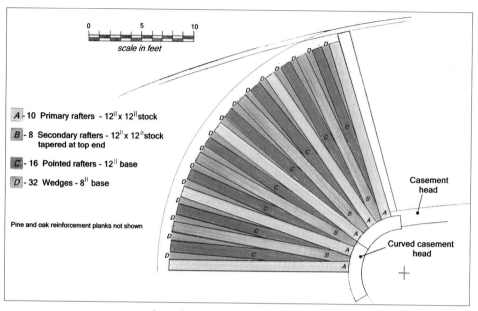

Spoke rafter pattern. *Drawn by author*

permeated with the correct amount of moisture, taken out of the steamer, and pinned down in the lofting jig, where it will dry and take on the desired shape. If the plank starts to dry before it is secured in the jig, the process is a failure and has to be redone. It takes hours to steam a piece of oak and only minutes before it dries to the point where it becomes rigid and refuses to bend. Like me, the restorers had never heard of bending five-inch pine boards into compound curves. Pine has a long, splinter-prone grain and also a knot problem—any knot along the length would cause the piece to splinter or snap at that point when being bent. A clear pine plank of the size required that was totally knot-free would be a rarity. Our final conclusion was that, unless the old carpenters had a secret that has not been passed along, the men working on the *Virginia* could not have bent any sixteen-inch-by-five-inch pine planks into compound curves. To maintain the uniform thickness of the shield, that layer of pine had to have been placed vertically, not horizon-tally. The oak that overlaid the pine could have been steamed and bent into compound curves for horizontal installation, but it probably wouldn't have made any appreciable dif-ference to the strength of the overall structure. If laid vertically, the eight-inch width given for the oak planks would not have been feasible on the vertical surface because planks that were less than twelve inches wide would come to a sharp point before reach-ing the top. To avoid confusion, there are no gun ports shown on my timber plan draw-ings. These will be discussed in detail later.

A lot of straight structural timber would be needed in the *Virginia's* casement, and all of which would not have been left lying around the Gosport Yard when the Union Navy evacuated. Numerous manufacturing facilities in the area would play a vital role in supplying parts and materials for the *Virginia*. The primary industry in the Portsmouth-Norfolk area was shipbuilding, the banks along the southern branch of the Elizabeth River hosting numerous shipyards and their satellite suppliers, two of which would play important roles in supplying materials for the *Virginia*. The Graves and Nash Ship Yard, owned by the naval architect William Nash and his associates, Graves and Stokes, would have been a prime source for lumber. In addition to building ships, the firm processed its own timber and had a large saw and planing mill that could easily supply all of the pineand oak lumber the *Virginia* would require. Atlantic Iron Works, which both fabricated iron products and built boats, would supply the two-inch-by-two-inch bars that Porter used to cover the *Virginia's* top deck. In addition to supplying bolts, small tools, and drill presses, the firm built templates used to form curved armor plates for the *Virginia*. Once again, we are left to wonder what kind of templates and which armor plates were curved.

FRAMING THE GUN DECK

With the casement walls in place, the carpenters could frame the gun deck. On Porter's gun deck plan, he shows the location of nine hatches, three amidships and three smaller ones on each side to service the guns. I assumed this would be a simple key that could show me the framing pattern, but I was wrong again; there was no set pattern. Porter's hatch locations turned out to be a jumble of total chaos and confusion. If the deck were built as the drawing shows, the accepted rules of ship deck frame construction would have to be ignored.

To understand the problem, we need to review the standard and accepted construction method. As mentioned earlier, a ship's beams were key elements in the shipbuilding process. They held together the sides of the ship and supported the deck planks. It was the general rule to make beams from a single piece of wood that would span the entire width, but two pieces could be scarfed vertically, if necessary. The beams were cambered (curved) to allow water to run to the sides of the ship. The beams that formed the engine and boiler platform of the *Merrimack* appear to have been flat. The size of the beams could vary from deck to deck. The 1856 dimensions for the *Roanoke* and *Colorado,* the *Virginia's* sister ships, give us their dimensions:

Berth deck beam moulded—1' 1½"
Berth deck plank—4"
Gun deck beam moulded—1' 2½"
Gun deck plank—5"

Beam spacing ranged from five to seven feet on canters. Hatches frequently interfered with the beam's run, and here the rule was that only one continuous beam could be eliminated to form a hatch opening. In that case a half beam ran between the side of the ship and a header that formed the side of the hatch. If a larger hatch was required, the beam actually ran through the hatch opening. To add further support to the deck planking, carlings were run in the space between the beams. The open space between beams where the carlings ran was called a berth. Carlings were about half the size of the beams and can be thought of as small beams. Individual carling pieces did not go across the ship as a continuous member like the beams. The general practice was to have the lateral carlings be

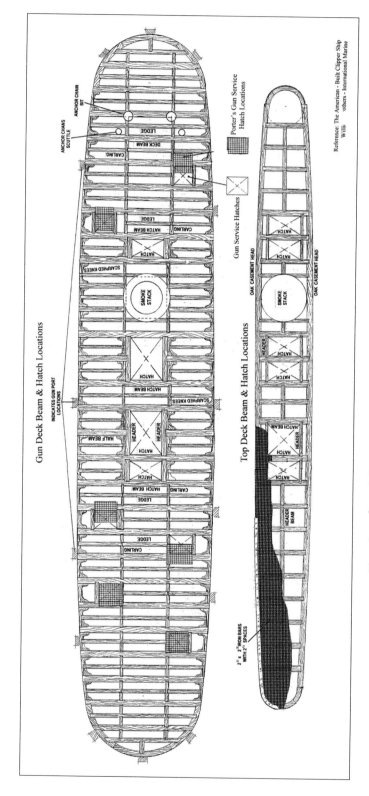

Framing plan of the gun deck and top deck. *Drawn by author*

a third of the width of the ship at its widest point. The carling's run was made continuous by being joined to the center of longitudinal members that ran across the berth space between the beams. Oak knees ran horizontally and vertically to attach the beams to the frame of the ship. The horizontal knees, called "lodging knees," were usually made from white oak. These knees could either touch toes at the center of the berth space or be butt joined or scarfed. The carlings were joined to one another or to the beams or knees with lap joints. Openings for hatches were framed on the sides facing outboard with headers.

From the *Colorado*'s dimensions and the *Merrimack* plans, I determined that the *Merrimack*'s beams were 15½ inches wide and averaged 6 feet on centers. I tried various combinations of these dimensions to make a gun deck framing plan that would both adhere to the rules and conform to Porter's hatch placements. Nothing worked. I tried to use a beam indicated in the opening of the largest of the center hatches on the gun deck as a point to work from both forward and aft that would indicate a constant, or nearly constant, spacing pattern. That didn't work either. Then I decided to draw two deck plans: one plan in accordance with the rules and placing the hatches as close as possible to the positions shown and a second plan conforming to Porter's hatch positioning. I bent the rule where necessary, but it took more than bending rules to conform to Porter's plan. No carpenter worth his salt would have framed a barn loft floor in such a haphazard manner. The major problems were caused by the random placement of the hatches and the fact that no two hatches were the same size. There was no consistency in the distance between the side hatches or the distance from the guns they would have served. I thought that something may have been happening on the lower decks that dictated where the hatches on the gun deck had to fall. Hatch placement above or near the magazines and shell rooms would be logical, but that was not the case. We don't know what compartments there may have been on the berth deck that might have had an effect. The hatches were over either water tanks or coal bunkers on the bottom deck, which had no bearing on anything. I finally had to settle on four possibilities for the beam pattern: First, Porter's drawing was hurriedly done and not accurate; second, the drawing was intended to show only approximate locations; third, the drawing was correct and required a strange and haphazard beam placement pattern to make it work; or fourth, my drawing that followed the rules was close to accurate but impossible to verify. Building a model of the gun deck based on the information I had developed would be appropriate but not historically verifiable. It was time to stop beating my head against the gun deck beams and move on to something else.

THE TOP DECK

As I struggled with the beam location problem on the gun deck, I was also looking at the location of the top deck hatches for useful information that could be applied to the gun deck. I found that the three hatches in the center of the top deck were in close alignment with the center hatches on the gun deck, but once again, there was no consistency in beam location. The distances on centers ranged from nine feet to four feet eight inches, and no two center measurements on the nine beams I could locate through hatch locations ever matched. The beam locations on the top deck were just as random as they were on the gun deck.

The top deck was a hybrid that did not necessarily have to conform to any standard ship construction rules for beam location. These beams were attached to the two headers that ran the length of the deck on port and starboard and had no bearing on the structure or stability of the hull. Their prime functions were to form the top of the casement, frame in the hatches, and provide a place for the two-inch-by-two-inch iron bars that formed the top deck. They could provide those functions and at the same time be scattered in a random pattern.

I have referred to the uppermost surface of the *Virginia* as the top deck because I can't find a more appropriate name to use. On sailing ships of the period, this deck would have been called the spar deck, but with no spars the term is inappropriate in this case. On riverboats and passenger steamers, it was the promenade deck where passengers could leisurely walk, which certainly doesn't apply. Porter refers to it as the shield deck, which to me implies something strong and protective, and that was not the case either. It was a large, open grillwork penetrated with three hatches. A plunging shot would have gone straight through. Porter may have meant that it was the deck above the casement that could be called a shield.

The decks fore and aft of the casement were made of twelve-by-twelve-inch timbers and four inches of iron. Those areas could be correctly considered shield decks. Porter describes the top deck as follows: "The upper shield deck was strongly framed with pine beams. Between these beams at their ends were placed oak timbers dovetailed to support the end of the rafters [casement heads]. An oak caffing or plank sheere was placed on top of the rafters and also on the beams which served as a bed for the iron grating which covered the entire shield deck. This deck was made entirely of two inch square bars and crossed, being riveted together."[18] On Porter's section drawings this deck scales to a length of 154 feet 6 inches and has a width of 14 feet at the widest point. It narrows down fore and aft to 10 feet. Porter's plan and cross-section drawings do not concur. The plan drawing shows a width of only about 11 feet at the widest point and then narrows down to 6 feet fore and aft.

The hatches on this deck were another bone of contention between Brook and Porter. In Brooke's April 3, 1862, letter to Porter, he writes, "The fifth alteration was the making of two additional hatches—your plan of detail provides for only one." The key words here are "plan of detail." The three-view drawing shows the three hatches, so Brooke would have been referring to the original twenty-seven-foot scroll of detail that has been lost. Obviously there were three hatches, but there is only one mysterious reference to them by J. W. Porter: "There were three hatchways in the top grating with pivot shutters."[19] What does he mean by pivot? Where and how were they pivoted, and more important, how were they constructed? If they were made of wood, which was the standard method of making hatch covers at the time, they would not have been shot resistant. If they were intended to provide protection and were constructed with two-inch iron bars in the same manner as the surrounding deck, they would have weighed more than seventy-seven pounds per square foot. The smallest of the six openings is shown as eight feet by four feet six inches, or thirty-six square feet. If the hatch cover was in two eighteen-square-foot sections, each section would weigh over a thousand pounds, so that approach must be eliminated. A simpler protective method would have been one-inch-thick iron plates. Here an eighteen-square-foot cover would weigh about seven hundred pounds, but that may still be too much weight to be moved by three or four crew members standing on the steps below. If the plate was drilled with a pattern of round holes, the weight could be reduced to about 360 pounds, still not a light weight but movable with some effort.

As for the pivot problem, it may be a mix-up in semantics. Whereas I think of something pivoted as being anchored at one point and moving from side to side, the *Virginia's* deck railings and awning stanchions would have prevented a cover from pivoting from side to side into a fully open position. Porter's son might have meant that there were pins at two corners of the covers, which can be construed as a pivot but act as a hinge. With hinges on the fore or aft side of eighteen-square-foot hatch covers, everything is simplified. There is always the possibility that the hatch covers were not armored and were constructed from wood, as on standard sailing ships. All of the drawings and models I have seen show the ship with uniformly sized and spaced hatches, but in a model or drawing made in accordance with Porter's plan, that would not be the case.

Other things shown on the top deck in pictures and models should be noted, most obviously the smokestack. The smokestack caused considerable problems in the *Virginia's* two engagements. After being shot full of holes, it no longer drew properly, which caused problems for the engines. On the *Merrimack*, it had been a telescoping affair so that it did not interfere with the sails. On the *Monitor*, there was no smokestack present during battle, only a hole in the deck and large blowers to expel smoke and gases.

Hand railings and awning stanchions were most likely on the ship, although Porter never showed them on his drawings or mentioned them. These are quite prominent on the Blackford drawing, which also shows two flagstaffs, galley smokestack, and a ventilator. Eyewitness descriptions of the ship mention the flagstaffs and describe the flags: Flag officer Buchanan's red flag toward the bow and the Confederate stars and bars toward the stern. The exact position of the flagstaffs is not known, so artists and model builders vary it from example to example. We know there was a galley smokestack but again not where it was, though it would have to have been back far enough from the forward pivot gun so as not to interfere with its operation. One of the more perplexing things Blackford shows is the ventilator. There is no mention or drawing of a ventilator in any of Porter's work. If one was in front of the stack, where Blackford shows it, it would have been in the middle of the forward hatch, so we can discount that location. Johnston showed a ventilator behind the stack. The engineers who designed the *Merrimack* saw no need for ventilators and did not include any. The *Merrimack* drawings show the beam framing around the smokestack in considerable detail. If the *Virginia's* builders had employed a similar pattern around the stack, the beams would have interfered with the ventilator pipe, and the pipe would have interfered with the steps leading to the hatches. For reasons never explained, as time went by *Virginia* models and drawings suddenly sprouted two ventilators. The *Virginia's* berth deck was completely open above the engines and boilers. The gun deck was perforated with numerous hatch openings, two directly above the engines and boilers, and with an open grillwork for an upper deck, there doesn't seem to be any reason for ventilators. But we must always return to those frustrating drawings done by Blackford and Johnston. If there were no ventilators, why did they show them? Artists and model builders have the choice of including ventilators or excluding them, and no one can prove that they are right or wrong.

THE PILOTHOUSE

With the top deck completed, it was time for Porter to add his finishing touch. Forward on the top deck, the overall width of the deck became narrower as the casement began to round out at the end. Above the center point of the casement curve, the width narrowed from fourteen feet to ten feet. Here Porter located his armored pilothouse. In times past, the captain, helmsman, or pilot stood exposed on the spar deck, which is not feasible on an armored ship designed for close-range pounding. Ericsson had given serious thought to this matter in designing the *Monitor*, even calculating the minimum width of the slot openings that would provide the greatest protection and at the same time allow an ample field of view. With the problem of a pilothouse near the front of the ship, his later designs had it on top of the turret.

Apparently a pilothouse was an afterthought on Porter's part—the conical device that he put on the *Virginia* was sketched in pencil on his drawing. For some unfathomable reason, neither his nor Brooke's original drawings show any place for a pilot or helmsman to stand, which is like designing a fighter aircraft and forgetting to provide a place for a pilot to sit. Porter's son describes the pilothouse as follows: "Mr. Porter sequentially had two cast iron conical shaped pilot houses made and put on each end."[20] We don't know why he said two pilothouses were put on the ship; there was only one, and it was toward the bow. Because of its size and weight, it was most likely made at the Tredegar Iron Works. He continues: "These were about twelve inches thick, with four loop holes for observation." As far as we know Porter's pilothouse was never used "by Commodore Buchanan during the engagement at Hampton Roads. He stood in one of the hatchways above referred to and communicated his orders to the wheelman from that position."

John Luke Porter's description is even less detailed, only confirming that there was one pilothouse and that the ship's wheel was on the gun deck under a hatchway: "A large pilot house of cast iron was placed on the forward end of the shield deck. It was never used for that purpose; the Captain and pilot choose to stand on a small peak in a hatchway over the steering wheel."[21] He does not explain what he meant by "a small peak in a hatchway" or give enough information for us to be able to make an accurate drawing of the pilothouse. Brooke's only comment on the subject is a negative one: "Porter has placed upon the end of the shield at the forward end of the opening a sort of look-out-house a hollow core of iron. . . . It will I think break into fragments if struck by a shot."[22]

Although Brooke should have known the pilot and helmsman would need a place to stand, he had not indicated any such provision in his earlier design drawing. He criticized what Porter did but, for once, didn't say what he thought should have been done. The only helpful part in any of these statements is the one dimension given: "about twelve inches thick." Based on that dimension and an analysis of what had to be done, we can make a scale drawing that shows a cone ten feet eleven inches wide at the base, four feet tall, and with a circumference of a little over thirty-four feet. With a thickness of twelve inches, the

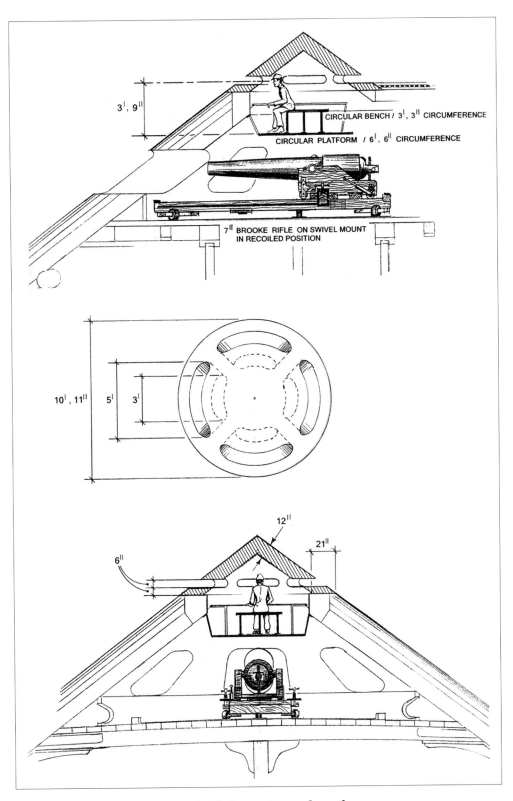

Porter's pilothouse. *Drawn by author*

hollow interior would have been about seven feet six inches across by two feet nine inches high in the center. The base width of ten feet eleven inches was required so that the iron bars and calfing that comprised the surface of the top deck, which was ten feet across, would not have been under the pilothouse but would have joined it in the rear. The uppermost interior point was eleven feet three inches above the deck. We are not given any location for the four loopholes. To arrive at a logical place, I had to start at the bottom and work up. On the gun deck, there was a pivot-mounted Brooke rifle directly under the pilothouse. The uppermost part of the gun would have been approximately four feet above the deck. For the crew to man the gun, there would have to have been at least sixteen inches of clearance between the gun and the bottom of a platform where the pilot would be. I estimated that the platform's floor would have been about two inches thick. A five-foot-six-inch-tall pilot, with a pointed head, could stand dead center on the platform, who would also need free movement to look out in all directions. That the interior wall was a circle on a 36-degree angle further complicated matters.

Ericsson's pilothouse design for the *Monitor* was less challenging. He was working with a straight rectangular box, with ample room for both captain and helmsman to stand. He describes his solution as follows: "Regarding the adequacy of the elongated sight-holes formed between the iron blocks in the manner described, it should be born in mind that an opening of five-eighth of an inch affords a vertical view of 80 feet high at a distance of only 200 yards. . . . Unfortunately the sight holes were subsequently altered, the iron blocks being raised and the opening between enlarged."[23]

Ericsson was concerned with only a few inches of horizontal iron. Because of the 36-degree angle, Porter was going to have to penetrate about twenty-one inches on the horizontal in a surface that was curving back on both sides. I tried numerous approaches and concluded that for optimal visibility and reasonable protection, Porter's loopholes could start at six inches above the base of the cone and be six inches high. If one foot of metal was left between each opening, the slots could be five feet wide on the outside and three feet on the inside. These dimensions may seem large, but two people were supposed to occupy the area, and because of the curve and slope of the walls, their eyes would be at least a foot away from the opening. If a man's head was touching the inside surface of this huge "bell" when it was hit by cannon fire, the concussion would have killed him.

As pointed out earlier, a man could not stand upright inside the cone. The center of the slot, as I suggested it might have been designed, was only three feet nine inches above the platform floor, which leaves only three possible positions for viewing: bend over as if spying through a keyhole, get down on his knees, or sit on a stool or bench. Some movies and illustrations show the ship's wheel located in the pilothouse, which because of its size and shape would have been absurd. A scenario with the captain, helmsman, and pilot in there together would make a great script for a Three Stooges movie. We can see why Buchanan chose to stand on the hatch steps. We don't know what Jones did during the *Monitor* engagement; he may have scurried back and forth looking out of the gun ports. This was Porter's first and last cast-iron conical pilothouse. He and other designers did continue placing armored rectangular structures with sloping walls and slots on the top of casements, and, for reasons I will never understand, they preferred placing them directly above guns.

THE GUN PORTS

With the casement timbers in place on the sides, fore, and aft and the gun deck in place, it would have been possible to cut the *Virginia's* gun ports. There are no detailed descriptions of how the gun ports for the *Monitor* were fabricated, but James Gibson's photographs, taken on board in July 1862, make the method quite apparent. After the metal plates that formed the circular wall of the turret were assembled, three overlapping holes were mechanically cut through the structure to form the opening for each port.

It is highly unlikely that anything of this nature could have been done on the *Virginia*. The work was almost certainly done by hand on the wooden casement with saws, mallets, chisels, draw knives, and adzes. Porter's drawings show the configuration of the ports in considerable detail. Each started two feet above the gun deck with a width of two feet and a height from the deck to the top of the opening of five feet. On the slope of the casement wall, the overall height of five feet and the top and bottom a semicircle. The outer planking of four-inch oak and five-inch pine was cut straight through horizontally, top and bottom and on the sides. The internal rafters were left with the straight horizontal cut top and bottom, but the sides flared out toward the interior of the ship at 25 degrees. This angle permitted the guns to be pivoted to increase the field of fire. The interior horizontal width was four feet. The quarter ports were on a point at 51 degrees off the center line of the ship. This placement was necessary to prevent the swivel carriage from interfering with the internal opening of the hawsepipe and anchor bitts. The quarter ports shown on Porter's gun deck plan were drawn somewhat haphazardly. They don't match the side ports, being lightly sketched in and out of square. This is further evidence to support Brooke's claim that they were not included in Porter's original *Virginia* plan.

THE ARMOR PLATE

With the wooden structure in place and the gun ports cut, the next step would have been the attachment of the armor plates. For years, I have tried to track down enough certified examples of *Virginia* armor plates to reproduce the pattern for drilling or punching the holes that took the bolts to hold the plates in place. Very few plates have a clear provenance, and because a hunk of iron with holes in it doesn't make a very exciting museum exhibit, those that are around are not often displayed. I was told that a plate at the Smithsonian is tucked away in a storeroom. The accompanying drawing shows what I found: The largest piece was at the Hampton Roads Naval Museum, protected in a display case along with a model of the *Virginia*. It was obviously underwater for a long time before it was recovered. The surface is severely pockmarked, and the bolt-holes are not much more than half an inch across because of the rust. The Portsmouth Naval Shipyard Museum's example, also pockmarked, is mounted on a plaque and covered with black paint. It can be touched by the public. The examples that are displayed in the open at Trophy Park on the grounds of the Gosport Navy Yard also show the ravages of time and

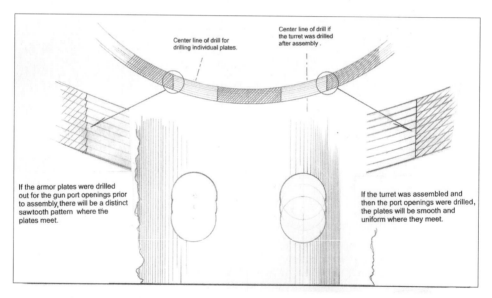

Monitor **gun port fabrication.** *Library of Congress photo; drawing by author*

weather. Their pockmarked surfaces are covered with coats of black paint, and because they are near the ground, they are kicked and prodded and walked on. Their "life expectancy" as historical artifacts may be short at this point. The small 13½-inch-by-8-inch piece at the Museum of the Confederacy in Richmond is the only piece that is preserved well enough to give us the size and shape of the holes in the outside plates. The dimensions derived from this piece are a close match to Porter's drawing.

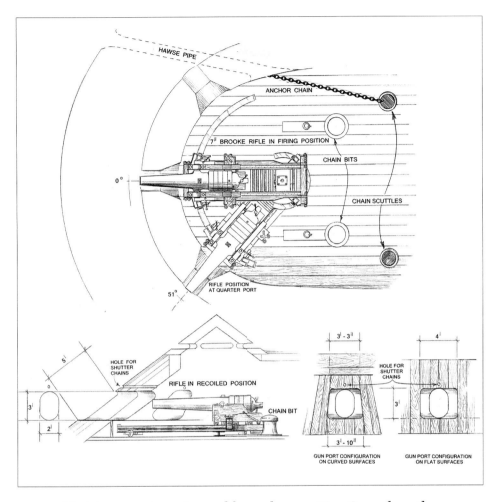

Virginia **gun port openings and forward gun position.** ***Drawn by author***

I quickly saw that I would never find any pattern in the examples I had located. I knew that the plates would range in thickness from one inch to two inches, but I was surprised to find the seven-inch plate at the Portsmouth Museum; everything I had ever read gave the width as eight inches. The comment from Tredegar that they were constantly relocating hole positions is good evidence that any plan of having a standard overall bolt pattern was soon compromised. The fact that the wooden casement was a minefield of hidden iron and brass bolts is a further reason that a standard pattern would have been extremely difficult to maintain throughout the ship. Even if Porter had known about the bolting method used on the CSS *Albemarle*, he probably could not have used it. Brooke would have objected to any changes in the installation method that had proven effective in the test he and Jones had conducted earlier. There is some slight evidence of uniformity in the few *Virginia* armor plates illustrated, but examination of dozens of certified examples would be necessary to arrive at any firm conclusion. The one certain conclusion to come from this research is that the myriad engravings, drawings, and paintings

Armor plates on public display. These armor plates, exposed to the elements and covered in black paint, are on display at the Gosport Navy Yard's Trophy Park. *Author's photo*

that show the *Virginia* with neat, straight columns of vertical and horizontal bolt heads are wrong.

Another artifact I could not find was a curved piece of armor plate that would have been used horizontally on the fore or aft curved sections of the casement. I am convinced that no pine planks were ever bent and put on the casement horizontally, and I doubt that it was ever done with oak. Blacksmiths at the yard could have formed curved armor plates more readily than carpenters could make them with wood. Jigs made for use in bending metal are mentioned, but not what metal was used. It is not surprising that there are no examples of curved plates in any museums. The necessary compound curve would make them difficult to handle, store, or display. The plates on the flat casement sides were installed horizontally and vertically in the theory that this arrangement would provide greater resistance to shot. Because of the compound vertical and horizontal curved surface of the fore and aft sections of the casement, plates there were less likely to suffer much damage when struck. It would have been more expedient to install both layers of these plates vertically. Unless some new evidence is found, we will never know which approach was actually used.

THE GUN PORT SHUTTERS

Blacksmiths would have had the job of forming the armor plates around the gun port openings and making provisions for the port shutters to be attached. On the morning of

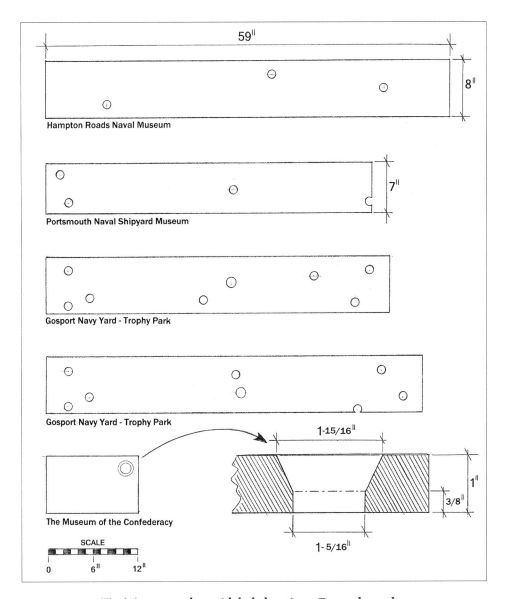

Virginia **armor plate with hole locations.** *Drawn by author*

March 8, 1862, all of the shutters had not yet been installed. In his article written in October 1887 for *Battles and Leaders*, John L. Porter wrote, "She had port shutters only at her four quarter port-holes." In *Records of Events in Norfolk County*, John W. Porter stated: "She was fitted with four inch, hammered iron, shutters on her four quarter ports. They were made in two pieces and closed like a pair of shears."

In John Luke Porter's *A Short History of Myself*, he wrote that the shutters were made at Tredegar from hammered iron, which raises an interesting problem: Fourteen sets of shutters made at Tredegar would most likely have been cast, not hammered. Regardless of how the shutters were made, they were either en route from Richmond or had arrived too late to be completely installed.

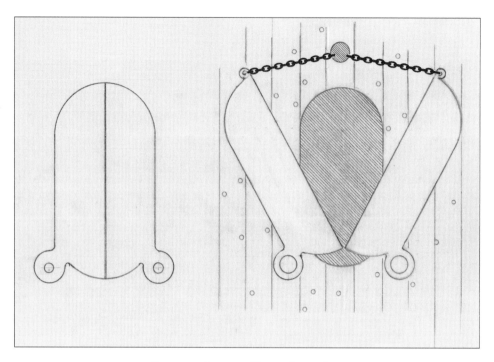

Gun port shutters. *Drawn by author*

The only illustrative information we have about the shutters is the rather confusing drawing on Porter's overall view of the ship. There are solid lines on the inside of the exterior line that defined the exterior shape of the shutter. At first glance, the oval and circles that are shown appear to be a part of the shutter. After further examination I determined that the oval was supposed to represent the port opening and the circles the muzzle of the gun. They should have been drawn in the traditional manner, as broken lines, to show that they were behind the cover and not part of it. The shutters are shown on their side, so it is impossible to tell which end is the top. We know that the shutters were in two pieces and operated like a shear, but we do not know if the pivot point was at the top or the bottom. The engraving of the wreck of the CSS *Albemarle* clearly shows that her single-piece shutters were pivoted at the bottom. Another Porter design, the CSS *Palmetto State,* also had one-piece shutters that pivoted at the bottom. In J. Anderson's description of the *Virginia,* he wrote that "the whole of the pivot and broadside ports can be closed in action, by means of shields, made of 3 inch iron [Porter claimed 4 inches], they are on the outside and worked from within by means of small chains."[24]

In this type of design the shutters were operated by releasing the chain that allowed the shutter to swing down. If a lucky shot broke a chain, the shutter could not be closed. If these shutters had been top mounted, a broken port chain would have been disastrous. The shutter would have swung closed, and the gun trapped inside the ship where it couldn't be fired. Another alternative was used on the USS *New Ironsides.* Her two-piece shutters were pendulum mounted at the top and were opened and closed from the inside by levers attached to axles that passed through the casement and were secured to

"Wreck of the CSS *Albemarle.*" The bottom attachment method used on these gun port shutters is clearly shown in this illustration by Davidson. The relatively even spacing of the bolts attaching the armor plates to the casement is also apparent. *Battles and Leaders of the Civil War*

the shutters.[25] Scissor-mounted shutters attached at the bottom and operated with a lever would have been the best possible way for Porter to have designed the *Virginia*'s shutters, but according to Anderson, he chose to use the small chains.

THE STEERING GEAR

The *Merrimack* would have had a traditional steering system in which the rudderpost went through the spar deck and then was attached by ropes to a large ship's wheel. This, of course, was impossible for the *Virginia*, for which an unusual arrangement was required because the rudder and all the connecting lines were to be underwater. The stern portion of the ship that would have protected the rudder had been cut away, so the rudder, the connecting attachment, and the propeller would have been vulnerable to both ramming and cannon fire. To compensate, Porter designed a fantail that would cover a large portion of the stern deck and the propeller, rudder, and its connections. Porter's drawings show the various parts, but there are no detailed descriptions of how everything was constructed. The *Merrimack*'s rudder was cut down to be flush with the aft deck. A yoke that had been on the *Pensacola* at one time was secured to the top portion of the *Virginia*'s rudder, and steering chains were attached to it.[26] The chains were

A ship's wheel purportedly from the *Virginia*. This large metal ship's wheel, on display at The Mariners' Museum in Portsmouth, was probably located under or near the steps to the forward top deck hatch where Buchanan stood during the first day of battle. With its fifty-eight-inch diameter, the wheel could never have fit into the confined space of the pilothouse. *The Mariners' Museum photo*

conducted over rollers under the fantail and then under the armor plate on the deck to the casement, where they passed through pipes up to the gun deck. "Her Rudder chains were let into the outside after deck flush under the iron, and passed up through the shield in pipes until they came above the waterline and were then conducted on rollers to the steering wheel."[27] Porter's plan had the chains going beneath the four inches of armor on the deck. Brooke objected to this plan, as he pointed out in his April 3, 1862, letter to Porter: "The fourth alteration was the removal of the wheel ropes—chains—from beneath the plates outside, where they were liable to be jammed by a shot. Mr. Robert Archer was present when I called your attention to this liability. The alteration was not made, however, until Lieutenant Jones called your attention to it a second time." Brooke's theory was that if an exposed chain was broken, it could be repaired, but if it became jammed beneath four inches of armor plate, it would be out of reach and beyond repair.

Porter's section drawing through the center of the ship shows that a wide plank was placed vertically at the sides of the gun deck that joined the casement just below the bottom line of the gun ports. This arrangement served two purposes: it prevented any part of the gun carriages, or loose objects, from rolling into the narrow space where the casement and deck met, and it provided an enclosed triangular "chase" on both sides of the deck. This was the area where rollers carried the chains to a point horizontally across from the ship's wheel. A large iron ship's wheel, fifty-eight inches in diameter, purported to be from the *Virginia*, is on display at the Mariners' Museum. As pointed out earlier, the wheel was somewhere on the gun deck near the forward hatch. In all likelihood, the chains and ropes that were connected to the wheel ran from the chase, under the gun deck planking, and then up to the wheel. The overall efficiency of this steering arrangement is somewhat in doubt. The ship needed an inordinate amount of space and time to make a 90-degree turn. This may have been due to a combination of factors involving the rudder, lack of sufficient power, and the anchors being dragged alongside.

The Anchors

The *Virginia* carried, or, more correctly, dragged, two large anchors. As was discussed above, one of her anchors may be on display at the Museum of the Confederacy. Two of

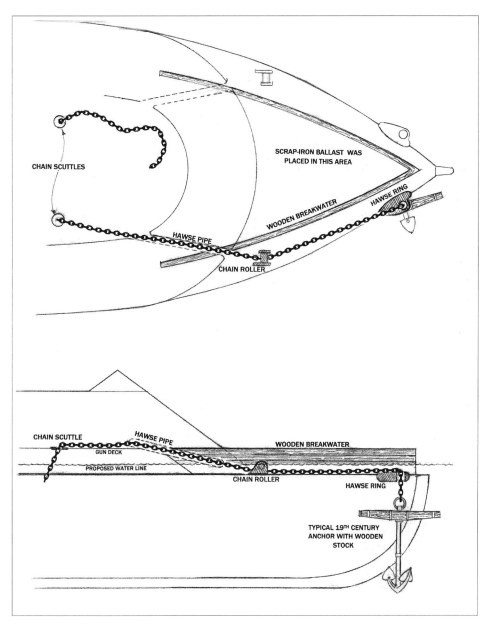

The anchor system. *Drawn by author*

these huge appendages, pulled through the water on both sides of the ship, would have had a considerable effect on her performance. The general practice on sailing ships at the time was to secure anchors alongside the ship's railing. After the anchor was raised out of the water and was hanging from the anchor cable under the hawsehole, it was lifted with lines that passed through the sheaves of a beam that extended out over the side of the ship, the cathead. With the anchor hanging from the cathead like a man on a gallows, additional lines were passed around a fluke. Crew members then "fished" it up with block and tackle until the shank was near a horizontal plane. It was then secured to the side of the ship and hung there until it was needed again. The configuration of the *Virginia* made this process impossible. The bow of the ship where this work would have been done was several feet underwater. Crew members would have either fallen overboard or been washed away if they went out to fish an anchor. As Porter's drawings show, he had two iron fixtures made that attached to each side of the bow where he wanted the anchors to hang. The anchor chains passed through a hole in the fixture, which I will call a hawse ring for lack of a better term, and then went across the deck through rollers to the submerged end of the hawse pipe in the forward part of the casement. The chains then went up the long hawse pipe to the gun deck. There, adjacent to the forward pivot gun, they went down through a scuttle to a windlass, probably on the berth deck. The chains were either stored there or passed down another scuttle to the lower boiler deck. There were two large single-post riding bitts adjacent to the scuttles where the chains could be secured. This arrangement made considerable clutter around the forward pivot gun for the gun crew to run into and fall over during the heat of battle. I have never seen a critique about the effect the hanging anchors would have had on the *Virginia*'s performance, but the drag and turbulence they would have caused at the bow could not have been helpful. They could also have caused problems when ramming a ship.

THE WOODEN BREAKWATER

Because the *Virginia*'s forward deck was underwater, the forward casement would have become a huge water brake. Not only would the ship be slowed but water would have piled up and poured through the forward gun ports. To compensate for this, Porter had a secondary prow in the form of a large, wedge-shaped wall built out from the casement on the forward deck. J. W. Porter mentions the breakwater only briefly in *Events in Norfolk County*: "there were two breakwaters but on the forward deck to throw off the water." The breakwater is shown in the profile view of the ship on Porter's three-view drawing, where it scales to four feet six inches high. On the plan view, it is shown as a single line with no indication as to how thick it was. Various texts and drawings give the width as twelve inches but with no explanation of how the author or artist arrived at that conclusion. We know that a lot of twelve-inch-by-twelve-inch timbers were used in the ship, so that guess is as good as any. To be efficient, it would have had to come to a point at the front, and that is how Porter shows it. Holes would have been drilled through the armor plate to bolt the first member to the deck, and subsequent pieces would have been bolted to one another. The finished structure wasn't meant to hold water when the ship rode high in the water, so there may have been scuppers along its length on both sides. When it was discovered that the ship rode too high in the water, ballast iron was placed inside this "corral" to bring the water level up to the desired depth. There are references to a similar structure on the aft deck, but that is highly unlikely.

THE SHIP'S BOATS

Porter doesn't give any detailed information about the *Virginia*'s boats. *Events in Norfolk County* only mentions that "her boats rested in chocks on her sides and were hauled out of the water." Other authors provide very little information. We learn that she had two boats and never had davits. No boats or chocks are shown on any of Porter's drawings. In all likelihood, the boats were "standard Navy issue" thirty-foot cutters and were probably never rigged for sea duty with a mast and sails. Their prime function would have been ship-to-shore transportation when the *Virginia* wasn't tied up at the shipyard dock. In any combat operation severe enough to require the crew to abandon ship, the boats would have been blasted into kindling long before they could have been used as lifeboats.

The Mariners' Museum drawing from Sumner Besse's book shows what the chocks might have looked like. The boats would have been cradled in the two-part chocks on the side of the ship between the gun ports on each side of the funnel. The chocks were constructed so that the inboard side was stationary and the outboard side was hinged and could swing down and away from the bottom of the cutter. At launch, a boat would be secured with lines and pulleys tied off near the top deck rail and then attached to the cutter's bow and stern, no doubt with John Brooke's patented boat hooks. On a given signal, two seamen would pull the chock lines, which would cause the outboard chock section to swing away, and the boat crew standing on deck could then lower the boat into the water. The process was reversed to bring a boat back on board. Ropes or rope ladders lying on the slippery, sloping casement side would have been required for crew members to go between the top deck and the boat.

THE DECK FITTINGS

There is no documentation or mention of the small parts and pieces that would have been scattered around the exterior decks. There would have been bitts for tying her up alongside the dock. We are told about flags but not where the flagstaffs were located. There were railings around the top deck, but their exact design must be left to our imagination. There were awning stanchions that most likely supported an awning draped over them and tied off at the railings. There is a mystery as to just how the deck hatches operated, possibly with some sort of fixtures attached to, or near, them.

By the first of March the scene around the *Virginia* was one of organized chaos. Catesby Jones and John Wood were frantically attempting to convert army artillerymen and riflemen into naval gun crews. While being drilled at the guns, the would-be sailors would have stumbled over carpenters and mechanics putting the finishing touches on the ship. Because they were landlocked in the Navy yard, the guns couldn't be fired. Gun drills were like children's war games, the gun crew going through the motions of loading and then pretending they were firing at the enemy. Any meaningful live ammunition practice had to be done on Craney Island. Mallory, Porter, and Brooke were in a panic over the late delivery of rifled guns and gun port shutters. The people at Tredegar were beginning to wish they had never heard of the *Merrimack*. Neither John Brooke, nor anyone else, was offering unsolicited construction advice to Porter at this time, even if they thought it might be warranted. Engineer Williamson had learned about that in the past: "As I am already in a scrape by objecting to Mr. Porter's plans and have really no right to interfere with them, I cannot do so again."[28]

The primary concerns by that time were twofold: How fast could the *Virginia* be made ready, and where was the *Monitor*? Northern newspapers and periodicals were smuggled south daily. An article in the *Scientific American*, dated November 23, had given Confederate naval officers a detailed description of the vessel they would soon have to fight. The newspapers gave a daily running account of the construction progress. With help like that, no one needed a naval intelligence service. The press reported that the *Monitor* was commissioned on February 25 and departed New York harbor on Tuesday, March 4. If the Union Navy ever had hoped for a surprise attack, it was now gone. Stephen Mallory knew that the *Virginia* was going into combat, ready or not.

Chapter Twelve

Two Days of Glory

While John Porter struggled to get the *Virginia* deeper into the water, where he had calculated she should be, Mallory was wrestling with a problem of politics and protocol. According to the old Navy rules of seniority, the highly prized and prestigious command of the *Virginia* was supposed to be decided by seniority. This meant that one of the abundant "ancient mariners" in the Confederate Navy could be taking Mallory's pride and joy into harm's way. This would never do. Sixty-six-year-old French Forrest, commandant of the Navy yard, wanted the post. The much younger Lt. Catesby ap Roger Jones also applied. Mallory probably preferred Jones above any of the other candidates, but of course such a prestigious command could not be given to a lieutenant. Mallory decided on Capt. Franklin "Old Buck" Buchanan, first commandant of the Naval Academy, who was then working with Mallory as head of the Office of Orders and Detail. Buchanan had a reputation as a fighting man, so Mallory considered him the best alternative. To get around the protocol hurdle, Mallory put Buchanan in charge of the James River Squadron with the rank of flag officer. This posting would allow Buchanan to select any ship in that squadron as his flagship. To no one's surprise, Buchanan selected the newly christened CSS *Virginia* with Lieutenant Jones as his executive officer. In addition to Jones, he had other excellent officers, including Lt. John Taylor Wood, nephew of Jefferson Davis's first wife, Sara Taylor, and grandson of Zachary Taylor. Wood had been sent out to neighboring Army camps to recruit crew members and was put in charge of the *Virginia*'s stern pivot gun.

Lt. John Taylor Wood.
The Century War Book

Lt. Charles C. Simms was in charge of the bow pivot gun that would be heavily engaged during the upcoming battle. Engineer Henry Ashton Ramsay, who had served on the USS *Merrimack* in 1856 under the direction of Chief Engineer Albin C. Stimers, would once again coax power out of the old *Merrimack's* sluggish engines. His old tutor, Stimers, was now in charge of the *Monitor's* engine room.[1]

Buchanan's flotilla would not be significant. There were the *Virginia's* escorts: the steam tugs CSS *Beaufort* with one 32-pound rifle and the CSS *Raleigh* with two 6-pound howitzers. The James River Squadron proper, commanded by Capt. John R. Tucker, was the side-wheel gunboat CSS *Patrick Henry* and her sister ship, the CSS *Jamestown.* They each carried one 10-inch smooth bore, one 64-pound smooth bore, six 8-inch smooth bores, and two pivot-mounted 32-pound rifles. Last, there was the small tug CSS *Teasar,* with one 32-pound rifle.[2] This was the flotilla that would attack the capital ships of the U.S. Navy. Mallory had exaggerated expectations of the *Virginia's* abilities and suggested to Buchanan that he might go up the Potomac and attack Washington. Buchanan politely explained that the river was too shallow for the *Virginia* at several places, that they couldn't buy the coal they would need from the Yankees, if they ever reached Washington, and that they would be under artillery and rifle fire from both banks all the way up and back. Mallory abandoned the notion.

Mallory had solved his personnel problem, but John Porter's mathematical problem was much weightier or, to be more accurate, not weighty enough. On or about February 14, water was let into the dry dock, and Jones saw that the *Virginia's* decks were not awash, although, according to Porter's drawing, they were supposed to be several feet below the surface. The knuckle that everyone thought was so vulnerable was barely submerged. It is a mystery as to how Porter, so proud of his mathematical abilities, could have made such a large error. He had built the *Colorado,* the *Merrimack's* sister ship, and should have known the parameters within which he had to work. It may have been a case of too much knowledge being a dangerous thing. Since he would have known the gross weight of the *Merrimack* off the top of his head, there would have no reason to take measurements and work out calculations. If he did his math based on the gross weight, he was in trouble before he started. He knew how much weight he had eliminated when he cut the hull down, but if he had subtracted only that figure from the gross weight, he may have forgotten to also subtract the huge weight of the mast, yards, rigging, and everything else on and above the spar deck. The *Virginia* was underweight and would not sit low in the water as required. There was some discussion about the weight of the coal, powder, and shot helping to correct the problem, but that was ludicrous because as they were expended, the ship would pop back up out of the water.

Time was of the essence, and there was only one solution. Porter went on a scavenger hunt to find all of the scrap iron scattered around the Navy yard. Tons of the stuff were dragged on board the *Virginia*. It was piled on the fore and aft decks and taken down into the bottom of the ship. (Artists and model makers seldom, if ever, show these piles of junk scattered all over *Virginia's* fore and aft decks.) The ship settled deeper into the water, but Brooke and Jones were not satisfied with the results and called for more. Porter became alarmed that the additional weight requested might go through the bottom of the ship and called a halt to the operation. What they had was as good as it was going to get.

Buchanan arrived at the shipyard on February 25, where men were scrambling to get the remaining coal on board and searching frantically for gunpowder. He may have been concerned about this chaos surrounding the *Virginia,* but he was not deterred. A land and sea attack plan had been worked out with flamboyant Gen. "Prince John" Magruder that was intended to stop George McClellan's end run up the peninsula to Richmond before it started. While Magruder moved down the north bank of the James River and captured the Union force in Newport News, Buchanan would cross the Hampton Roads with the *Virginia,* the *Buford,* and the *Raleigh* to attack and sink the *Cumberland* and the *Congress* anchored off Newport News, plus any other Union victim he came across, and also to pound the shore batteries. At the same time, the James River Squadron, *Patrick Henry, Jamestown,* and *Teaser,* would come down the river and join the fight. This three-prong attack would put Confederate forces in command at Newport News. Their guns would be in command of both banks of the James, and the ironclad would be in command of Hampton Roads. The Union forces would be checked and driven out to sea, the blockade would be lifted, supplies would come in from Europe, and the Confederacy would win the war! At least that was how the plan appeared on paper.

But Magruder was getting cold feet. He had little or no confidence in the *Virginia* and was incorrectly convinced that the enemy had heavily reinforced Newport News and Fort Monroe to hopelessly outnumber him. He also thought the roads were bad, and besides, he had already contributed eighty of his men to the *Virginia's* crew. Buchanan knew that the *Monitor* was somewhere over the horizon, and he planned to be ready to move by the evening of the 6th. But the *Virginia* was still short 18,200 pounds of powder, and the last of the 150 tons of coal was still being loaded.

One of my early questions about the *Virginia* was: How did they get the coal on board? The *Merrimack* had had numerous coal scuttles situated on all of the decks above the coal bunkers but because of the slope of the casement and the *Virginia's* deck configuration, it was impossible to incorporate any of those coal scuttles in the conversion. Most likely it was a slow, labor-intensive process. Sacks of coal would have been brought onto the top deck and then passed down, bucket-brigade fashion, by slaves through the hatches and dumped in the bunkers.

Gun port shutters were installed fore and aft, but the rest were either still en route or had arrived too late to be installed. Both the Navy and the Army needed gunpowder; the Army got its powder, while the Navy waited week after week. To further hinder progress, a fierce late-winter storm swept down on March 6, pounding the Navy yard and the entire Atlantic coast with gale-force wind, torrential rain, and sleet. The storm ended, but by then the *Virginia's* construction and logistics problems became meaningless as far as the three-pronged land and sea battle plan was concerned. The storm gave General Magruder the final excuse he needed not to participate or offer any kind of support: "the roads were too muddy." The same storm that interfered with Confederate battle plans came within a hair's breadth of sinking the *Monitor* off the coast of New Jersey and totally changing history.

The *Virginia's* departure date kept being delayed, but time had run out. Buchanan's plan to leave on the evening of the 7th was foiled when the pilots informed him they could not take the ship through the Elizabeth channel in the dark because there were no buoys or lights to guide them. That night an exasperated Buchanan gave Jones the final orders. The *Virginia* would depart the next morning, no excuses accepted. Jones had already had tallow poured over the armored sides of the casement to further enhance the deflection of shot.[3]

SATURDAY, MARCH 8, 1862

Porter does not give a detailed account of where he was that fateful morning. He may have watched the action from Sewell's Point. Brooke had wanted desperately to go with the ship and be a part of the action, but Mallory was opposed because he knew that Brooke's imagination and management skills were too valuable to risk. The problem was solved a few days before departure. Word came that Lizzie's health had taken another turn for the worse. Mallory told Brooke that he had done all that was necessary for the *Virginia* and that he should be with his wife.

The workmen came on board early and quickly went to work to finish some final details, while the crew prepared for what they thought would be a shakedown cruise. There are no records that show exactly how many men were on the *Virginia* during the two days of combat. Existing records list the names of 431 men who were assigned to the ship but no accurate head count for the two days of battle. Catesby Jones complained that because of the poor ventilation and unhealthy living conditions, "there was an average of fifty or sixty [men] in the hospital in addition to the sick list on board."[4] If that is so, far fewer than 400 men actually went into combat. Engineer Ramsay said that there were about 350 men and four pilots on board when Buchanan ordered the construction workers off the ship a little after 10:30 AM. At 11 Buchanan hoisted his red pennant, the Navy yard's signal gun fired, and the mooring lines were cast off. Progress down the ten-mile river channel was slow and tedious. Word was soon out that the *Virginia* was on the move, and the riverbanks were filled with awestruck spectators. Strangely, there was no cheering. The mood was one of concerned anticipation, not jubilation. Chief Engineer Ashton Ramsay's friend, Capt. Charles MacIntosh, had bid him a final goodbye; he and many others were convinced that the *Virginia* would be the crew's tomb and that none of them would ever be seen again.

The *Virginia* crept along the river channel with considerable difficulty. She was slow to answer the helm. The *Raleigh* and *Beaufort* rode along at her flanks, nuzzling her to keep her in the channel. The *Beaufort* finally had to pass a towline and go on ahead to keep her in the center of the river.[5] The crew was under the impression that this was a shakedown cruise, so there was not the tension there would have been had they been anticipating a battle. The cooks prepared the noonday meal.

Carefully, the *Virginia* passed the obstructions at Craney Island that had been placed there the year before. They went down the south channel to Sewell's Point and into Hampton Roads, where they turned west toward Newport News.[6] It was a bright, sunny day with the temperature about 50 degrees. A light breeze from the south hardly caused a ripple on the water.[7] Strung out in order along the horizon from Newport News Point to Fortress Monroe were the *Cumberland*, *Congress*, *Minnesota*, *Roanoke*, and *St. Lawrence*. High tide would come at 1:40 PM, so the *Virginia* would have the advantage of working in

"The *Virginia* Passing the Craney Island Battery." ***The Century War Book***

deep water. Buchanan planned to start his run of destruction at the west end of the line of ships and work his way east. He also knew that the *Cumberland* might prove to be his biggest challenge because of the pivot rifle on her stern, so he would take her on first. He assembled the crew and announced that they were going into battle.

Despite the fact that it was a bright, sunny day, the gun deck was a dark and dreary place. Because the top deck was literally a sieve, the gun deck would have been soaked by the recent storm. To break the gloom, a checkered pattern of small rectangles of light would have drifted across the gun deck around noon, as sunbeams slipped between the top deck's grillwork. When that was gone, there would have been only some light filtering in through the open gun ports and the open hatch where Buchanan and the pilot stood. Other than that, the only constant illumination would have come from the lanterns gently swinging from the overhead beams. The casement walls may have been whitewashed to enhance illumination, or they may have been left their natural pine color. There is no mention of the old Navy customs of painting the area around the guns red to camouflage blood splatters and sanding the deck to prevent slipping. The guns were loaded and run out. The crew was ordered to keep totally silent; they were not even to whisper.[8] The only sounds came from the engines and an occasional order called down by Buchanan or the pilot to the helmsman. The tension mounted.

Around 2 PM the crew heard a single shot fired off to their port beam. The *Virginia* was flanked by her escorts, the *Raleigh* and the *Beaufort.* The *Beaufort,* without Buchanan's permission, had fired the first Confederate shot in the Battle of Hampton Roads. A little later, there was the distant rumble of artillery off the stern. It was the Confederate guns on Sewell's Point trying to annoy the line of Union ships, but the range was too great to have any effect.[9] The silence and gloom returned, except for the throb of the engines, as the *Virginia* approached the *Congress.* The next sound the crew heard was that of a single gun somewhere off the bow. This was followed by a new noise, a blow like a sledgehammer on the forward casement, quickly followed by the sound of a splash, as a solid shot bounced harmlessly off the casement and hit the water. That was the

Congress's first attempt to defend herself, and it had the same effect as most of the shots that would be fired at the *Virginia* over the next twenty-two hours.

At approximately 2:20 PM the crew heard what they had been hoping for: Buchanan's order to fire the forward gun, immediately followed by Lieutenant Simms's order to his gun crew, and then a roar that reverberated through the gun deck. That first shot was a canister of grape that struck the *Congress* and killed about twelve of her gun crewmen. At a few hundred yards, as the *Virginia* cruised westward past the *Congress,* there came a tremendous roar when the *Congress* let go with a full twenty-five-gun broadside.[10] The roar was followed by numerous hammer blows off the casement and splashes as shots ricocheted into the water. If there had ever been any doubt, it was now gone; the *Virginia* was virtually impregnable. The Union men and officers on ships and shore looked on in trepidation. It was obvious what was about to happen. Now at point-blank range off the *Congress's* stern, the *Virginia* returned the broadside with canister and hot shot from her starboard and forward pivot guns. Dr. Edward Shippen, the *Congress's* surgeon, described the scene on the gun deck: "One of her shells dismounted an eight-inch gun and either killed or wounded every one of the gun's crew, while the slaughter at the other guns was fearful. There were comparatively few wounded, the fragments of the huge shells she threw killing outright as a general thing. Our clean and handsome gun deck was in an instant changed into a slaughter-pen, with lopped-off legs and arms and bleeding, blackened bodies scattered about by the shells."[11]

The *Virginia's* gun crews, encased in their dark, smoke-filled iron cocoon, had no knowledge of what was actually happening on board the other ship. The gun captains on the starboard side were shouting orders to reload. There would have been some relief on board the *Congress* as the *Virginia* did not follow up on the attack but continued straight ahead toward the *Cumberland.* The *Congress's* commander, Lieutenant Smith, knew that his ship, now burning, was doomed. He ordered the tug *Zouave* to tow them into the shoals near shore so the ship could be grounded there in the seventeen-foot water and not sink.[12]

The *Virginia* continued to close on the *Cumberland.* The *Cumberland* fired with some 9-pounders and its large rifled pivot gun, while her marines blasted away with small-arms fire. The Confederate crew heard more hammer blows on the casement as they returned fire at the frigate and also at some annoying shore batteries at Camp Butler. The ships continued to exchange fire, but the efforts of the *Cumberland* were fruitless. Buchanan, standing with his head sticking out of the forward hatch, called out for the *Cumberland* to surrender. The answer came back, "Never." The men at *Virginia's* forward pivot gun watched as the distance between the *Virginia* and the *Cumberland's* starboard beam was reduced to a few yards. A warning was shouted out: "Stand fast!"

"We are going to run into her!" In the damp, dark cavern of the engine deck, Engineer Ramsay heard two bells, his signal to stop engines. Almost before the shaft could stop turning, there came three bells: "reverse engines." Two of Ramsay's men began struggling with the reversing gear that didn't want to engage. Ramsay had had advance warning of what was going to happen. Just before they left the Navy yard, Buchanan had asked him what would happen to the engines and boilers if there was a collision. Ramsay assured him that everything was properly secured and nothing would happen. Buchanan then informed him that he was going to ram the *Cumberland.*[13] The crew in the engine

"The *Virginia* **Ramming the** *Cumberland*." *The Century War Book*

room heard the splintering and crashing of timbers as the *Virginia* was shaken in every fiber. At the same instant, the *Cumberland* fired a point-blank broadside, and the *Virginia*'s bow pivot gun fired back, sending a shell crashing into the *Cumberland*'s berth deck, where it exploded. The gun recoiled, and the sponge man, Charles Dunbar, sprang to the front of the muzzle to sponge the barrel. In doing so, he leaned partway out of the gun port. At that moment, he was either shot in the head or was hit when a shell exploded near the sill of the gun port. He died instantly, the first Confederate casualty.[14]

The ship came to an abrupt, shuddering stop, and according to Ramsay, everyone standing in the engine room was almost thrown to the deck. There is a discrepancy in testimony here. Catesby Jones said that there was a noise of crashing timbers but that the blow was "slight"; Lt. Taylor Wood described it as "hardly perceivable."[15] Physics 101 tells us that there is an opposite reaction to every action. When a mass of iron and timber weighing 3,200 tons comes to a sudden grinding stop, inertia sets in, and anything that is not tied down moves. Ramsay's recollection of the event seems more logical. With the *Virginia* motionless, and its beak and several feet of its prow stuck into the side of the *Cumberland,* the *Cumberland*'s crew blasted away with every gun they could bring to bear. Ramsay suddenly thought one of the boilers had exploded but was relieved to discover that it was the roar of a shell detonating inside the funnel. The reversing gear was finally engaged, and the propeller began turning, but nothing was happening. The *Virginia*'s crew heard the din of shot bouncing off the casement and the tearing of metal as the funnel was pulverized. They exchanged anxious glances as the deck slowly began to tilt forward.[16] The *Cumberland* was sinking as water poured into the gaping hole in her side, and as she settled, it appeared that she was taking the *Virginia* along for the ride to Davy Jones's locker. While the two ships were locked in a deadly embrace, they pounded one another with every gun that could be brought into play.

The propeller churned the waters as it strained to pull the *Virginia* free. The current began to turn the ship, and her starboard side moved toward that of the *Cumberland*. Slowly, she began pulling away, and the bow rose to its original position. Here again, we have another instance when a dozen things can be speculated but nothing proven. The consensus is that the *Virginia*'s ram broke off as she pulled away from the *Cumberland*. The problem is that there were no witnesses. No one on board the *Virginia* could see anything other than the forward-most point of the breakwater, which was some five feet above the ram. There were no surviving witnesses from the *Cumberland*'s berth deck where the ram and shell had gone through. The ram may have broken off inside the *Cumberland,* it may have broken off as the *Virginia* pulled away, or it could have broken free at any time after it rammed the *Cumberland* and before the *Virginia* tied up that night off Sewell's Point. With the two ships practically touching, the broadside bombardments continued until the tallow that Jones had poured over the casement sides began to sizzle and burn.

Buchanan's demand that the *Cumberland* surrender was refused. He now backed away about a hundred yards and positioned his ship parallel to the wounded *Cumberland* and continued pounding away with his starboard and bow guns. Both the *Cumberland* and the *Congress* and numerous shore batteries had the *Virginia* in range. Shells, solid shot, and rifle bullets rained down on the ironclad. A shot cut one of the anchor chains.[17] When the

"On the Gun Deck of the *Merrimac*." Northern artists preparing illustrations for publication didn't have the time or inclination to do a lot of research; consequently, mistakes were common. The gun ports shown here are incorrect, and these Rebel artillerymen are all wearing Yankee sailor uniforms. *The Century War Book*

anchor fell away, the free end of the chain whipped back through the hawse pipe and injured several more men near the forward pivot gun. The deck railings and awning stanchions were swept away, along with the small top-deck howitzers, like the one shown in Johnston's sketch.[18] The starboard cutter was converted into kindling, and more and more holes were put in the funnel, which was damaged to the point where it would hardly draw, and the ship filled with sulfurous coal smoke. The coal, gun, and grease smoke was so thick on the gun deck that the crews could hardly see or breathe.

Realizing that they were wasting shot and powder by simply firing in the general direction of the *Virginia*, the gun crews on the sinking *Cumberland* and grounded *Congress* began aiming for the gun ports. One of the aft 9-inch Dahlgrens had part of its muzzle shot away. A hotshot gun was hit and had its muzzle broken off almost back to the trunnions. Gunner Louis Waldeck was killed, and several others were wounded in that explosion. The good thing about smooth-bore muzzle-loading cannons is that they can still fire with part of the muzzle missing, so the *Virginia*'s guns continued to be fired. This did present a new problem, though—every time the guns discharged, they set the inside of the gun ports on fire.[19]

The flagstaff was shot away, and the colors fell to the deck. Flags in the Civil War had a strange effect on men's minds—they were badges of honor that became more important than life itself. On a battlefield where men charged the enemy in rolling waves of humanity, the flag was at the center of the line. The flag bearer was the target of choice, so bearer after bearer would crumple to the ground, and without hesitation, another man would grab the colors before they touched the ground, knowing full well that he, too, had probably just taken his last breath. On shipboard, if the colors were struck, it was the signal that the ship had surrendered, but no one in Hampton Roads that day would have thought that the *Virginia* was surrendering just because her flagstaff was shot away. Apparently Lt. John Randolph Eggleston took the fact the flag was down as a personal affront and decided to do something about it. He went onto the top deck in the heat of battle, and while more than a thousand people tried desperately to kill him with rifle fire, cannonballs, and shells, he picked up the flag and lanyard. He managed to secure the lanyard to some of the numerous holes in the funnel, and the flag flew from the battered funnel for the remainder of the day. Confederate veteran Eggleston died in bed in 1915.[20]

The cannon fire from the *Cumberland* slackened as more and more of her men and guns were swept away by the *Virginia*'s shells. At about 3:35 PM the order to abandon ship was given. As her gun deck slipped beneath the water, one last broadside boomed out. When the smoke cleared, the *Cumberland*'s main mast and top yard formed a crude cross above the watery grave of 121 men. In all of naval history, no ship had ever taken a pounding like the *Virginia* and survived. Not only had she survived but she was also about to cause more carnage as Buchanan turned his attention to the *Congress*. But before he could attack the *Congress*, which was now off his stern, he would have to get to her. With a steering system that was as stubborn as a mule and engines and boilers that were wheezing and gasping for air, the *Virginia* began the laborious task of turning from west to east.

The James River Squadron had come down and sailed past the Newport News Point batteries at about 3:30. The *Patrick Henry* temporarily stopped to repair her steam drum that had been hit. The crew of the *Congress*, thinking the *Virginia* was retreating, gave a cheer when they saw her going west toward the James River to make the slow left turn. Lieutenant Wood and his gun crew had been frustrated all day. The *Virginia* had never been in a position where they could fire at the *Cumberland* or *Congress*, but that was about to change. After the tug *Zouave* had taken the *Congress* to shallow water, the *Congress* grounded with her bow toward Newport News. As the *Virginia* crept west past her, Wood got his chance. Three shells went crashing into the frigate's stern, damaging two guns and wounding or killing a number of cooks and boys, who were passing powder from the aft magazine.[21]

The James River Squadron passed the *Virginia* as she continued her half-hour-long turn to get into position to attack. A little after 3:45, the *Virginia* was some two hundred yards off the grounded *Congress*'s stern, and the carnage began in earnest. The other ships were already in position and were blasting away. In short order, *Congress*'s stern was demolished, and wreckage and bodies covered the deck. Henry Reaney, on the tug *Zouave*, reported that blood poured from the *Congress*'s scuppers and onto his deck like water. The tug also fell victim, taking several shots, but cut the towline and managed to limp far enough away to be ignored. The *Congress* fought back as best she could, but about the only injury she did was to put one of the *Raleigh*'s howitzers out of commission. By 4:20 most of her guns were out of action, and a quarter of the crew was dead. Lt. Austin Pendergrast, one of the few officers left standing, knew the situation was hopeless, so he ordered the *Congress*'s surrender.[22] At the sight of the white flag, Buchanan immediately ordered the *Raleigh* and *Beaufort* to go alongside, pick up the officers and wounded, allow the able to make their way to shore, and then set the ship on fire. With the *Raleigh* on one side and the *Beaufort* on the other, the Confederates started to remove some sixty wounded men from the ship.

Watching from shore, Brig. Gen. Joseph Mansfield did the unimaginable. Ignoring the white flag, he ordered the men of the 20th Indiana and 1st New York to open fire on the Confederates evacuating the wounded Union sailors. When questioned about firing on the white flag, he snapped back: "The damned ship has surrendered, but I haven't."[23] The shots from shore leveled ten men on the *Beaufort*'s deck. Lt. William Parker, in command, ordered the *Beaufort* away with only about thirty wounded men on board. Sheltered on the far side the frigate, the *Raleigh* pulled away without incident. Not realizing that the Union troops were firing on the flag of truce, Buchanan was furious with Parker because his orders to set the ship on fire had not been carried out. Parker was already in Buchanan's doghouse for having fired the first shot of the battle without permission. Lieutenant Minor volunteered to take the *Virginia*'s surviving port cutter over to the *Congress* and set the fires. Before they could reach her, his boat was raked with rifle fire, and he and two of the oarsmen were wounded. The *Teaser* came to their rescue, picking up the men and the boat. Buchanan then realized what was happening and went into a rage. The *Virginia* was pulled in as close as possible, and hotshot and shells were poured into the *Congress* as fast as the crews could load and fire. Any wounded men left on board were doomed. Buchanan stormed around on the *Virginia*'s top deck with rifle in hand, popping away at the troops on shore. The Union troops were not about to ignore that target of opportunity, and in short order, Buchanan went down with a bullet in his thigh that narrowly missed his femoral artery. He was carried below, and Catesby Jones assumed command.[24]

Soon after 5 PM the *Congress* was burning from stem to stern, and Jones wanted to go stalking his next victim, the *Minnesota*. Earlier in the day, the *Minnesota* had attempted to go to the aid of the *Cumberland* and *Congress* but managed to ground herself instead. Despite all of the efforts of the tugs, she had not budged. With the tide going out, she was now stuck fast and helpless. As Jones approached, he managed to get some long-range hits on his victim, but nature interceded. The ebbing tide that was holding the *Minnesota* would also keep the *Virginia* at bay. With the light fading and the tide going out, the pilots warned Jones that if he didn't hold to the center of the channel he would soon be in the same fix as the *Minnesota*. The other ships of the James River Squadron had been pounding

"The *Congress* Burning."
The Century War Book

the Union fleet that day as well. Jones surveyed the havoc and decided to call it a day. Besides, the *Minnesota* and the other wooden targets would still be there in the morning.

A little after 8 PM a battered and bruised *Virginia* dropped her remaining anchor under the guns at Sewell's Point. The crew began cleaning up the gun deck and making things shipshape. The magazines were secured, and the cooks set about preparing a late supper.[25] With the adrenaline rush over, many of the men who had been in action since eleven o'clock that morning simply lay down by their guns and slept. Jones conducted a cursory battle damage examination by lantern light while Chief Surgeon Dinwiddie Phillips tended to the wounded. Lieutenant Wood wrote that twenty-one men had been wounded and two killed, Charles Dunbar and Louis Waldeck. Buchanan and Lieutenant Minor were the most seriously wounded, but they both wanted to stay on board. Only eight other men had been wounded seriously enough to be listed in Phillips's medical report. They were taken ashore at Sewell's Point. Phillips and Jones finally persuaded Buchanan and Minor that they could contribute nothing to the coming battle and should be taken to the naval hospital. In the early hours of the morning, Phillips had the two lowered down the sloping casement sides and put in a boat. He accompanied them as far as Sewell's Point,[26] from where it was only a short trip to the Navy hospital grounds on the Elizabeth River.

Before going back on board, Surgeon Phillips did a more extensive survey of the ship's damage. He counted ninety-eight indentations in the armor plate, and the funnel was so riddled that, as he put it, "a flock of crows could fly through without inconvenience." The ship's railings and awning stanchions were twisted and broken, the flagstaffs had been shot away, one launch was blown to pieces and the other left with the *Teaser,* the deck howitzers were gone, and two Dahlgren guns had their muzzles blown off. Because of the darkness, neither Phillips nor Jones could see the condition of the ram or even know if it was still there though Jones thought it might have been twisted but still attached. A small leak in the bow was considered insignificant.[27] No one came down from the Navy yard to survey the damage or assist. The only thing of any real importance was the perforated funnel. Its condition had caused the boilers considerable trouble and almost suffocated the crew, but if any cursory attempt was made to patch the holes, it was never mentioned. For the required work to be effective, men and materials would have to be brought from shore. To provide the Union fleet with a new target for the next day, a temporary flagstaff of some sort was jury-rigged. We know that the old *Merrimack* engines required 2,880 pounds of coal per hour, and they had been running for twelve hours or more. Of the 150 tons she had started with, at that rate of consumption she would still have had in excess of 134 tons of coal on board. We don't know how much powder and shot was expended, but it, in combination with the coal, wasn't enough to have any appreciable effect on the overall weight of the ship. The vulnerable knuckle was still underwater. The *Virginia* was not in her prime but still dangerous and in good fighting condition.

The James River Squadron had some minor damage, and a few men from the *Beaufort* had been wounded, but the damage done to the Confederates was insignificant compared with that inflicted on the Union. It would be seventy-nine years in faraway Hawaii before the U.S. Navy would again suffer such losses. Two transports were destroyed, a schooner captured, a steam frigate damaged, a tug damaged, and shore installations shot up. The *Congress* was gone, and of the 434 men on board that day, 110 were dead or missing. Of the twenty-six wounded that were rescued, only sixteen survived. The *Cumberland's* losses, as best as could be determined, were nearly 120 men killed, over 30 wounded, and 23 taken prisoner by the *Beaufort* during the aborted rescue attempt. Though he would never admit it, Union General Mansfield's order to fire on the Confederate rescue boats was partly responsible for those losses. The grounded *Minnesota* and *St. Lawrence* struggled for their freedom, while their crews anticipated the next day's events, when they would probably meet the same fate as the crews of *Congress* and *Cumberland.*[28]

As Franklin Buchanan lay in the Naval Hospital that night, his thoughts would have been not only about the day's battle but also about the whereabouts and condition of his brother, McKean Buchanan. McKean was the paymaster on board *Congress.* Franklin later learned that McKean lived to fight another day.

On the *Virginia* some men, too wrought with emotion and exhaustion to sleep, stood on deck and watched the burning *Congress,* which would soon explode and shower Hampton Roads with fiery debris. At about 11 PM by the glow of the burning ship and a second-quarter moon, a pilot saw something strange that he brought to the attention of Lieutenant Jones. Jones later wrote, "looking in the direction of the *Congress* when there passed a strange looking craft, brought out in bold relief by the burning ship, which he [the pilot] at once proclaimed to be the Ericsson."[29]

"The *Monitor* Arrives at Hampton Roads." *The Century War Book*

SUNDAY, MARCH 9, 1862

Before dawn, the *Virginia*'s weary crew was awakened by the boatswain's pipe. The cooks were already up and had prepared a hearty breakfast that included two shots of whiskey per man.[30] There would have been very little trepidation among the crew that morning. As far as they were concerned, they were going out to continue the carnage they had dealt the day before. The most powerful gun they had faced had been the rifle on the stern of the *Cumberland,* and it was now on the bottom of Hampton Roads. The gun crews had learned to stay as far clear of the open gun ports as possible. By doing that, the odds of avoiding injury or death were excellent. There is no mention of Jones or the pilot discussing the supposed arrival of the *Monitor* with anyone.

Ramsay had the steam up, and Jones gave the order to weigh anchor. The *Virginia* moved off into a light early-morning fog, accompanied by her entourage: *Patrick Henry, Jamestown,* and *Teaser.* The *Raleigh* had limped back up the Elizabeth for repairs. In addition to the official participants, the waters were filled with civilian boats out to enjoy the coming Confederate victory. The banks were again lined with soldiers and civilians. Unlike the previous day, everyone was now in a holiday mood. A warm morning sun burned off the fog, the sky was clear and blue, and everyone watched with great anticipation.

About 140 miles north the city of Washington was also waking up to a beautiful spring morning. Despite encouraging news coming in from the war front, a somber mood hung over the White House. On February 24 Abraham and Mary Todd Lincoln had buried their twelve-year-old son, Willie. The president was inconsolable and carried the grief to his grave.[31] The telegraph line linking Fort Monroe and Washington had not been completed, so official Washington had no knowledge of the events that had taken place in Hampton Roads. At 9:30 AM the passenger steamer *Adelaide,* which had left Point Comfort Saturday evening, docked in Baltimore. A messenger, sent from Fort Monroe by General Wool, dashed to the Baltimore telegraph office with a message for Secretary Stanton. In a few minutes, the telegraph operator David Bates, on Sunday duty at the Washington War Department telegraph room, received the message that shook him and would shatter the calm in Washington and throughout the North.[32] A runner was sent to Stanton's residence. A little before ten o'clock, a pale and trembling Stanton burst into the White House with the telegraph message in hand. Lincoln read about the carnage the CSS *Virginia* had inflicted on the Union Navy and about the terrible things that could be anticipated. Messengers were dispatched to assemble the cabinet members.

Lincoln wanted to talk to someone who could provide concrete information, not speculation, so he went to the Navy yard to confer with Captain Dahlgren. Back at the White House, Stanton tried to panic the arriving cabinet members with a "Chicken Little" performance. He pranced about the room, going from window to window so he could see the *Virginia* when it opened fire on the Capitol and announced to one and all that at any minute a cannonball would come crashing into the room. Lincoln soon returned to the White House, accompanied by Dahlgren. There he found Secretary of State Seward, Treasury Secretary Chase, Assistant Secretary of War Peter Watson, Secretary of the Navy Welles, General McClellan, and Gen. Montgomery Meigs. Dahlgren explained to the group that the *Virginia*'s draft was too great to ascend the Potomac all the way to Washington, and even if that wasn't sufficient, ships and barges could be sunk in the channel to further block the way. Welles and McClellan objected to this suggestion because the river was to be the path the Navy would use to transport the Army of the Potomac south to launch the Peninsular Campaign.[33] It was further explained that the best intelligence stipulated that the *Virginia* was not seaworthy and would never go beyond Hampton Roads. Even this information couldn't calm Stanton. He sent telegrams to the governors and mayors of the East Coast states and cities to warn them of the *Virginia*'s impending approach. This nonsensical hysteria would continue in one form or another throughout the day. No one knew, or could imagine, what was happening in the real world at Hampton Roads.[34]

The *Virginia* steamed north across Hampton Roads toward the *Minnesota* with the intention to make quick work of her and then taking on the next available target. Jones and the pilot soon spotted a strange little craft that sat along the side of the *Minnesota*. It had a deck that hardly cleared the water and a single large canister perched in its center. It looked harmless, so Jones kept to the original plan. At approximately a one-mile distance, the *Virginia* and *Minnesota* opened fire on one another, almost simultaneously. The *Virginia*'s shell crashed into the side of the *Minnesota*. The strange little vessel came to life and steered straight at the *Virginia*. As the range closed, a single shot fired by the little intruder crashed into the *Virginia* near the waterline. Annoyed by this audacity, the *Virginia* responded with a full broadside intended to blow the antagonist into a thousand pieces. The exploding shells rattled the turret and deck plates and shrapnel splashed harmlessly into the water. As the *Virginia* passed, the *Monitor*'s turret turned to track her, and another shot boomed out. At that moment, naval history was changed forever. The *Virginia*, with her broadside guns, was suddenly as obsolete as the wooden ships she had pounded the previous day. She still had her armor, but to fight, she, and not her guns, had to be "aimed." It would be the descendants of Ericsson's revolving armored turret that would dominate the oceans of the world.

It was now a little after 8 AM, and a battle had begun that would last until shortly after noon. This four-hour fight would be like a heavyweight championship boxing match between two equally matched fighters. The fight would end in a draw, and the supporters on each side would forever claim victory. These two combatants circled and jabbed. Throughout the morning, heavy blows were landed, but little damage was done. Frustrated by the futility of firing at one another, the two captains tried ramming. That, too, failed. The ships only scraped one another's sides, though the *Monitor* did do some minor damage to the *Virginia*'s fantail. One solid blow against the *Virginia*'s stern would have crippled the already inept steering system, but because it was submerged, her most vulnerable point was concealed. The ramming attempts by the poorly maneuverable *Virginia* grounded her for the second time in two days. Ramsey's engines would once again have to struggle and strain to break her free. Everything that would burn fiercely was thrown on the fires. The gauges on the boilers were well into the red danger zone when she finally broke free. A lucky punch from the *Virginia* blinded the *Monitor* temporarily—a shell exploded on the forward viewing slot in the *Monitor*'s pilothouse. Her captain, Lt. John Worden, was blinded by the blast, and Lt. Samuel Green took over. Both the *Virginia* and the *Monitor* would end the fight with their executive officers in command.

Approximately half an hour passed between the time Worden was wounded and Green took over and when the *Monitor* headed back toward the battle site. During that time, Jones turned his attention back to the destruction of the *Minnesota*. Once again, he was going to be foiled by nature. The tide was ebbing, and the pilots told him that if he went within a mile of the *Minnesota*, he would probably be grounded again. Both ships were now running low on ammunition, and the *Virginia*'s gun crews were exhausted. Having accomplished nothing, a frustrated Catesby Jones decided it was time to retire and head for Sewell's Point. Wood suggested that they go to Fort Monroe and blast the frigates anchored there. Jones rejected that idea because of the tide and the dwindling ammunition supply. When Worden was wounded and the *Monitor* backed off, Jones thought she was quitting. Before Green could continue the fight, Jones steamed away, and Green thought Jones had retreated.[35] The fight itself was a draw, but the assignments given to each vessel had been accomplished. The *Monitor* was supposed to defend the *Minnesota* and any other vessels the *Virginia* might attack. She had done that. The *Virginia*'s assignment was to block Union access to the James River. That had also been accomplished. For all practical purposes, the military situation at Hampton Roads on Sunday afternoon was a temporary stalemate. The Union Army couldn't advance up the peninsula, and the Confederates couldn't put to sea.

Two primary factors led to the final outcome of that day's battle. The Confederates went out to destroy wooden ships. To do this, they would need explosive shells, which they had, but they were virtually useless against the *Monitor*. The only solid shot on board were the cannonballs for the hotshot guns, and they were also useless in this situation. After the battle, John Brooke immediately set to work to have armor-piercing bolts made for his rifles. The other factor was that Union gunners were handicapped by misinformation. The Navy regulations called for powder charges of fifteen pounds to be used in the 11-inch Dahlgren guns. Unbeknownst to them, Captain Dahlgren had conducted experiments at the Washington Navy Yard, successfully using thirty-pound charges. They could have safely double-charged their guns and doubled their destructive power. If either side had been using the proper ordnance procedures, the outcome could have been quite different.

The *Monitor* had taken twenty-three hits. The most serious was the one to the pilot-house, the only telling shot that landed all day. Two of the dents on her turret were from friendly fire, when the *Minnesota* was trying to hit the *Virginia*. The *Virginia* had some twenty new dents from the forty-one shots the *Monitor* fired at her. When the *Monitor's* shots hit the *Virginia*, they ricocheted upward and cleaned off anything remaining on the top deck. The stanchions and railings were completely gone, there were numerous cracked plates, and the funnel was a mass of twisted metal. There is no mention of any ship's boats—the *Virginia's* boat that was picked up by the *Teaser* may or may not have been taken back on board. The only serious battle casualty on Sunday was Union Lieutenant Worden. In time, he recovered his sight, but his face was permanently scarred. There were walking wounded on both sides, primarily concussion victims who were standing too close to, or leaning against, the armored walls when shots struck.[36]

As the *Virginia* began her return trip to Portsmouth for repairs, the banks of the Elizabeth River were filled with cheering crowds. Shore batteries boomed out salutes. Small boats, filled with more cheering and shouting admirers, followed in her wake. Crew members stood on the top deck waving back to the cheering throngs. As one sailor said: "No conqueror of Rome ever enjoyed a prouder triumph than that that greeted us." It was a triumphal return that no one there would ever forget.[37] For days after the battle, a delighted public would pore over exuberant newspaper accounts of the *Virginia's* two days of glory.

On the north shore of Hampton Roads, other spectators had watched breathlessly as the fight progressed. The *Monitor* looked so small beside the Goliath that had inflicted such pain the day before. As the smoke of battle began to clear, the anxious audience saw the *Virginia* heading for home, and the little *Monitor* standing undamaged and firing one last shot toward the departing *Virginia*. Another chorus of cheers filled the Sabbath air, and Union guns boomed out salutes. The telegraph link connecting Fort Monroe and Washington was completed at 4 PM Sunday afternoon. A jubilant Assistant Secretary of the Navy Gustavus Fox sent a message to Secretary Welles: The battle had lasted all morning; the *Merrimack* retired; the *Monitor* was undamaged and ready for another fight. Official Washington gave a collective sigh of relief. As soon as possible, the public that Stanton had successfully terrified was told to relax. New York and Boston would not be destroyed that night.

When the *Virginia* docked, Lieutenant Wood, accompanied by Captain Forrest, went immediately to the naval hospital to tell Buchanan and Lieutenant Minor about the day's events. After hearing the glorious tale, Buchanan dictated a brief report to Wood and instructed him to deliver it immediately to Secretary Mallory. Wood went to the Norfolk & Petersburg Rail Road station in Norfolk and took the next train out to Petersburg, where he found connections to go on to Richmond. Wood said that, all along the way, people wanted to be told about the battle. At the president's residence, where he arrived on Sunday evening, he retold the story again in detail to the president, Mallory, Attorney General Judah Benjamin, and some other guests who were there visiting Davis. He had also brought the flag that had been captured in the battle with the *Congress*. He unfurled it on the floor, where it was discovered to be bloodstained. The flag was quickly refolded and later taken to the Navy Department office, never to be seen again.[38]

On Monday, March 10, the repair work began on the *Virginia*. This would prove to be another exercise in frustration. Tempers would flare, and the euphoria of the 8th and

9th would begin to fade. For the protection of the James and Elizabeth rivers, the *Virginia* had to be back in fighting trim as soon as possible. It was hoped that if given a second chance, she could sink the *Monitor*. The repair work was not highly technical, and both the military and the politicians were clamoring to complete it as fast as possible.

Many of the people closely associated with the *Virginia* were of the opinion that it was the naval vessel of the future. Mallory was expecting inquiries from foreign navies about the structural details of the ship. If foreign governments wanted design information, there was a possibility of selling plans, but no foreign government ever inquired. There was nothing new or secret about the design and engineering of the *Virginia;* the foreign press had already carried the descriptions of its design. Brooke's patent was probably more of an ego boost than a real attempt to protect a concept of value. In reality, all that was there was a wood and iron fortification sitting on the hulk of a burned-out sailing ship. But John Porter was locked into the *Virginia* concept. For the remainder of the war, he would continue to build copies of the *Virginia* which in essence were nothing more than a slight modification of his 1846 floating battery. He didn't realize that a ship that depended on broadside guns was as obsolete as the wooden ships the *Virginia* had destroyed on March 8. If he had ever had an opportunity to see the *Monitor* in action, he might have found a way to improve on his design, but as it was, he remained in the same rut.

While the navies of the world were ignoring the *Virginia,* they were pestering the Union Navy Department and Ericsson for drawings and detailed information about the *Monitor.* What they wanted most were facts about the gun turret. All requests were denied, and naval architects and engineers around the world went to work to figure it out for themselves. Of Ericsson's forty patented features on the *Monitor,* it was the gun turret design that caused a naval revolution. In a few years gun turrets would be on the deck of every major fighting ship in the world.

Chapter Thirteen

Ironclad Down

The Confederate press and public may have been impressed with the mighty *Virginia,* but all was not sweetness and light back at the Navy yard. John Brooke had never been an admirer of John Porter. He criticized practically everything Porter did in the design and conversion of the *Merrimack* and was forever telling Mallory about poor design decisions and what he thought should be done to correct them. While working with Catesby Jones, he constantly expressed his dissatisfaction with the constructor. After Jones had been on board the *Virginia* for a few days, he shared Brooke's opinions. When John Taylor Wood joined the *Virginia's* crew in November, Brooke and Jones gave him an earful about the *Virginia's* shortcomings, and as soon as Buchanan came on board, he joined the chorus, all quick to express their opinions to anyone who would listen. It was only a few days after the battle that the war of words between Brooke and Porter appeared in the press. At a critical time when cooperation was essential, the principals responsible for getting the *Virginia* back into action were squabbling. People in Richmond and at the Navy yard began choosing sides. At this critical juncture, internal bickering was the last thing the Confederate Navy needed.

On Monday, March 10, everyone in military and civilian life were asking the same question: When would the *Virginia* go back into Hampton Roads and destroy the *Monitor*? On Saturday the 8th, when Mallory had heard that the battle was under way, he had immediately sent orders to Tredegar to start producing armor plates to replace any that might be damaged. Brooke soon went to work supervising the production of armor-piercing bolts for his rifles, and the search was on for much-needed powder. Porter examined the ship and reported that, other than the destroyed funnel and some steam pipes, the structural damage was minor. While a new funnel and pipes were being installed, damaged armor plates were being replaced. According to Porter, "I found 8 to 10 plates broken in the shield by the shots from the Monitor, but none had been entirely knocked off. I soon replaced these without much difficulty."

The strange contradictory information about the ram came up again. Porter wrote, "After the engagement in the Roads, I made a new ram of wrought iron entirely having got the material from Tredegar Works for that purpose. The bow with the addition of the new ram was 14 feet longer. I also placed a steel tip on the end that was forged under the steam hammer at the Gosport Yard. It was fitted very snugly to prevent it from breaking off." After explaining exactly what he had done, Porter continued with why he shouldn't have: "I am of the opinion that projections of any kind beyond a ships bow will not stand as a ram, but that the bow should be used as a ram."[1] Porter was the constructor in charge. If he didn't think it would work, why did he do it? A few paragraphs later, Porter continued: "I put a new piece into the stem, and put on a bolted ram of wrought iron and steel extending back about 14 feet from the bow."

This ram sounds like that odd device E. R. Archer sketched in 1906, but this picture of the *Virginia's* ram as a swordfish beak was modified by Brooke: "The original cast-iron ram had been too long and was replaced by one of steel and wrought iron *two feet in length*. The new ram was made square rather than pointed at Brooke's suggestion."[2] The logical conclusion here is that an absurdly long lance was made at Tredegar and sent to Portsmouth. There it was cut down and modified to a reasonable size. The most interesting question is who had designed it in the first place. I have seen one account that credits Brooke with the design, but that is highly unlikely.[3]

While repair work was under way, the hull was being reinforced at and below the knuckle; the layer of one-inch iron going partway down on the hull was considered insufficient. This new modification required Tredegar to manufacture 440 armor plates 8¾ inches wide by 48 inches long by 2 inches thick. The plates had to be drilled to take copper or composition bolts in specific places and then crimped at the top to conform to the shape of the knuckle and hull and to descend 42 inches below the knuckle. Holes were drilled in the hull, and then the plates were bolted on.[4] There is no record to show if the plates were bent and drilled at Tredegar or at the Navy yard. When the work was finished, the plates would cover 160 feet on both sides of the ship. The old problem of having the plates rolled at Tredegar shipped to Portsmouth recurred.

The press, the public, and government officials were demanding to know from Mallory when the *Virginia* would be back in action. He also had a new personnel problem. There were complaints based on the general understanding that the Confederacy would be in a much better position if the *Virginia* had gone into combat earlier. Jones, Wood, and the others most closely associated with the project blamed all problems, past and present, on John Porter. They expressed dismay over the poor quality of the improvements to the armor reinforcement that they claimed were inadequately completed. Paymaster James Semple told Flag Officer Minor that "the project was plagued by John Porter's poor workmanship."[5] If Porter was the cause, then Mallory had a big problem because Porter was his only certified naval constructor.

Porter himself had more concerns than the *Virginia*. Mallory was pushing him hard to design and supervise the construction of more and more ironclads. He was responsible for the construction of the gunboats *Nansemond* and *Elizabeth* in Portsmouth and the steamer *Richmond* that was being completed in Richmond at the Rocketts yard. He was also supervising the draftsmen who had other ships on the drawing board.[6] If Porter was actually the problem, Mallory couldn't do anything about it. He couldn't replace him, he had no practical advice to give him, and he knew that criticizing Porter would only make a bad situation worse. The political pressure was growing on Mallory daily. He was in desperate need of a sacrificial lamb, and on March 20, a victim presented himself. Mallory sent a frantic message to Commandant French Forrest to ask if the *Virginia* was ready for sea and "if not, when would she be?" Apparently Forrest couldn't find anyone at the yard who knew the answer. Instead of blowing smoke, he simply told Mallory the truth: He didn't have a clue.[7] Mallory's problem was solved: "This man was not providing proper leadership. He was obviously the source of the problems and would have to go." On March 24 Mallory appointed Capt. Sidney Smith Lee, Robert E. Lee's brother, to the vacant post. Lee, an Army man, was certainly no better qualified to run a Navy yard than Forrest, but for the moment that didn't matter because, for a while, the pressure would be off. Mallory's orders to Lee were quite simple: have the *Virginia* ready to move at a moment's notice. Lee started scrambling to find the needed materials and advertised for carpenters and mechanics.

Buchanan was still recovering from his wound and in no condition to return to command. In appreciation for his service, he was promoted to admiral. The consensus was that Catesby Jones should take his place, but once again Jones was denied. On March 21 Mallory appointed sixty-seven-year-old Josiah Tattnall as commander of all naval forces in Virginia. Tattnall first saw action in 1812 and had served in the Algerian and Mexican wars. Stationed in China, he had been in command of the East India Squadron. After resigning his Union commission in 1861, he was placed in command of the Confederate Savannah Squadron until called to take over in Virginia.[8] The only thing he wanted was action and, like Buchanan, getting the *Virginia* ready to go to Hampton Roads and sink the *Monitor*.

The *Virginia* was finally pulled out of dry dock on April 4, but some of the repair work was still unfinished. The new armor was in place, and damaged guns had been replaced. There was a new anchor, and the port shutters and ram were attached. The deck fittings, railings, stanchions, boats, and boat chocks were being in place. There was a new funnel that would help the furnaces breathe, but Ramsay reported that the engines were undependable and, because of the ship's increased weight, the best they could hope for was about four knots. Lieutenant Wood noted that a hundred tons of ballast on the stern had improved the draft, but nothing was done to further protect the propeller and rudder. For six days after the *Virginia* was out of dry dock, Lee had carpenters and mechanics swarming all over her. The work would be completed.[9] Bad weather further hindered Tattnall's plans, but at 6 AM on April 10 the *Virginia* and her entourage steamed down the Elizabeth River channel for the second time. She was going hunting for the *Monitor*, to either blow her out of the water or board and capture her.

Since March 9 the *Monitor* had seen some changes, too. The pilothouse had been reinforced and had come to resemble a pyramid with the top lopped off. Commanding officers had been coming and going. Like Catesby Jones, the *Monitor's* executive officer, Samuel Green, an ambitious twenty-two-year-old, was denied command. On March 10 Fox appointed Lieutenant Selfridge of the *Cumberland* to take charge, and on the 12th Selfridge was replaced by a twenty-two-year veteran, Lt. William N. Jeffers.[10] Lincoln had personally given the orders for the disposition of the *Monitor*. She was to protect the Union ships and facilities at Hampton Roads against the *Virginia* and prevent the *Virginia* from going to sea, but in no way was her safety to be compromised. She was too valuable to go far into harm's way until the new fleet of Ericsson *Monitor*-class ships being built was ready.

The Union Navy had been watching the reports on the *Virginia's* repair work in the southern press and knew approximately when to expect her. When the *Virginia* steamed out into Hampton Roads, the *Monitor* steamed toward her. Then a game of cat and mouse began that would drag on for weeks. The *Virginia* tried to entice the *Monitor* into the deep water in the center of the Roads, where the *Virginia* could maneuver. The *Monitor* wanted the *Virginia* near the shore, where she would ground and could be pounded at will. The two steamed back and forth but not across the imaginary line the captains had drawn. Tattnall was not going to run his ship aground in pursuit of the *Monitor,* and the *Monitor* was not going to fight on his terms. Meanwhile, the *Jamestown* captured two brigs and a schooner from under the nose of the *Monitor.* At 4 PM, April 11, Tattnall gave up in disgust. Flying the flags from the captured Union vessels upside down under his own, he steamed away and took up station off Craney Island for the night.[11]

Franklin Buchanan and Josiah Tattnall after the war. *The Century War Book*

A plan proposed to capture the *Monitor* proved to be another hopeless venture. For some unexplained reason, on April 8 the Norfolk *Day Book* told everyone, including the Union Navy, that: while the *Virginia* and the *Monitor* were engaged, two tugboats would sneak up and position themselves on either side of the *Monitor.* Boarding parties would cover the pilothouse with sailcloth, throw flaming tar balls and chloroform-soaked rags down the ventilators, and drive wedges between the deck and turret, and then the prize would be towed to Norfolk. Because of the chloroform, the *Monitor*'s crew was supposed to be asleep while all this was going on. The boats and boarding crews had gone out with the *Virginia* that morning, but needless to say, they never got within a mile of the *Monitor,* and if they had, they would have been blown to bits.[12]

Meanwhile, the press and public in the North were also indignant about the situation in Hampton Roads. After all the talk about the vast superiority of the *Monitor,* they could not understand why she just didn't go sink the *Virginia.* Why was she cowering under the guns of Fort Monroe?[13] By contrast, Commo. Louis Goldsborough, in command of the North Atlantic Blockading Squadron and therefore responsible for the *Monitor,* had begun taking Lincoln's concern about the *Monitor* to extremes. His orders to Jeffers were quite specific: do not attack the *Virginia* under any circumstance unless she tries to go past Fort Monroe and into Chesapeake Bay.[14]

The situation in Hampton Roads was static, but the conditions on the ground were beginning to change. On April 5 Gen. George McClellan landed the 105,000-man Army of the Potomac at Fort Monroe and began moving northwest toward Richmond. Confederate general Magruder, with 10,000 men, would try to block his path at a narrow point on the Virginia peninsula between the James River on the south and Yorktown on the north. The Union Navy was in command of Chesapeake Bay and the York River and would support McClellan's right flank halfway up the peninsula toward Richmond.[15] Even before the *Virginia* was out of dry dock, Gen. Robert E. Lee had asked Mallory if she could be sent to attack the Union transports and gunboats stationed at the mouth of the York River adjacent to Yorktown, and Mallory had forwarded the message to Tattnall. They both understood the urgency of the request but were concerned about the possible final outcome: that the *Virginia* might have engine trouble far from any assistance or could be blocked from returning to Hampton Roads or be sunk.[16]

Since the first engagement with the *Monitor,* some new, dangerous antagonists had entered the scene: the ironclads USS *Galena,* USS *Naugatuck,* and the iron-hulled ocean liner USS *Vanderbilt.* The *Vanderbilt* had been donated by her owner, Cornelius Vanderbilt, specifically to destroy the *Virginia.* This 1,700-ton side-wheeler, with a speed of approximately fifteen knots, had a reinforced prow especially designed to cut through the *Virginia.* If the *Virginia* was lost, Norfolk, Portsmouth, and the James River would be open to Union forces.[17] The key to solving the Confederates' problem was the ironclad CSS *Richmond,* being built at the Portsmouth Navy Yard. When the *Richmond* could come out to patrol Hampton Roads and spar with the *Monitor,* then *Virginia* could take more aggressive action. But the military situation wouldn't remain on hold until the *Richmond* was completed.

The Confederate Navy was stuck in a waiting game, and Tattnall's patience grew thinner by the day. He wanted to end his naval career with a victory, not playing chicken in Hampton Roads with a "cheese box on a shingle." If things for Tattnall weren't already bad enough, they were about to get worse. Jefferson Davis put Gen. Joseph E. Johnston in command of the military situation on the peninsula, and that included the Hampton Roads region. Both Army and Navy would report to him. Special Order No. 6 on April 12 fell on Tattnall like a hammer blow. He would no longer report to the secretary but to an Army general. He immediately sent a communiqué to Mallory: "I am to be placed under the command of an army officer, and, being a seaman, am to hold my action and reputation subject to the judgment of a landsman, who can know nothing of the complicated nature of naval service. I earnestly solicit to be relieved from my command." Somehow Mallory found a way to calm him, and Tattnall stayed on,[18] a decision he would regret.

As the situation on the peninsula worsened, Tattnall went to Richmond and met with Mallory and Davis to discuss their best course of action. As General Lee had requested, in order to take some pressure off his besieged troops, they decided to send the *Virginia* to harass the Union Navy at Yorktown.[19] A few nights later, well after sunset, the *Virginia* entered Hampton Roads and headed for the channel between Fort Monroe and a small island named Rip Raps. In the darkness, she was to slip past the guns into Chesapeake Bay, turn north, and head for Yorktown. As the blacked-out ship approached the channel, however, Jones saw a lantern signal flashing from the Sewell's Point battery. The Army commander in Norfolk, Gen. Benjamin Huger, was ordering them to return to Sewell's Point. Huger was more concerned with the protection of Norfolk and Portsmouth than the relief of Yorktown and had persuaded the powers that be to abort the mission. Engineer Ramsay reported that Tattnall at first acted as if he might ignore the order by pretending not to hear. When Jones asked for orders, Tattnall informed him in disgust that he was going to bed and that Jones was in command and could do whatever he pleased. The *Virginia* returned to the Elizabeth River.[20]

Back at the naval yard, the *Virginia*'s crew stood by. Ramsay's men tinkered with the engines, and the officers tried to find busywork for the crew. Inside the ship, there was little light or ventilation and stifling humidity. Hordes of mosquitoes made sleeping on the top deck impossible. At nightfall, officers and men slept on dry land if they could find a place. As spring turned to summer, the midday sun turned the iron casement into an efficient oven, and Ramsay declared a modern prison to be more comfortable. The only place to walk was under the awnings on the top deck, where the two-inch iron bars separated by two-inch gaps required a man to keep his eyes on his feet or run the risk of a broken ankle. Sometimes men would wade in the shallow water covering the fore and aft decks, and slaves on shore came to the conclusion that the *Virginia* was (as recorded in the vernacular) a "debble ship" with a crew that could walk on water.[21]

Catesby Jones noted that Commodore Tattnall had been in command for forty-five days, including only thirteen days when the *Virginia* was operational and not under repair.[22] About the only thing that broke the monotony was the arrival of one of the daily papers. Fighting men are seldom told about the overall situation of the war they are fighting; like the general public, they depend on the press, and the articles the *Virginia*'s crew members were reading were not encouraging. On Sunday, May 4, Johnston fell back from the Yorktown line to Williamsburg. His left flank was now anchored at Queen's Creek on the north and his right at College Creek on the south, a span of a little more than seven miles. On May 5 McClellan's forces fell on Williamsburg, and after a bloody two-day battle that cost the Confederate forces 1,603 casualties and the Union 2,239, the line broke, and Longstreet and D. H. Hill began a rearguard delaying action to try to keep the Union Army away from Richmond. The guns Jones had positioned on Jamestown Island, where he and Brooke had conducted the *Virginia* armor test, were now turned against the Confederates. This meant that Union artillery controlled more than thirty miles of the north bank of the James River, and river traffic between Richmond and Norfolk would have to run a gauntlet of Union cannons. Still, the *Virginia* sat on station as a guardian in the Elizabeth River between the naval hospital and Norfolk while Tattnall awaited orders. A bad situation became worse when the Union forces moved into Albemarle Sound to the south and, on April 29, up the Pasquotank River to South Mills. There, only thirty miles south of Norfolk, the advance was stopped, but it was obviously a temporary stay.[23] They could soon force their way up the Chesapeake & Albemarle Canal through Dismal Swamp to the Elizabeth River and into Norfolk or swing east and advance north between the swamp and the ocean. Either way, the end looked near for the Confederate towns of Norfolk and Portsmouth.

On April 28 Lee gave Porter new orders[24]: he was to disassemble all of the Navy yard machinery that could be moved and load it onto boats. Lumber, metal, fittings, cannons, and anything else that could be used to construct ships was to go to the Rocketts shipyard in Richmond. During the first days of May, the *Virginia*'s crewmen could stand on the top deck in the twilight and watch the procession of machine-laden ships slide past them and the Yankee guns under the cover of darkness and go up the James to Richmond. On Tuesday, May 6, they watched the *Jamestown* and *Patrick Henry* tow the unfinished *Nansemond* and *Elizabeth* past on their way to the Rocketts yard. On the 9th a joint Army-Navy conference decided that the *Virginia* would continue to hold the mouth of the Elizabeth River until all supplies were moved out of the Navy yard and the Army could make an orderly evacuation. Then the *Virginia's* weight would be reduced to bring her up to a draft of eighteen feet so she could follow the path of the *Nansemond* and *Elizabeth* up the James to assist in the defense of the capital. When it was time to leave, a signal gun would be fired from the Navy yard.[25] At this point, the *Virginia* was in a peculiar position. She was still on guard duty and expected to fight any Union vessels that attempted to approach Norfolk. To be fit to fight, she had to maintain her fighting weight; to run, she had to get skinny. There is no evidence that anyone calculated just what would have to be done to guarantee a draft of eighteen feet.[26]

On Monday, May 5, 1862, as the Union Army was on the way to Richmond, President Lincoln decided to go to Hampton Roads and hurry things along. He had long lamented that just when things looked most promising, General McClellan was prone to acquire a "case of the slows," and he wanted to personally make sure that didn't happen on the way up the peninsula. He also wanted to know what was holding up the capture of Norfolk. On board the U.S. Revenue cutter *Miami*, Lincoln, Stanton, Secretary of the Treasury Chase, and Brig. Gen. Egbert L. Viele set out for Fort Monroe, where they landed a little after 8 PM.[27] Tuesday's highlight was an inspection tour of the *Monitor* and the *Galena.* On Thursday morning, the 8th, word came through the lines that Norfolk was being evacuated. Lincoln wanted Goldsborough to order his ships to see if the report was true. Orders quickly went out for the *Galena* and some other ships to shell the batteries on the south bank of the James, while the *Monitor* did the same at Sewell's Point. Lincoln, Stanton, and Chase went over to Rip Raps, newly named Fort Wool, to watch the show. The *Virginia* had been at the shipyard but got up steam and, for the last time, went down the Elizabeth River to see what all the noise was about. When she reached Sewell's Point at about 2:45 PM, Tattnall's heart must have leaped when he saw the *Monitor* directly ahead of him.[28] On board he had metal-piercing projectiles, explosive shells, and 1,800 pounds of powder. He was looking for a fight, but Goldsborough wasn't. The minute the *Virginia* showed up, he ordered the fleet back under the protection of the guns at Fort Monroe. Tattnall was not going to chase his quarry into an untenable position in shallow water, and Goldsborough wouldn't let the Union ironclads go out to fight. The *Monitor's* crew, embarrassed, had numerous uncomplimentary names for their officers; Lieutenant Wood said that Goldsborough and Jeffers had committed "the most cowardly exhibition he had ever seen." Fuming, Tattnall steamed around in the deep water until after 4 PM and then stalked back to his old moorings at Sewell's Point.[29] The second battle of the *Monitor* and the *Merrimack* would never happen.

On Thursday evening Lincoln and his party looked south across the entrance to Hampton Roads toward the Confederate side and wondered just what was going on over there. A little over a mile south by southeast of the gun parapets at Fort Monroe was a minuscule island called Rip Raps. This small speck of land was the southern border of the boat channel that connected Hampton Roads to Chesapeake Bay and the Atlantic Ocean. A mile and a half south by southeast of Rip Raps, across shallow water, was Willoughby's Point, the closest Confederate real estate to Fort Monroe. Rip Raps, an eighth of a mile long from east to west and about a hundred yards wide, was heavily fortified with huge Union guns.[30] Willoughby's Point was a small peninsula that formed Willoughby's Bay. Because the point and the bay were within range of both Rip Raps and the Confederate gun positions on Sewell's Point, they became a no-man's land. On

Friday morning Lincoln decided he should go over to take a look. Everyone around him quickly squelched that idea: The commander in chief was supposed to command from afar, not take a casual sightseeing tour into no-man's-land. On Friday, May 9, for the first and probably the last time in American history, the secretary of the treasury led a military expedition. Lincoln instructed Chase, accompanied by generals Wool and Viele, to look around Willoughby's Point and report what they found. The trip was quick because they found nothing but a stretch of open shoreline waiting to be invaded. There were no troops or guns to offer any resistance. The naval bombardment of the day before had convinced the Rebels that it was time to go. They were moving away toward Norfolk and ignoring any Yankee activity at their rear. Lincoln returned with Chase to have a look for himself and, with the help of a pilot, found an ideal place to make a landing.

On Friday night the *Virginia*'s crew had something new to watch. The sky over Portsmouth began to glow red. The Portsmouth Naval Shipyard was burning. The fire was not as spectacular as the one that burned the yard in the preceding year because the two huge ship houses were no longer there, and there were no capital ships in flames. Everything that could be evacuated was already in Richmond. This time there had been time to plan the destruction of the shipbuilding facility more carefully, and the damage done to future ship construction was probably more severe. Everything that could burn was burned with one exception: once again sentiment saved the decrepit old *United States*. For reasons never explained, there was no successful attempt to destroy the dry dock.

On Saturday morning, May 10, Union transports began unloading troops, under the command of General Wool, adjacent to Sewell's Point without opposition. Because this operation was being carried out on the direct orders of the commander in chief, Wool took great delight in not informing McClellan. As far as he was concerned, the upstart could read about it in the newspapers. Around 10 AM Tattnall looked over toward Sewell's Point and wondered why no flags were flying. When he received no answer to his signal, he sent Lieutenant Pembroke to Craney Island to find out what was going on. Pembroke returned with disturbing news. He had been told that the Confederates had abandoned Sewell's Point without firing a shot. Tattnall found this hard to believe, so he sent Catesby Jones up to Norfolk for confirmation. By the time Jones arrived in Norfolk, military supplies were in flames and the evacuation was in full swing. Jones got back to the *Virginia* at 7 PM, and by then, the garrison on Craney Island was also gone. The signal shot from the Navy yard, which should have alerted Tattnall that morning, had never been fired. The *Virginia* stood alone.

In her short history the *Virginia* had never had a draft as shallow as the eighteen feet she needed to make the trip all the way to Richmond. Her initial dash would have to carry her well beyond Williamsburg Island in order to stay clear of the Union guns that were now on the south side of the peninsula. For months mechanics, carpenters, and slaves had done everything imaginable to get the *Virginia* to sit as deep in the water as possible. Now, between nightfall and dawn, Tattnall's crew was supposed to undo what had originally taken thousands of man-hours. By now physically ill, Tattnall went to his cabin and left Catesby Jones in charge of the frantic scramble to throw tons of ballast overboard from the fore and aft decks and drag up more out of the hold. Everything that wasn't essential, wasn't nailed down, and could be lifted, went over the side. For this short trip coal was also expendable, but the heavy shot and powder were a different

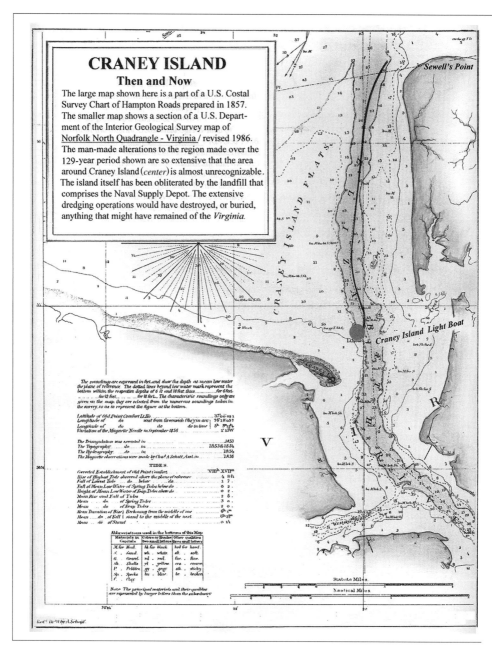

Craney Island then . . .

matter. At some point, she might have to fight her way past Union guns or through a naval blockade on the river.

For months the lack of armor at and below the knuckle had been a bone of contention. In late April John Porter had finally fixed that problem, but Porter's fix would now spell the end for the *Virginia*. The tons of iron that were added to the knuckle were partly below the water and impossible for the crew to reach or remove. By 2 AM on May

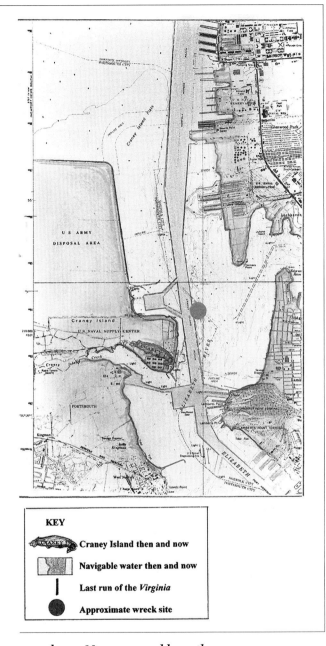

KEY

Craney Island then and now

Navigable water then and now

Last run of the *Virginia*

Approximate wreck site

. . . and now. *Maps prepared by author*

11, 1861, those who were on board stated that the *Virginia* had two feet of the hull exposed below the knuckle.[31] If that was correct, her draft was approaching the necessary eighteen-foot mark. She would have to have been in dry dock at the Navy yard to reduce her weight much further. Just as there appeared to be hope, weather attacked. Wind can pile up water the way it piles up snow. With a good breeze off the Atlantic, the water in the Roads and at the mouth of the James River could have piled up deeper and offer an advantage to the *Virginia*, but the wind had shifted, and the leeward was now back toward the sea. The pilots told Catesby Jones that they would need a draft of less than eighteen feet to clear even the sandbar at the mouth of the James. Jones woke Tattnall and gave him the bad news.[32] The *Virginia* sat with her knuckle two feet above the water and her rudder and propeller exposed, a sitting duck.

The captain was furious. His plans were constantly being foiled by pilots who found excuses not to guide him where he needed to go. He came to the conclusion that it was all deliberate. They were either cowards who didn't want to go into harm's way or were in league with the enemy. Tattnall must have thought back to that day when he had asked to be relieved of duty from the *Virginia* but had acquiesced to Mallory's request to stay on. He thought of McCauley and Forrest and the way any association with the Portsmouth

Navy Yard transformed dedicated men into scapegoats. He knew full well that his quest for glory had ended because he would be blamed for the impending Confederate tragedy. The ship's officers assembled to discuss the situation. Come dawn, two Yankee ironclads would pounce on the helpless ship, shoot the rudder and propeller away, and at their leisure slam shots into the hull at the waterline. At that point, the crew would have only three options: surrender the ship to the Union Navy and become prisoners of war, go down with the ship and become dead Confederate heroes, or scuttle and burn the *Virginia* and then get the crew as far from the scene as possible. The last option was the only sensible thing to do, one they all reluctantly agreed upon.

To successfully destroy the ship and then enable the crew to escape into Confederate territory, they would first have to pick a place as far from the Union forces as possible, where the work could be carried out in the dark without interference. It would have to be as close to shore as possible so the crew could either wade ashore or be taken there by boat in a reasonable amount of time. The landing would have to be at a place where the crew could bypass or slip through enemy lines. The only place that met these requirements was Craney Island. There are no records that give the coordinates of the *Virginia* when Tattnall was informed that the run up the James was hopeless. If she had been at her old mooring off Sewell's Point, she would have slipped her cables and gone toward the entrance to the Elizabeth River channel to start a run at Craney Island. Once there she would go about three miles in the center of the channel, veer slightly to the southwest, and then aim slightly to the right of the channel light that sat northeast of Craney Island. At that spot on the channel's western edge, the water abruptly changed from a depth of some twenty-four feet to less than six feet, and they could run aground about a half-mile from the eastern end of the island. Taking that approach, the ship would list slightly to port when she came to a stop, stuck fast on the bottom.

Shortly after 2 AM the crew was told to discontinue the load-lightening project. The boatswain's mate piped the crew to "splice the main brace." The men gladly responded to the order and went fore or aft, where there were tubs of grog awaiting them. This was a ceremony that usually took place just prior to going into battle or to celebrate a victory, but this would be a far different occasion. Dejectedly, they drank their grog and listened as they were told what was about to happen and assigned their new duties. The majority began preparations to abandon ship by gathering up all of the small arms, ammunition, and other portable items that might be useful in their attempt to reach the Confederate lines. Eight men, under the command of Catesby Jones and Taylor Wood, were assigned the dubious honor of destroying the ship. With Ramsay's engines throbbing, the CSS *Virginia* began her death journey up the Elizabeth River channel.

As soon as the *Virginia* came to rest, slightly northwest of the channel light, her two boats would have been lowered and taken to a position alongside the bow. The crewmen waiting on the gun deck would then squeeze through the forward gun port, go down the sloping face of the casement to the deck, walk over to the bulwark, climb over it to the edge of the deck, and then step down into a waiting boat. When a boat was full, it would be rowed a little over half a mile to Craney Island and unloaded and then return to pick up the next group of men. While this was happening, Jones and Wood were supervising the preparations to destroy the ship. The forward and aft magazines were opened. Some of the powder bags were carefully cut open, and powder was sprinkled over the floor and onto the unopened boxes and kegs of powder. Other bags and kegs of powder would have been taken to the berth and gun decks. Apparently the powder magazines were then closed. Lumber and other flammable substances were piled up to make indoor barn fires on the decks. Powder trains were laid connecting the various fire locations, the final one laid toward the forward gun port. Just before leaving the ship, Midshipman Littlepage noticed the ship's flag lying on the gun deck. He immediately dumped out his clothing on the deck and stuffed the flag into his haversack. It was time to abandon ship. With the demolition crewmen loaded into the boat, Jones lit the powder trains at the forward gun port and joined the others. As they made their way to shore around day-break, the ship began to burn.[33]

As they stood on shore, about three hundred sailors were transformed into land sol-diers and began a hike to Suffolk, some five miles away as the crow flies, to board a train for Petersburg. The last hour of the *Virginia's* existence is not well documented. If the run to Craney Island had started at a little after 2 AM, it would have taken at least two hours for the ship to reach its destination, for the crew to go ashore, and for the fires to be set. It was reported that as the crew began walking toward Suffolk, they heard the dis-tant roar of an occasional cannon as the fire reached the various gun locations and the guns discharged.[34] If this is so, then the guns would have been loaded the day before in anticipation of having to fight to and up the James River. In all likelihood, the guns would have been tied down in their inboard position with the port shutters closed. As each gun discharged, it would have blown the shutters away and recoiled across the deck. The gun deck would have become an inferno, with flames pouring out of the open ports and through the top deck grating. But no Confederates were left behind to record the ship's destruction. The only detailed eyewitness account was written by a young Union naval officer, Samuel R. Franklin, stationed on the USS *Dacotah*. The report seems to be filled with errors, but because it is all I could find, I will repeat it here (the parts of Franklin's statement that I think are erroneous are in italics):

> *I was called at midnight, and it was reported to me that the Merrimac was on fire.* I went on deck and *there she was, all in flames.* The Confederates had decided to abandon her, and, to prevent our getting possession, they wisely set her on fire. It was a sight to us in more senses than one. She had been a thorn in our side for a long time, and we were glad to have her well out of the way. I remained on deck for the rest of the night watching her burn. *Gradually the casement grew hotter and hotter, until it became red hot, so that we could distinctly mark its outline, and remained in this condition for fully half an hour,* when, with a tremen-dous explosion, the Merrimac went into the air and was seen no more.[35]

According to the numerous Confederate reports of the night's activities, the *Virginia* was still sitting off Sewell's Point at midnight and being stripped down to reduce her weight. We know that Jones lit the powder train just before daylight, probably around 4 AM, so Franklin could not have watched the ship burn all night. Because of the 18,000 pounds of powder on board, the ship would never have burned long enough for the case-ment armor to glow red. We know that her crewmen heard the explosion at a little be-fore 5 AM, and this seems logical. The fires were set so that they would burn as fast and as intensely as possible, so the flames would certainly have reached one of the magazines by the time the ship had been burning for an hour.

Regardless of the errors in Franklin's report, we know that sometime between five and six on the morning of Monday, May 11, 1862, the CSS *Virginia* was blown into oblivion. The ironclad was down.

Chapter Fourteen

Epilogue

Union troops occupied Norfolk on May 11, 1862, and Lincoln, Stanton, and Chase toured the city and inspected the smoldering ruins of the Navy yard. The *Monitor* steamed up the Elizabeth River and docked at the *Virginia's* old berth. On the way she had stopped beside some of the skeletal remains of the *Virginia's* casement that protruded out of the water so crew members could collect souvenirs. In Richmond things were progressing exactly as Tattnall had predicted. He was the villain, the coward who had needlessly lost the *Virginia*, the shining hope of the Confederate Navy. Mallory wrote in his diary, "May God protect us and cure us of weakness and folly." Tattnall was court-martialed, but when the facts were examined, he was exonerated. The *Virginia's* crew fought shoulder to shoulder once more when they manned heavy guns on a high point called Drewry's Bluff, overlooking the James River eight miles south of Richmond. On the morning of May 15 Goldsborough ordered the Union ironclads *Monitor* and *Galena*, accompanied by three wooden ships, to go up the James and attack Richmond. In the narrow channel below Drewry's Bluff, the little fleet took a terrible pounding the *Monitor's* guns could not elevate high enough to reach the artillery on the bluff. The *Monitor* was not harmed, but the devastating fire virtually destroyed the *Galena*. After four hours of being pounded, they retreated to City Point. Midshipman Littlepage had unfurled the *Virginia's* tattered flag over the guns, and for the last time, the men of the *Virginia* rained shot and shell on the USS *Monitor*.

On May 30 the Army of the Potomac was within seven miles of Richmond, but as Lincoln had feared, McClellan snatched defeat from the jaws of victory, and the Peninsula Campaign turned into a disaster. In the long run, it was even more disastrous for the Union than Lincoln could have imagined at the time. On May 30 the commander of the Confederate forces, Gen. Joseph Johnston, was seriously wounded at Seven Pines and had to be replaced. As his successor, Davis selected friend and military adviser, whom the press had derided as Old Granny Lee, the King of Spades. On the first day of June, 1862 Robert E. Lee took command of the Army of Northern Virginia.[1] His star was in ascension, and soon, throughout the South, unbounded praise replaced criticism. In campaign after campaign, Union soldiers and generals would fall before him like wheat before the scythe.

The crew of the *Monitor* spent the summer frying in their iron skillet anchored at Hampton Roads. Their living conditions were more intolerable than the circumstances that had plagued the *Virginia*'s men. The *Virginia*'s top deck grating had allowed hot air to escape, and gun ports could be opened to let the breezes blow through. The *Monitor*'s men were sealed like sardines in a can, where the stagnant, humid air always hovered above a hundred degrees. If they went on deck, during the day they would fry and at night be eaten alive by mosquitoes. To add to their misery, they served under Lt. William N. Jeffers, a commander they detested. On August 15 both officers and men rejoiced when Cdr. Thomas H. Stevens replaced Jeffers.[2] More good news came at the end of September, when the ship was ordered to the Washington Navy Yard for repairs. For a month the crew enjoyed a well-earned leave. In early November the *Monitor* returned to Hampton Roads, anchored just off Newport News. On Christmas day orders were received directing her to be taken under tow by the USS *Rhode Island* to Beaufort, South Carolina. Once again her unseaworthiness came into play. About 1 AM on December 31, 1862, she foundered in heavy seas sixteen miles off Cape Hatteras, North Carolina, and went down with sixteen of her crew. For more than a hundred years her location was unknown, but in 1974 the wreck was located. Successful efforts began, and are continuing, to recover her turret, guns, anchor, propeller, and other artifacts before they are claimed by the ravages of the sea. Today, what remains of the USS *Monitor* can be viewed in a special facility dedicated to her memory at the Mariner's Museum in Newport News, Virginia, just a short distance from her last anchorage in Hampton Roads.

There will never be a CSS *Virginia* museum. Even if all of the certifiable pieces that remain of her were gathered together in one place, they would be far too few to warrant a museum. The ship's channel in the Elizabeth River has been dredged numerous times, and what was once Craney Island is now a landfill, covered by U.S. Navy fuel storage tanks. Recovery of any meaningful remains of the *Virginia* would be close to miraculous. Even her name has faded from memory. Only people with more than a casual interest in the American Civil War know what the CSS *Virginia* was. In American schools, some students become acquainted with a sea battle between the *"Monitor* and the *Merrimack."* As for the men of the *Virginia*, most of them have also been tucked away in the dark corridors of history, where, on rare occasions, some historian visits.

STEPHEN RUSSELL MALLORY

Mallory was deeply disturbed by the loss of the *Virginia* and the Portsmouth Navy Yard. He knew that a way could be found to build more ironclads, but the Navy yard was irreplaceable. As "Lincoln's anaconda" tightened its grip, he had to face the fact that, as long as the war lasted, the Confederacy could not have a blue water fleet. The best he could hope for was to buy ships in Europe that could be made into Confederate raiders and to build shallow-water ironclads on inland rivers and ports that might find a way to harass the Union blockade. The raider program met with success, but for all practical purposes, the ironclad projects were failures. Mallory was always plagued by the inefficiencies of the government: The Navy's bills were never paid on time, Davis held cabinet meetings incessantly that dragged on for hours and accomplished nothing, and, of course, Congress and the press blamed Mallory for the loss of the *Virginia* and for the demise of practically every other ship lost during the war. After the loss of Pensacola and New Orleans, the only coastal cities where ships of substance could be built were Charleston, Wilmington, Savannah, and Mobile, and they were locked tight in the vise of the blockade. After Memphis fell, inland shipbuilding efforts took place on small-town riverbanks and in cornfields. As the war dragged on, Mallory's ironclads and raiders dropped away, one by one. The ram *Albemarle* was lost, the raider *Florida* went down off the coast of Brazil, and the USS *Kearsarge* sank the *Alabama* in sight of Cherbourg, France. Some Southerners thought that the devastating losses the Confederate raiders were inflicting on the U.S. maritime fleet might actually end the war, but all it ended was the dominance of the American shipping industry, which was never regained. The U.S. government considered the crews of the raiders to be pirates and wanted them treated as such if captured. Some were captured, but there were no hangings.

By January 1865 it was obvious to anyone who would accept the truth that the cause was lost. Foolish pride and stubbornness prevented the South from admitting the obvious and suing for peace. There were still too many young men willing to go to their graves and too many old men willing to send them there. Sherman marched to the sea, and Mallory was in charge of a Navy that had no ports. But the pretense dragged on. On Sunday, April 2, 1865, Mallory was summoned to a hastily called cabinet meeting. Jefferson Davis calmly informed them that General Lee's defenses around Petersburg were crumbling and that Richmond must be abandoned. That evening, the president, his cabinet, and other government officials and their families met at the Richmond & Danville station to go south and find a safe place to set up the government. At 11 PM their special train pulled out of the station and crossed the James River bridge. As the train rumbled over the James, Mallory looked down on the last remnants of his Navy, the James River Fleet, soon to be put to the torch. They reached Danville, Virginia, on the afternoon of the 3rd and languished there for five days awaiting news from Lee. On Sunday afternoon, April 9, the news came from Appomattox that Lee had surrendered.

That night the president's entourage departed for Greensboro, North Carolina, and were shocked to learn that they were not welcome there. The officials of the Confederate government might not have known that the war was over, but the Confederate people did, and they knew it was not wise to associate with acknowledged enemies of the U.S. government. Due to lack of accommodations, the Confederate government had to operate out of a railway car. On the night of the 12th the generals Johnston and Beauregard advised Davis to contact Sherman and ask for terms. Davis was cool to the idea but willing to listen to a proposal, but events at Ford's Theater on Friday night in Washington precluded new plans. With the assassination of Lincoln, Confederate officials were in as much danger of being shot as of being captured. They continued their wanderings south through North Carolina down to Charlotte, where they learned of Lincoln's assassination. The peace negotiations that had started were quickly ended. The only terms available were unconditional surrender, and Confederate president Davis had a $100,000 price on his head. Ill and desperate, he refused to accept the obvious and decided to go west of the Mississippi to set up his new government. Traveling by train was no longer safe, so the band of fugitives now made their way in wagons and on horseback. The

Confederate cabinet members were not deluded and began dropping away like autumn leaves. Treasury Secretary Trenholm was the first to go, followed on May 2 at Washington, Georgia, by Mallory and then Judah Benjamin. The remnants of Davis' party, including his nephew John Taylor Wood, made its way to the Oconee River near Dublin and, by the evening of the 9th, were camped near the village of Irwinville, Georgia, where, in the predawn hours of May 10, the Davis party and the last remaining cabinet member, Postmaster General Reagan, were captured by the 4th Michigan Cavalry. By stealth or by bribery, Wood managed to get away and headed for Cuba. There was talk of trying the Confederate president for treason, but that never materialized. Jefferson Davis spent two years as a prisoner at Fort Monroe and then moved near Biloxi, Mississippi, where he died on December 9, 1889.

Angela Mallory and the children had gone to La Grange, Georgia, months before the fall of Richmond, so after leaving Davis at Washington, Georgia, Stephen made his way to Atlanta and then down to La Grange, where he awaited the inevitable. As expected, he was soon arrested and on his way to prison. On Sunday, June 4, he arrived at Fort Lafayette, New York, with no notion of how long he might be there, what the charges against him would be, or that there were northern politicians and financiers who wanted him tried for treason and executed. In solitary confinement, Mallory spent most of his time writing to Angela, the children, and old political friends he thought might help his cause. He reminded everyone that he had been among the last to abandon the Union and had done everything in his power to preserve it. He volunteered information he thought might help the Union Navy find the raider CSS *Shenandoah*, whose commander, James Waddell, was not aware that the war was over and was still causing havoc in the north Pacific.

To be near him, Angela and the children moved to Bridgeport, Connecticut, and visited Stephen from time to time. Angela succeeded in getting an appointment with President Andrew Johnson to plead her husband's case, but nothing came of it. On two occasions, Mallory wrote to the president himself, but Johnson was too involved in matters like his impeachment to care about the plight of a former Confederate cabinet member. Summer turned to fall and fall to winter, and Stephen languished in limbo. He had not been charged with any crime and therefore could neither confess guilt nor plead innocence. Early in December, he received word that Secretary Stanton wanted him to be tried for treason and knew that, at the time, such a trial would be a mere formality before execution. Other Confederate officials were being pardoned, while Lee and the other generals had taken the oath of allegiance and returned to civilian life. Why was he singled out for such harsh treatment? Stephen never realized that his decision to launch a fleet of merchant raiders had done more political and economic damage at home and abroad than all of the Confederate armies that ever took the field. The raiders had caused industries and financial institutions to fail; Lloyds of London would not insure a ship that carried the American flag. Valuable cargo languished in ports. New England whalers all but vanished from the seas. Unfinished merchant ships sat on the ways as old, established American shipping companies ceased to exist. Mallory's "pirate ships" did not change the outcome of a single battle, but they did impoverish men on both sides of the ocean, and these men correctly blamed their fate on the Confederate raiders and Stephen Mallory.

Angela made another desperate dash to Washington to see President Johnson. Just as things looked darkest, an old friend came to Stephen's aid. Judge William Marvin, his old law instructor, had become governor of Florida. He convinced both Seward and Stanton that any further persecution of Mallory would serve no good purpose. If the government started hanging ex-Confederates, it would be hard to find a place to stop, and guerrilla warfare would flare up across the South. Stanton informed the president that they no longer wished to proffer charges, and Johnson immediately issued the order of parole. On March 10, 1866, a free Stephen Mallory walked out of prison, unaware that he was a hated man in many quarters.

Mallory returned to Pensacola and established a successful law practice. As a Democrat, he expressed his opinions on reconstruction and other political affairs in person and in print but stayed clear of direct political involvement. He wrote essays and letters about current affairs and family matters but not about himself or his part in the Confederate Navy, and there was little or no correspondence between him and the men who had served under him—almost as if he had been a casual observer of the Civil War. Either he didn't understand the impact he had had on world and naval history or through modesty never wrote about it. He left the American Civil War in his prison cell in New York and never looked back. Stephen Russell Mallory died at his home in Pensacola on the morning of November 12, 1873.

JOHN MERCER BROOKE

Brooke did not seem particularly upset by the loss of the *Virginia.* His numerous run-ins with Porter and the project's endless transportation and construction nightmares must have made the entire episode unpleasant for him. His greatest strength was the design of artillery pieces and their projectiles, so on March 31, 1863, he became commander of the Office of Ordnance and Hydrography. Richmond was the hub of the ordnance department. Through Brooke's leadership and Tredegar's production capabilities, heavy artillery was supplied to the Navy, the coastal batteries, and the Army. Brooke also had the ordnance workshop producing projectiles and gun carriages in Atlanta, Charleston, Charlotte, and a foundry and ordinance shop in Selma under the supervision of his old friend, Catesby Jones. As the war dragged on, the shortage of skilled workmen became critical, and the quality of the raw materials dwindled dramatically. Brooke's railroad transportation problems never ended. By 1864 the engines and the cars were falling apart, and the rails were little more than ribbons of rust. The war years also brought much personal unhappiness to John Brooke. Of the four daughters he and Lizzie had had, only one survived. Lizzie's last surviving brother, and John's cousin, Gen. Richard Brooke Garnett, was killed at Gettysburg in Pickett's Charge, and on June 14, 1864, Lizzie lost her long battle with tuberculosis. In the midst of the chaos of war, John became a widower with a young daughter to care for.[3]

As Sherman marched to the sea, he swept away Brooke's naval ordnance facilities. John's Navy had ceased to exist. On May 2, 1865, the day Richmond was evacuated, John and three companions acquired a horse-drawn ambulance and started an aimless trek similar to that of President Davis and company. They passed through Appomattox Court House on Thursday the 6th and reached Danville the day after the president's group had left. Brooke soon left his companions and set off on his own. He went to Greensboro, where on May 1 he took the oath of allegiance, based on the earlier agreement between Johnston and Sherman. He was now a civilian, but a destitute civilian with no money, no home, and no prospects. All he owned was a $5,000 Confederate bond. He found his way back to Richmond, where he learned, on May 29, that the earlier oath he had taken was meaningless. President Johnson had written a proclamation of amnesty that excluded him on several counts. He was a Naval Academy graduate, had resigned his commission, and had been a high-ranking official in the Confederate government. To gain amnesty, he would have to submit a personal appeal directly to the president, and that could produce numerous problems. Brooke, like Mallory, was among the most hated surviving Confederates. Adm. David Dixon Porter had labeled Brooke as causing "more harm than any other man in the south." In later years, unbiased experts declared the rifled cannons Brooke designed to be the finest produced during the Civil War, but for now, without a pardon, he was a man without a country. He could not own property, vote, procure a patent, or do much of anything to make a living. He submitted his request to the president and asked old friends in the North to put in a good word.

During the first of the darkest days back in Richmond, old friends and relatives gave him a little money from time to time so he could survive. Lizzie's relatives cared for his daughter while he desperately tried to find work. In October 1865 he received wonderful news. He had been appointed to the newly created chair of astronomy, geodesy, meteorology, and physical geography at the Virginia Military Institute (VMI) in Lexington, a state-run institution that had been burned by the Union general David Hunter in 1864.[4] Brooke was suddenly thrown back into a situation that would challenge his imagination and management skills and enable him to play an important part in raising the school from the ashes. He needed books and instruments and charts, and he contacted old friends at the Chicago Academy of Science and the Smithsonian, who provided what they could. Finally, in August 1866, he received his pardon. With that accomplished, he contacted the Naval Observatory and Coastal Survey to request their assistance in providing instruments and books. He improved the school's situation, but his own prospects were not as good because his small salary forced him to lead a hand-to-mouth existence. He therefore considered his teaching job as an interlude until something better came along. Brooke applied to be captain of a new merchant ship running between California and Japan, but nothing came of that. He, Jones, and Robert Minor, an old Naval Academy schoolmate, explored establishing a company to provide supplies and ordnance to foreign navies, particularly Japan; there was much planning but never any real success, and by the summer of 1869 the would-be partners put that idea to rest. Meanwhile Brooke was slowly becoming more comfortable with academic life. At VMI he was making new friends, and old ones were reappearing. His old mentor, Matthew Fontaine Maury, became its professor of meteorology in 1868. For a while, the work provided no drama or excitement, but it did provide steady, dependable employment for a man who had a young daughter to raise. In 1870 he turned down an opportunity to become a colonel of ordnance for the Egyptian government.

Circumstances being what they were, John Brooke settled down to live in two worlds—the academic world of VMI and a world of invention. He improved the boat hook device he had invented years earlier and discussed his ideas about mines, torpedo boats, and submarines with the German government. He had designed a submarine for the Prussian government that was never built, but he had kindled a spark of interest in Germany that would not be extinguished. Brooke also devised a new system for electronically mining harbors and invented a new gun sight as well as a gun that could be fired underwater. Despite his efforts and those of some rather inept agents, Brooke never made a sale. In 1867 he began courting Mrs. Kate Corbin Pendleton, the widow of Lt. Col. Alexander Pendleton. John soon proposed marriage, but Kate, twelve years younger than John, didn't quickly decide to remarry and take on a teenage stepdaughter. They were eventually married on March 14, 1871, and settled down in a new house the school built for them. In May 1875 George Mercer Brooke Jr. was born, and Rosa Brooke came along in October 1876.

In the early 1870s VMI fell on hard times and for a while faced bankruptcy. Instructors' salaries were cut and temporarily suspended in 1872. Brooke and many other instructors felt the school's curriculum was antiquated and needed an overhaul, but the administrators were still trying to live in the antebellum South and refused to change anything. Frustration had become a permanent part of John Brooke's life: His inventions met with little or no success, he could make no changes to a faltering curriculum, and his quests for a better future always met with failure. He actively sought the presidency of the Virginia Agricultural and Medical College and then the superintendency of the Coastal Survey office, to no avail. His only opportunities were in foreign countries, and he turned those down. John corresponded with old friends and made a little money by writing articles about naval ordnance and meteorology for various publications. He was interested in weather patterns and believed that weather could be predicted, given the proper observations and scientifically recorded background information. In 1879 he was invited to be a member of the Board of Visitors at the Naval Academy, a group of eleven men, military and civilian, who for nine days every year would review the academy's curriculum and examination procedure and suggest improvements. While Brooke was attending the conference, the academy's superintendent, Commo. F. A. Parker, died, and Brooke was asked to be one of his pallbearers.[5] His Confederate transgressions had been forgiven. For the rest of his life, he was invited to join distinguished groups in various projects and even named president of the Naval Academy's Board of Visitors.

Little changed at VMI because of stagnation at the top until 1890, when Gen. Francis Smith, the school's founder and superintendent, reluctantly retired. Under new direction from Gen. Scott Shipp, things slowly began to change. By this time, Brooke was reconciled to spending the remainder of his productive years as a teacher of young men. Thoughts of building bigger and better cannons and sailing the seven seas became occasional daydreams, and his energies went toward obtaining much-needed modern laboratory equipment and updated textbooks for his department. At one point, the library had so few chairs that cadets had to sit on the windowsill to study. A group of cadets were reprimanded for requesting that classes not be held on Saturday, and free speech was frowned upon. A cadet could not have articles or letters published or give a speech that was not first approved by the academic board. Because of the hardships of Reconstruction, attracting qualified instructors at the low salaries offered by a state institution was difficult.[6]

The Spanish-American War brought new recognition to the institution: 136 cadets served as officers in the war and 24 VMI men held commissions in the Regular Army, including Lt. George Mercer Brooke Jr., U.S. Infantry, VMI class of 1896. The lieutenant's father was then seventy-two years old, and the school's June 1899 annual report included the following: "Colonel John M. Brooke, Professor of Physics and Astronomy, was relieved from active service and appointed Emeritus Professor." The school awarded him a lifetime annual salary of $1,200, and he and Kate continued to live on campus in the house that had been built for them years before. Brooke puttered in his garden, read in his study, and, on rare occasions, wrote a letter, but there were fewer and fewer people around for him to write to. Robert Minor was gone, in February 1873 Matthew Maury had died, Catesby Jones had been shot and killed in a quarrel with a neighbor in June 1877, and John Wood immigrated to Canada, became a successful businessman, and died in Halifax on July 19, 1904. Brooke was still famous in naval and scientific circles and still received letters from all over the world, but his own writing slowed to a trickle.

On the morning of December 14, 1906, four days before his eightieth birthday, John Mercer Brooke suffered a stroke and was gone before the day was over. On a bleak and rain-swept day in December, he was buried with full military honors and the VMI corps of cadets in attendance. Orations and obituaries described his adventurous early life and the honors and medals he had received at home and abroad for his scientific achievements. He was lauded for his contributions to the Virginia Military Institute. We can only wonder what he might have accomplished if there had never been a Confederate States of America.

JOHN LUKE PORTER

Porter seems to have never had any great happiness or received much praise for his life's work. We don't know where he was on the day the Gosport Navy Yard fell to the Virginia militia or where he was on the day in May when it was recaptured. Soon after the fall of Norfolk, he was busy reestablishing a passable Navy shipyard at the Rocketts yard on the James River in the southern outskirts of Richmond. The equipment and supplies brought up from Portsmouth had to be sorted and set up to start building ships. Rocketts was a far cry from the Gosport facility: a few permanent buildings and a scattering of sheds where several hundred carpenters worked.[7] At another facility across the river with the inauspicious name of "Yard Opposite Rocketts," other ships that became part of the new James River Squadron were built. Throughout the war, Porter and James Mead assembled Porter-designed ironclads patterned after the *Virginia*. Across the river acting constructor William Graves built the *Virginia II*. All of these ships had a shallow draft and a *Virginia*-type casement. For three years, no one came up with a new or original idea. Basically, the ships of the James River Fleet were all failures. They were lighter than the original *Virginia* but still too heavy and clumsy to easily navigate the waters of the James. Only on the Mississippi, particularly around Vicksburg, did the river ironclads play an important part in the war. The James River ironclads were primarily floating batteries to defend Richmond. The Union destroyed only one commissioned Confederate ironclad, the CSS *Albemarle*. Of the twenty-one others, three were captured, and the rest destroyed by their crews or retreating Confederate forces to prevent their capture.[8]

Porter spent the war designing ironclads in Richmond and traveling all over the South to inspect ships he had designed that were being built in various ports and on riverbanks. He was in Wilmington, North Carolina, when he was informed that it was time to retreat. He tried to get his work crew and equipment to some safe place but was blocked by Union troops in every direction. When he learned that Richmond, where his family then lived, was about to fall, he immediately took off alone for Raleigh, where he learned that Lee had surrendered and that Davis and the cabinet were on the run. He arrived at Greensboro at about the same time as Davis and the remnants of the cabinet. He was anonymous enough to manage renting a room and stayed there for a month. One day on the railroad siding, he discovered the ill and miserable Chief Engineer Williamson living in a boxcar and took the sick man back to his room. General Johnston surrendered to Sherman on May 1, and Porter quickly made arrangements to take the oath of allegiance and gain parole.

Porter immediately went to Richmond, where he learned his family had returned to Portsmouth. Back in Portsmouth, he found hardship and unhappiness. The government had confiscated his home and sold it for $700. People he had helped in the old days who could have given him work now shunned him. He said: "I often regretted that I ever gave up my situation which had offered me a good living for life."[9] In 1877 he was finally hired as a carpenter in the Norfolk Navy Yard (formerly the Gosport Shipyard). At sixty-four, as he walked through the gates each morning carrying his lunch pail, he must have been reminded of the old days when he had been king of the shipyard.

Constantly reminded of the past, he began to dwell on the terrible wrong he felt Brooke, Jones, and the others had done to him by denying that he was the inventor of the CSS *Virginia*. Righting this wrong became the windmill he would at which tilt for the rest of his life. With the aid of his son, he published the story of how John Luke Porter designed and built the *Virginia* and how the stories told by Brooke and the rest of his ilk were distortions of the facts. These challenges prompted Brooke to get back into the fray. Much of the correspondence between Brooke and Catesby Jones is on this subject. If the war of words had never started, we would know next to nothing about the *Virginia*. Because of this obsession, the Porters preserved the only reliable pictorial references about the structure of the ship. John Luke Porter's anguish over the subject of who invented the *Virginia* became an irreplaceable gift to Civil War historians.

In time, Porter was hired as the superintendent of construction at the Baker's Barkley shipyard. In 1883 seventy-year-old Porter became the superintendent of the Norfolk County Ferries. In addition to supervising the ferry system's operations, he returned to the drawing board and designed several ferries. By the time he retired in 1888, he had purchased his wife's old family home, and the Porter family was once again on firm financial ground. John Luke Porter died on December 14, 1893, at age eighty, exactly thirteen years to the day before John Brooke died.

Civil War buffs in particular love to play the game of "what if": What if Joseph Johnson hadn't been wounded at Seven Pines? What if the naval officers had voted not to accept Ericsson's proposal for an ironclad ship? Anyone can conceive of countless events where the outcome of the Civil War could have been altered. But the history does not change. We can only marvel at the lives sacrificed to a lost cause by the men who built and served on the *Virginia,* and wonder what lives they might have lived if they had not been swept up in a disastrous civil war.

As for my model of the exterior and interior of the CSS *Virginia,* I have not built it and probably never will. The super-detailed cutaway model I now envision would have to be twelve or fifteen feet long, not the sort of thing to put on the living room coffee table. I hope a museum somewhere would like to have such an accurate model. If so, the information in this book provides the groundwork to begin building it.

Notes

Chapter One: The Secretary: *Stephen Russell Mallory*

1. J. Thomas Scharf, *History of the Confederate States Navy* (1868; Avenel, NJ: Gramercy Books, 1996).
2. Bern Anderson, *By Sea and by River* (New York: Alfred A. Knopf, 1962).
3. Joseph T. Durkin, *Stephen R. Mallory: Confederate Navy Chief* (Chapel Hill: University of North Carolina Press, 1954).
4. Ibid.
5. Ibid.
6. Ibid.
7. Ibid.
8. James M. McPherson, *Battle Cry of Freedom* (New York: Oxford University Press, 1988).
9. Durkin, *Stephen R. Mallory.*
10. Ibid.
11. Mary Chestnut, *A Diary from Dixie* (1905; New York: Random House Publishing, 1997).
12. Robert G. Elliot, *Ironclad of the Roanoke* (Shippensburg, PA: White Mane Books, 1999).
13. Durkin, *Stephen R. Mallory.*
14. Ibid.

Chapter Two: The Constructor: *John Luke Porter*

1. Alan B. Flanders, *John L. Porter: Naval Constructor of Destiny* (White Stone, VA: Brandylane Publishers, 2000).
2. Ibid.
3. Ibid.
4. John W. H. Porter, *A Record of Events in Norfolk County, Virginia, from April 19th, 1861, to May 10th, 1862, with a History of the Soldiers and Sailors of Norfolk County, Norfolk City and Portsmouth Who Served in the Confederate States Army or Navy* (Portsmouth, VA: W. A. Fiske, Printer, 1892).
5. Geoffrey M. Footner, *USS* Constellation*: From Frigate to Sloop of War* (Annapolis, MD: Naval Institute Press, 2003).

6. Ibid.

7. Flanders, *John L. Porter.*

8. K. Jack Bauer and Stephen S. Roberts, *Register of Ships of the U.S. Navy, 1775–1990* (Westport, CT: Greenwood Press, 1991).

9. Flanders, *John L. Porter.*

10. James L. Nelson, *Reign of Iron* (New York: HarperCollins, 2004).

11. McCauley family papers, Navy Dept. correspondence to Capt. C. S. McCauley, April 10, 1861.

12. Nelson, *Reign of Iron.*

13. Ibid.

14. Gideon Welles' diary, vol. 1, p. 43.

15. Capt. Edward McCauley, short biography of C. S. McCauley, written April 1938.

16. John Luke Porter, *A Short History of Myself* (Portsmouth, VA: Portsmouth Naval Shipyard Museum, 1878).

Chapter Three: *The Inventor: John Mercer Brooke*

1. James M. Morgan, *Midshipman in Gray* (1917; Shippensburg, PA: Burd Street Press, 1997).

2. Geo. M. Brooke Jr., "John Mercer Brooke: Naval Scientist" (PhD diss., University of North Carolina, 1955).

3. Charles L. Lewis, *Matthew Fontaine Maury: Pathfinder of the Sea* (Annapolis, MD: United States Naval Institute, 1927).

4. Brooke, "John Mercer Brooke."

5. Dean King, *A Sea of Words* (New York: Henry Holt, 1995).

6. Brooke, "John Mercer Brooke."

7. Geo. M. Brooke Jr., *John Mercer Brooke: Naval Scientist and Educator* (Charlottesville: University Press of Virginia, 1980).

8. Ibid.

9. Ibid.

10. Ibid.

11. Ibid.

12. Ibid.

Chapter Four: A Changing Technology

1. James P. Baxter, *The Introduction of the Ironclad Warship* (1933; Hamden, CT: Archon Books, 1968).

2. Donald L. Canney, *The Old Steam Navy*, vol. 2, *The Ironclads, 1842–1885* (Annapolis, MD: Naval Institute Press, 1993).

3. Donald L. Canney, *The Old Steam Navy*, vol. 1, *Frigates, Sloops and Gunboats, 1815–1885* (Annapolis, MD: Naval Institute Press, 1993).

4. Ibid.

5. Canney, *Old Steam Navy*, vol. 2.

6. Ibid.

7. Howard I. Chapelle, *History of the American Sailing Navy* (New York: Konecky & Konecky, 1949).

8. Canney, *Old Steam Navy,* vol. 1.

9. Ibid.

Chapter Five: The USS *Merrimack*

1. Merrimack River Watershed Council, *The Voice of the Merrimack,* http://www.merrimack.org.

2. Albert Leroy Bartlett, *The Story of Haverhill in Massachusetts.* Typed manuscript on file at the Haverhill Public Library.

3. Robert K. Cheney, *Maritime History of the Merrimac Shipbuilding* (Newburyport, MA: Newburyport Press, 1964).

4. John J. Currier, *Ship Building on the Merrimac River* (Newburyport, MA: William H. Huse & Co., 1877).

5. Richmond Hobson, *The Sinking of the "Merrimac"* (1899; Annapolis, MD: Naval Institute Press, 1987).

6. U.S. Navy information site, http://navysite.de/ao/179.htm; accessed July 2005.

7. Canney, *Old Steam Navy,* vol. 1.

8. Ibid.

9. Flanders, *John L. Porter.*

10. Edward E. Barthell, *The Mystery of the* Merrimack (Muskegon, MI: Dana Publishing Co., 1959).

11 Canney, *Old Steam Navy,* vol. 1.

12. Ibid.

13. Granville Bathe, *Ship of Destiny* (Philadelphia: Press of Allen, Lane and Scott, 1951).

14. Ibid.

15. Ibid.

16. Ibid.

17. Ibid

18. George F. Amadon, *Rise of the Ironclads* (Missoula, MN: Pictorial Histories Publishing Co., 1988).

19. Bathe, *Ship of Destiny.*

20. Ibid.

21. Canney, *Old Steam Navy,* vol. 1.

Chapter Six: Whose Idea Was This Anyway?

1. Brooke, *John Mercer Brooke.*

2. Richard N. Current, ed., *Encyclopedia of the Confederacy,* vol. 4 (New York: Simon & Schuster, 1993).

3. Durkin, *Stephen R. Mallory.*

4. Scharf, *History of the Confederate States Navy.*

5. Durkin, *Stephen R. Mallory.*

6. Ibid.

7. Ibid.

8. Brooke, "John Mercer Brooke."

9. William N. Still Jr., *Iron Afloat* (Columbia: University of South Carolina Press, 1985).

10. Ibid.

11. Scharf, *History of the Confederate States Navy.*

12. Brooke, *John M. Brooke.*

13. Ibid.

14. J. W. Porter, *A Record of Events.*

15. The War of the Rebellion: A Compilation of the Official Records of the Union and Confederate Navies, 1881–1902 (OR).

16. Ibid.

17. Kenneth W. Dobyns, *The Patent Office Pony* (Fredericksburg, VA: Sergeant Kirkland's Museum and Historical Society, 1997).

18. The War of the Rebellion (OR).

19. Ibid.

20. Ibid.

21. J. L. Porter, Letter to *Examiner,* April 8, 1862, reprinted in *Oldetimes Magazine,* Spring 1987.

22. J .M. Brooke, Letter to Catesby Jones, 1874, reprinted in George M. Brooke Jr., "John Mercer Brooke: Naval Scientist" PhD diss., University of North Carolina, 1955.

23. J. L. Porter, Letter to *Examiner*, April 8, 1862. Reprinted in *Oldetimes Magazine,* Spring 1987.

24. Baxter, *The Introduction of the Ironclad Warship.*

25. J. W. Porter, *A Record of Events.*

26. J. M. Brooke, letter to Catesby Jones, reprinted in G. Brooke, "John Mercer Brooke."

27. The War of the Rebellion (OR).

28. J. L. Porter, *A Short History of Myself.*

29. J. W. Porter, *A Record of Events.*

30. J. L. Porter, *A Short History of Myself.*

Chapter Seven: Words, Plans, Pictures, and Pieces

1. Keith Kurr, e-mail sent May 21, 2003, from Cartographic Section, Special Media Archives Service Division, National Archives and Records Administration, College Park, MD.

2. Fred Freeman, *Duel of the Ironclads* (New York: Time Life Books, 1969).

3. Clancy, *Virginian Pilot,* July 22, 2003.

4. J. Graml, The Mariners' Museum, e-mail to author, 2003.

5. Mariners' Museum Web page, accessed August 6, 2003.

6. Barisic, *Virginian Pilot,* August 2, 2003.

7. Peter H. Falk, ed., *Who Was Who in American Art* (Madison, CT: Sound View Press, 1985).

8. Angus Konstam, *Duel of the Ironclads* (Oxford: Osprey Publishing, 2003).

9. Meagher, David J., [CSS *Virginia*] drawing, 1986, available by order through Tatum Plans Service, Jersey City, NJ.

10. History Channel, *Great Ships: The Ironclads* [television series] (New York: A&E Television Networks, 1996).

11. Turner Pictures, *Ironclads* [DVD] (New York: Turner Home Entertainment, 1991).

12. National Archives, Record Group 45 Naval Subject File, stack 11W4 14/12/6 box 67, Desc: fol 4 *Virginia/Merrimack*.

13. Patricia L. Faust, ed., *Encyclopedia of the Civil War* (New York: Harper & Row, 1986).

14. National Archives, Record Group 45 Naval Subject File, stack 11W4 14/12/6 box 67, Desc: fol 4 *Virginia/Merrimack*.

15. Faust, *Encyclopedia of the Civil War*.

16. Ibid.

17. National Archives, Records Group 45 Naval Subject File, stack 11W4 14/12/6 box 121 fol. 1 of 7, Salvage of *Cumberland*.

18. National Archives, Record Group 45 Naval Subject File, stack 11W4 14/12/6 box 67, Desc: fol 4 *Virginia/Merrimack*, F. M. Smith letter.

19. Jeff Johnston, *The Fate of the CSS* Virginia, http://home.att.net/%7eiron.clad/thefateofthecssva.html.

20. Ibid.

21. Ibid.

22. National Archives, Record Group 45 Naval Subject File, stack 11W4 14/12/6 box 67, Desc: fol 4 *Virginia/Merrimack*.

23. Johnston, *The Fate of the CSS* Virginia.

24. Ibid.

25. Ibid.

26. Ibid.

27. Ibid.

28. Ibid.

29. John J. Ahladas, Curator, the Museum of the Confederacy, Richmond, VA, letter written August 18, 1997.

30. John M. Coski, Historian and Library Director, Museum of the Confederacy, Richmond, VA, e-mail correspondence, December 2003.

31. Molly Hutton Marder, Assistant Registrar and Collections Database Manager, Chrysler Museum of Art, Norfolk, VA, e-mail correspondence, December 2003.

32. Ibid.

33. John M. Coski, Historian and Library Director, Museum of the Confederacy, Richmond, VA, e-mail correspondence, February 7, 2004.

34. John S. Wise, *The End of an Era* (New York: Thomas Yoseloff, 1965).

35. National Archives, Record Group 45 Naval Subject File, stack 11W4 14/12/6 box 67, Desc: fol 4 *Virginia/Merrimack*, Willard letter.

36. Army Corps of Engineers, Norfolk Division Reference Library, telephone conversations, February 13, 2004, and February 19, 2004.

37. National Archives, Records Group 45 Naval Subject File, stack 11W4 14/12/6 box 121 fol. 1 of 7, Salvage of *Cumberland*.

Chapter Eight: Iron for the Ironclads

1. Charles B. Dew, *Ironmaker to the Confederacy* (New Haven, CT: Yale University Press, 1966).
2. Ibid.
3. Ibid.
4. Ibid.
5. Ibid.
6. Brooke, "John Mercer Brooke."
7. Kathleen Bruce, *Virginia Iron Manufacturing in the Slave Era* (1930; New York: Augustus M. Kelley, 1968).
8. Dew, *Ironmaker to the Confederacy*.
9. Porter, *Record of Events*.
10. Brooke, "John Mercer Brooke."

Chapter Nine: The Guns

1. Canney, *Old Steam Navy*, vol. 1.
2. Robert J. Schneller, *A Quest for Glory* (Annapolis, MD: Naval Institute Press, 1996).
3. Ibid.
4. Ibid.
5. Ibid.
6. Victor Vifquain, *The 1862 Plot to Kidnap Jefferson Davis* (Mechanicsburg, PA: Stackpole Books, 1998).
7. Schneller, *A Quest for Glory*.
8. Encyclopedia Britannica, vol. 2, *Early Artillery*.
9. Carel de Beer, ed., *The Art of Gunfounding* (East Sussex, England: Jean Boudriot Publishers, 1991).
10. Ibid.
11. Faust, *Encyclopedia of the Civil War*.
12. Dew, *Ironmaker to the Confederacy*.
13. Ibid.
14. Ibid.
15. Ibid.
16. Ibid.
17. Ibid.
18. Ibid.
19. Ibid.
20. Schneller, *A Quest for Glory*.
21. Faust, *Encyclopedia of the Civil War*.
22. Ibid.

23. Eric Ortner, *The Patriot and The Parrott Rifle*, http://www.mrduckscannons.com/parrot_refle.htm.
24. Jack W. Melton and Lawrence E. Pawl, *Guide to Civil War Artillery Projectiles* (Kennesaw, GA: Kennesaw Mountain Press, 1996).

Chapter Ten: The Long Road to Portsmouth

1. Dew, *Ironmaker to the Confederacy.*
2. Robert C. Black, *Railroads of the Confederacy* (Chapel Hill: University of North Carolina Press, 1952).
3. Bache, Map of the City of Richmond.
4. Black, *Railroads of the Confederacy.*
5. Ibid.
6. Vifquain, *Plot to Kidnap Jefferson Davis.*
7. John V. Quarstein, *C.S.S. Virginia: Mistress of Hampton Roads* (Appomattox, VA: H. E. Howard, 2000).
8. Brooke, "John Mercer Brooke."
9. Quarstein, *C.S.S. Virginia: Mistress of Hampton Roads.*

Chapter Eleven: Building the Virginia

1. Porter, *A Short History of Myself.*
2. Ibid.
3. Eugenius A. Jack, *Memoirs of E. A. Jack Steam Engineer, CSS Virginia* (White Stone, VA: Raddylane Publishers, 1998).
4. Charles G. Davis, *The Ship Model Builders Assistant* (1926; New York: Dover Publications, 1988).
5. Virginia S. White, *Live Oaking: Southern Timber for Tall Ships* (Annapolis, MD: Naval Institute Press, 1995).
6. Ibid.
7. Ibid.
8. Ibid.
9. William L. Crothers, *The American-Built Clipper Ship* (Camden, ME: International Maritime/Ragged Mountain Press, 1997).
10. Robert T. Packard, ed., *Ramsey/Sleeper: Architectural Graphic Standards*, 7th ed. (New York: John Wiley & Sons, 1981).
11. Crothers, *The American Built-Clipper Ship.*
12. Ibid.
13. Ibid.
14. Dew, *Ironmaker to the Confederacy.*
15. Porter, *A Short History of Myself.*
16. Ibid.
17. Ibid.
18. Ibid.
19. J. W. Porter, *A Record of Events.*
20. Ibid.

21. Porter, *A Short History of Myself.*

22. John Mercer Brooke, Richmond Diary, 1861–62.

23. Ericsson, quoted in *Battlers and Leaders of the Civil War* (New York: Century Co., 1887).

24. Baxter, *Introduction of the Ironclad War Ship.*

25. Canney, *Old Steam Navy*, vol. 2.

26. Porter, Notebook.

27. J. W. Porter, *A Record of Events.*

28. R. G. Elliot, *Ironclad of the Roanoke.*

Chapter Twelve: Two Days of Glory

1. Quarstein, *C.S.S. Virginia: Mistress of Hampton Roads.*

2. Freeman, *Duel of the Ironclads.*

3. A. A. Hoeling, *Thunder at Hampton Roads* (1976, New York: Da Capo Press, 1993).

4. Ibid.

5. Ibid.

6. Woods, quoted in *Battles and Leaders.*

7. Quarstein, *C.S.S. Virginia: Mistress of Hampton Roads.*

8. Freeman, *Duel of the Ironclads.*

9. Ibid.

10. Ibid.

11. Hoehling, *Thunder at Hampton Roads.*

12. Ibid.

13. Ibid.

14. Quarstein, *C.S.S. Virginia: Mistress of Hampton Roads.*

15. Hoehling, *Thunder at Hampton Roads.*

16. Ibid.

17. Quarstein, *C.S.S. Virginia: Mistress of Hampton Roads.*

18. Ibid.

19. Ibid.

20. Ibid.

21. William C. Davis, *Duel between the First Ironclads* (1975; Baton Rouge: Louisiana State University Press, 1981).

22. Quarstein, *C.S.S. Virginia: Mistress of Hampton Roads.*

23. Ibid.

24. Ibid

25. Davis, *Duel between the First Ironclads.*

26. Ibid.

27. Quarstein, *C.S.S. Virginia: Mistress of Hampton Roads.*

28. Ibid.

29. Ibid.

30. Davis, *Duel between the First Ironclads.*

31. Hoehling, *Thunder at Hampton Roads.*

32. Ibid.

33. Ibid.
34. Ibid.
35. Davis, *Duel between the First Ironclads.*
36. Amadon, *Rise of the Ironclads.*
37. Davis, *Duel between the First Ironclads.*
38. Ibid.

Chapter Thirteen: Ironclad Down

1. Porter, *A Short History of Myself.*
2. G. M. Brooke, *John Mercer Brooke.*
3. Quarstein, *C.S.S. Virginia: Mistress of Hampton Roads.*
4. Ibid.
5. Ibid.
6. Porter, *A Short History of Myself.*
7. Quarstein, *C.S.S. Virginia: Mistress of Hampton Roads.*
8. Ibid.
9. Ibid.
10. Davis, *Duel between the First Ironclads.*
11. Quarstein, *C.S.S. Virginia: Mistress of Hampton Roads.*
12. Hoehling, *Thunder at Hampton Roads.*
13. Davis, *Duel between the First Ironclads.*
14. Quarstein, *C.S.S. Virginia: Mistress of Hampton Roads.*
15. Faust, *Encyclopedia of the Civil War.*
16. Quarstein, *C.S.S. Virginia: Mistress of Hampton Roads.*
17. Davis, *Duel between the First Ironclads.*
18. Quarstein, *C.S.S. Virginia: Mistress of Hampton Roads.*
19. Davis, *Duel between the First Ironclads.*
20. Ibid.
21. Ibid.
22. Quarstein, *C.S.S. Virginia: Mistress of Hampton Roads.*
23. Ibid.
24. Davis, *Duel between the First Ironclads.*
25. Ibid.
26. Ibid.
27. Ibid.
28. Ibid.
29. Ibid.
30. United States Coastal Survey Office, Preliminary Chart of Hampton Roads and Elizabeth River, Virginia, A. D. Bache, Superintendent, and John J. Almy, Lieutenant Commanding Asst., United States Navy, 1857.
31. Davis, *Duel between the First Ironclads.*
32. Ibid.
33. Ibid.
34. Ibid.
35. Hoehling, *Thunder at Hampton Roads.*

Chapter Fourteen: Epilogue

1. William J. Miller, *The Peninsula Campaign of 1862,* vol. 1 (Campbell, CA: Savas Publishing Co., 1997).
2. William Marvel, ed., *The Monitor Chronicles* (New York: Simon & Schuster, 2000).
3. Brooke, "John Mercer Brooke."
4. Faust, *Encyclopedia of the Civil War.*
5. Brooke, "John Mercer Brooke."
6. Ibid.
7. John M. Coski, *Capitol Navy: The Men, Ships and Operations of the James River Squadron* (Campbell, CA: Savas Woodbury Publishers, 1996).
8. Ibid.
9. Porter, *A Short History of Myself.*

Bibliography

Books and Articles

Amadon, George F. *Rise of the Ironclads.* Missoula, MN: Pictorial Histories Publishing Co., 1988.

Anderson, Bern. *By Sea and by River.* New York: Alfred A. Knopf, 1962.

Bache, A. D. *Atlas to Accompany the Official Records of the Union and Confederate Armies.* Washington, DC: Government Printing Office, 1891–95.

———. *Map of the City of Richmond, Virginia.* Washington, DC: U.S. Coastal Survey Office, 1864.

Barthell, Edward E. *The Mystery of the* Merrimack. Muskegon, MI: Dana Publishing Co., 1959.

Bathe, Granville. *Ship of Destiny.* Philadelphia: Press of Allen, Lane and Scott, 1951.

Bauer, K. Jack, and Stephen S. Roberts. *Register of Ships of the U.S. Navy, 1775–1990.* Westport, CT: Greenwood Press, 1991.

Baxter, James P. *The Introduction of the Ironclad Warship.* 1933. Hamden, CT: Archon Books, 1968.

Black, Robert C. *Railroads of the Confederacy.* Chapel Hill: University of North Carolina Press, 1952.

Bourne, J. K., Jr. "Iron vs. Oak.," *National Geographic Magazine* 209 (2006): 134–47.

Brooke, Geo. M., Jr. "John Mercer Brooke: Naval Scientist." Ph.D. diss., University of North Carolina, 1955.

———. *John Mercer Brooke: Naval Scientist and Educator.* Charlottesville: University Press of Virginia, 1980.

Brooke, John M. "*Virginia*, or *Merrimac*: Her Real Projector." *Southern Historical Society Papers* 19 (1891) [unpaginated].

Bruce, Kathleen. *Virginia Iron Manufacturing in the Slave Era.* 1930. Reprint, New York: Augustus M. Kelley, 1968.

Campbell, R. Thomas, and Alan B. Flanders. *Confederate Phoenix: The CSS* Virginia. Shippensburg, PA: Burd Street Press, 2001.

Canney, Donald L. *The Old Steam Navy,* Vol. 1, *Frigates, Sloops and Gunboats, 1815–1885.* Annapolis, MD: Naval Institute Press, 1993.

———. *The Old Steam Navy,* Vol. 2, *The Ironclads, 1842–1885.* Annapolis, MD: Naval Institute Press, 1993.

Chapelle, Howard I. *History of the American Sailing Navy.* New York: Konecky & Konecky, 1949.

Cheney, Robert K. *Maritime History of the Merrimac Shipbuilding.* Newburyport, MA: Newburyport Press, 1964.

Chestnut, Mary. *A Diary from Dixie.* 1905. Reprint, New York: Random House Publishing, 1997.

Coski, John M. *Capitol Navy: The Men, Ships and Operations of the James River Squadron.* Campbell, CA: Savas Woodbury Publishers, 1996.

Crothers, William L. *The American-Built Clipper Ship.* Camden, ME: International Maritime/Ragged Mountain Press, 1997.

Current, Richard N., ed. *Encyclopedia of the Confederacy,* Vol. 4. New York: Simon & Schuster, 1993.

Currier, John J. *Ship Building on the Merrimac River.* Newburyport, MA: William H. Huse & Co. 1877.

Davis, Charles G. *The Ship Model Builders Assistant.* 1926. Reprint, New York: Dover Publications, 1988.

Davis, William C. *Duel between the First Ironclads.* 1975. Reprint, Baton Rouge: Louisiana State University Press, 1981.

de Beer, Carel, ed. *The Art of Gunfounding.* East Sussex, England: Jean Boudriot Publishers, 1991.

Dew, Charles B. *Ironmaker to the Confederacy.* New Haven: Yale University Press, 1966.

Dobins, Kenneth W. *Patent Office Pony.* Fredericksburg, VA: Sergeant Kirkland's Museum and Historical Society, 1997.

Durkin, Joseph T. *Stephen R. Mallory: Confederate Navy Chief.* Chapel Hill: University of North Carolina Press, 1954.

Elliot, Robert G. *Ironclad of the Roanoke.* Shippensburg, PA: White Mane Books, 1999.

Falk, Peter H., ed. *Who Was Who in American Art.* Madison, CT: Sound View Press, 1985.

Faust, Patricia L., ed. *Encyclopedia of the Civil War.* New York: Harper & Row, 1986.

Flanders, Alan B. *John L. Porter: Naval Constructor of Destiny.* White Stone, VA: Brandylane Publishers, 2000.

Footner, Geoffrey M. *USS* Constellation*: From Frigate to Sloop of War.* Annapolis, MD: Naval Institute Press, 2003.

Freeman, Fred. *Duel of the Ironclads.* New York: Time Life Books, 1969.

History Channel. *Great Ships: The Ironclads* [DVD]. New York: A&E Television Networks, 1996.

Hobson, Richmond. *The Sinking of the* "Merrimac." 1899. Reprint, Annapolis, MD: Naval Institute Press, 1987.

Hoeling, A. A. *Thunder at Hampton Roads.* 1976. Reprint, New York: Da Capo Press, 1993.

Jack, Eugenius A. *Memoirs of E. A. Jack Steam Engineer, CSS* Virginia. White Stone, VA: Raddylane Publishers, 1998.

Jones, Catesby ap Roger. "Service on the *"Virginia" (Merrimac)."* *Southern Historical Society Papers* (1917). Vol 11, 65–75.

King, Dean. *A Sea of Words.* New York: Henry Holt, 1995.

Konstam, Angus. *Duel of the Ironclads.* Oxford: Osprey Publishing, 2003.

Lewis, Charles L. *Matthew Fontaine Maury: Pathfinder of the Sea.* Annapolis, MD: United States Naval Institute, 1927.

Luraghi, Raimondo. *A History of the Confederate Navy.* Annapolis, MD: Naval Institute Press, 1996.

Marvel, William, ed. *The Monitor Chronicles.* New York: Simon & Schuster, 2000.

McPherson, James M. *Battle Cry of Freedom.* New York: Oxford University Press, 1988.

Melton, Jack W., and Lawrence E. Pawl. *Guide to Civil War Artillery Projectiles.* Kennesaw, GA: Kennesaw Mountain Press, 1996.

Miller, William J. *The Peninsula Campaign of 1862,* Vol. 1. Campbell, CA: Savas Publishing Co., 1997.

Mondfeld, Wolfram zu. *Historic Ship Models.* 1977. Reprint, New York: Sterling Publishing Co., 2006.

Morgan, James M. *Midshipman in Gray.* 1917. Reprint, Shippensburg, PA: Burd Street Press, 1997.

Nelson, James L. *Reign of Fire.* New York: HarperCollins Publishers, 2004.

Packard, Robert T., ed. *Ramsey/Sleeper: Architectural Graphic Standards*, 7th ed. New York: John Wiley & Sons, 1981.

Porter, John Luke. *A Short History of Myself.* 1878. Reprinted in *Oldetimes Magazine* (Spring 1987).

Porter, John W. H. *A Record of Events in Norfolk County, Virginia, From April 19th, 1861, to May 10th, 1862, with a History of the Soldiers and Sailors of Norfolk County, Norfolk City and Portsmouth Who Served in the Confederate States Army or Navy.* Portsmouth, VA: W. A. Fiske, Printer, 1892.

Quarstein, John V. *C.S.S. Virginia: Mistress of Hampton Roads.* Appomattox, VA: H. E. Howard, 2000.

Scharf, J. Thomas. *History of the Confederate States Navy.* 1868. Reprint, Avenel, NJ: Gramercy Books, 1996.

Schneller, Robert J. *A Quest for Glory.* Annapolis, MD: Naval Institute Press, 1996.

Still, William N., Jr. *Iron Afloat.* Columbia: University of South Carolina Press, 1985.

Turner Pictures. *Ironclad.* [DVD]. New York: Turner Home Entertainment, 1991.

Vifquain, Victor. *The 1862 Plot to Kidnap Jefferson Davis.* Mechanicsburg, PA: Stackpole Books, 1998.

White, Virginia S. *Live Oaking: Southern Timber for Tall Ships.* Annapolis, MA: Naval Institute Press, 1995.

Wise, John S. *The End of an Era.* New York: Thomas Yoseloff, 1965.

Official Documents and Archival References

National Archives. Records Group 19 Bureau of Ships. Reference Report for USS *Merrimack*/CSS *Virginia*.

———. Records Group 19 Bureau of Steam Engineering. Merrimack File, Van Nostrand Folder.

———. Record Group 45 Naval Subject File. Stack 11W4 14/12/6 box 67, Desc: fol 4 *Virginia/Merrimack*.

———. Records Group 45 Naval Subject File. Stack 11W4 14/12/6 box 121 fol. 1 of 7, Salvage of *Cumberland*.

Porter, John Luke. Technical notebook and journal kept 1860–72.

United States Coastal Survey Office. Preliminary Chart of Hampton Roads and Elizabeth River, Virginia. A. D. Bache, Superintendent, and John J. Almy, Lieutenant Commanding Asst., United States Navy, 1857.

The War of the Rebellion: A Compilation of the Official Records of the Union and Confederate Navies, 1881–1902 (OR).

Other Sources

Ahladas, John J., Curator, the Museum of the Confederacy, Richmond, VA. Letter written August 18, 1997.

Army Corps of Engineers, Norfolk Division Reference Library. Telephone conversations February 13 and 19, 2004.

Barisic, Sonja. "Mariners' Museum Acquires Original Drawing of CSS *Virginia*," *The Virginia Pilot – Pilot Online* (Hampton Roads, VA), August 2, 2003.

Bartlett, Albert Leroy. *The Story of Haverhill in Massachusetts.* Typed manuscript on file at the Haverhill Public Library.

Brooke, John Mercer. Richmond diary, 1861–62.

Clancy, Paul. "Museum Buys Rare Drawings of Ironclad Virginia," *The Virginian-Pilot – Pilot Online* (Hampton Roads, VA), December 10, 2002.

Coski, John M., Historian and Library Director, Museum of the Confederacy, Richmond, VA. E-mail correspondence, December 2, 2003–February 7, 2004.

Johnston, Jeff. *The Fate of the CSS Virginia,* http://home.att.net/%7eiron.clad/thefateof thecssva.html (accessed November 30, 2006).

Kurr, Keith. E-mail sent May 21, 2003, from Cartographic Section, Special Media Archives Service Division, National Archives and Records Administration, College Park, MD.

Marder, Molly Hutton, Assistant Registrar and Collections Database Manager, Chrysler Museum of Art, Norfolk, VA. E-mail correspondence, December 2003.

McCauley, Capt. Edward. Short biography of C. S. McCauley, written April, 1938.

McCauley family papers. Navy Dept. correspondence to Capt. C. S. McCauley, April 10, 1861.

Meagher, David J. "CSS *Virginia*" [ship plans]. Jersey City, NJ: Tatum Plans Service, 1986.

Merrimack River Watershed Council. *The Voice of the Merrimack.* http://www.merrimack.org (accessed November 30, 2006).

Ortner, Eric. *The Patriot and The Parrott Rifle.* http://www.mrduckscannons.com/parrot_refle.htm (accessed September 19, 2003).

Porter, John Luke. Notebook. Portsmouth Naval Shipyard Museum.

Ramsay, Henry Ashton, Acting Chief Engineer CSS *Virginia,* January 1, 1862. Letter to J. H. Morrison, May 17, 1906. The Mariners' Museum Archives, Ms6.

Tyson, Mabry, and Martha H. Tyson. CSS *Virginia* Home Page, http://www.cssvirginia.org (accessed Dec. 12, 2006).

U.S. Navy Information Site. http://navysite.de/ao/179.htm (accessed 2002).

INDEX

About the Author

Carl D. Park was born in Tennessee and has been a lifelong Civil War history buff. After serving in the Army, he studied design at the Layton School of Art and studied fine art at Lake Forrest College.

His professional life has been spent in the advertising industry. He has worked as a commercial artist and art director and has written copy for ads, brochures, and historical pamphlets. He has owned and managed display companies where he designed and built industrial trade-show displays and museum exhibits. Model building has been both a vocation and avocation. His experience in model building, writing, and architectural drafting led him to write and illustrate numerous "how-to" articles for *Fine Scale Modeler* magazine.